Cultivating Customers

Women and Change in the Developing World

Series Editor
Mary H. Moran, Colgate University

Editorial Board

Cultivating Customers

Market Women
in Harare, Zimbabwe

Nancy E. Horn

LYNNE
RIENNER
PUBLISHERS

BOULDER
LONDON

Photographs by Nancy E. Horn

Published in the United States of America in 1994 by
Lynne Rienner Publishers, Inc.
1800 30th Street, Boulder, Colorado 80301

and in the United Kingdom by
Lynne Rienner Publishers, Inc.
3 Henrietta Street, Covent Garden, London WC2E 8LU

Library of Congress Cataloging-in-Publication Data
Horn, Nancy E.
    Cultivating customers : market women in Harare, Zimbabwe / by
Nancy E. Horn.
        p. cm.—(Women and change in the developing world)
    Includes bibliographical references and index.
    ISBN 1-55587-472-X (alk. paper)
        1. Women merchants—Zimbabwe—Harare. 2. Markets—Zimbabwe—
Harare. I. Title. II. Series.
HF3902.Z9H375 1994
331.4'8138118'096894—dc20   94-4426
                                                                                              CIP

British Cataloguing in Publication Data
A Cataloguing in Publication record for this book
is available from the British Library.

Printed and bound in the United States of America

The paper used in this publication meets the requirements
of the American National Standard for Permanence of
Paper for Printed Library Materials Z39.48-1984.

▲

Contents

v

Illustrations

Tables

Figure

▲
Acknowledgments

The joy an author takes in finishing a manuscript is to be shared with the many people who have been supportive and who have contributed to the development of the ideas, the conduct of research, analyzing the data, and writing the volume. For me, that list begins with the many faculty and friends in the Department of Anthropology, the Department of Agricultural Economics, and the African Studies Center at Michigan State University. Of particular note are those who served on my dissertation committee—Bill Derman, my chair, Larry Robbins, Harold Riley, and Scott Whiteford—and Dave Wiley, director of the African Studies Center, for his financial support during my graduate school years.

I am indebted to all the hundreds of women who became a part of my research in the field. Their interest and participation made my fieldwork experience a high point in my professional life. My research assistants, Elijah, Eddie, Taka, Florence, and Junior, added an extremely insightful dimension to my understanding of the fresh produce trade in Zimbabwe. Faculty at the University of Zimbabwe were very supportive of my research, and special thanks go to Kingston Nyamapfene (then chair of the Department of Land Management) for providing me office space and the opportunity to share my ideas with faculty; to Marshall Murphree, director, Center for Applied Social Science, for bringing together a number of interested colleagues to listen to and critique my ideas; and to Jim Rosenberger, then statistician in the Department of Land Management (now chair, Department of Statistics, Penn State University).

Very heartfelt thanks go to three anthropologists who read my dissertation and encouraged me to publish my findings: Gracia Clark at the University of Michigan, Linda Stone at Washington State University, and Mary Moran at Colgate University. The time they spent reading and critiquing this opus was a gift of confidence in my ability.

The book would not have been written without the cooperation of two colleagues at Washington State University: Jan Noel with the International Development Cooperation Office, and Jim Henson, director, International

Programs. They allowed me to take the time from my professional activities to write the draft and finalize the manuscript.

Dear friends who led me to countless resources in Zimbabwe deserve special mention: Kuda and Irvine Mariga, and Florence and Gladman Kundhlande. Their open hearts and homes provided the moral support I needed while in Zimbabwe and provided me with many professional opportunities to obtain a deeper understanding of women and the fresh produce trade in Zimbabwe.

The opportunity to conduct the research presented in this volume was made possible by Fulbright-Hayes and National Science Foundation grants. My return visit in 1993 was made possible through the Peace Corps; I am grateful to them for allowing me the time while on assignment in Botswana to return to Zimbabwe.

Finally, I would like to thank my son, Andrew, for being quiet when I needed to work, for being understanding when I was short-tempered, and, during his teenage years, for saying "lighten up" as often as it needed to be said. The many friends—especially Sue and Bob Herner—who played surrogate mom when Andrew was younger and I was immersed in the activities of the market women deserve the greatest of thanks because they allowed me to develop professionally while being a single parent.

N. E. H.

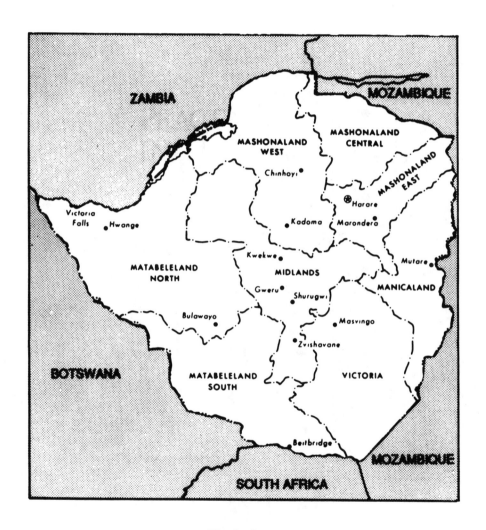

Zimbabwe

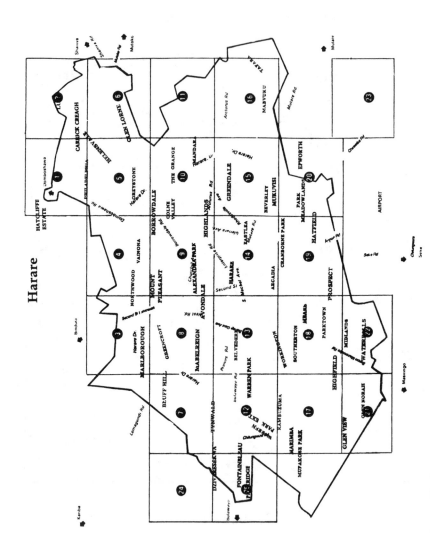

Source: The Greater Harare A to Z Street Guide Including Buildings and Industrial Areas, 1991 (Harare: Munn Publishing). Reproduced with permission of the Surveyor-General of Zimbabwe: copyright reserved.

▲ 1

The Ethic and Tradition
of Women's Economic Roles

Shandira! Hapana chinouya chega!—"Work! Nothing comes without it!"—is a song women fresh produce vendors sing from time to time as they toil in the market sites of Harare, Zimbabwe.[1] Work is the underlying ethic that defines women's economic roles, produces money for household survival, sends children to school, provides a niche in a sometimes hostile urban environment, and gives status.

The research findings presented in this book are based on data collected in Zimbabwe from September 1985 through December 1986 under Fulbright-Hayes and National Science Foundation grants, and on data obtained during July 1993. The analysis tells a story of commitment on the part of Zimbabwean women to the ideal of development—self-sufficiency. To overcome economic vulnerability in the city and to ensure family provisioning, women fresh produce vendors take risks to conduct trading enterprises that constitute the end point in a production-marketing chain of perishable commodities.

The main question answered by this writing is: Why do Zimbabwean women establish and maintain fresh produce marketing enterprises in the face of great uncertainty? Elements of the complex response to this question are found in the context of culture, history, geography, political economy, and assumptions about what constitutes business.

▲ Tradition, Changes, and Adaptations

From the origins of women's economic roles—their ethnic heritage—to present day adaptations of these roles, women's activities in Zimbabwe have been guided by their socialization into systems of patriarchy. A rural, gender-based division of labor rooted in the allocation of land at marriage developed in women an indigenous knowledge system of the cultivation and distribution of garden crops. When women migrated to urban areas with their spouses or alone, they brought the knowledge of horticultural crops with them. They were faced with a dilemma, however: how to main-

1

tain their culturally-ascribed roles without the means to do so, or how to grow food and provision their families without a plot to cultivate. To resolve this dilemma, many women utilized their skills in establishing a fresh produce marketing enterprise.

The context in which this adaptation was made was the colonially-engineered labor reserve economy. The early creation of African reserves, the imposition of taxes payable in coin, and the alienation of land for white commercial agricultural production created a need for Africans to generate an income. Unwilling to leave their homes to find cash, Africans increased their marketable agricultural output. In succeeding years, however, with declining productivity in the reserves and the imposition of laws designed to decrease African competition, African males sought employment in settler-developed towns, mines, and commercial farms. Wages paid were too low to provide full urban support to migrants; it was assumed that female spouses would continue agricultural production back home and provision men as needed.

White settlers completely misconceived women's economic roles, basing their assumptions in their own cultural traditions of patriarchy. On the one hand, African women's agricultural production skills were integral to the maintenance of the labor reserve economy; on the other hand, settlers were blind to the broader marketing implications of women's surplus production. Consequently, women's movement was not curtailed, and they were allowed to sell their crops in towns.

Trade in horticultural crops in Salisbury developed along two streams: white and African. White traders with kin connections to growers in South Africa imported a variety of nonindigenously grown fruits and vegetables to satisfy the white palate, while rural African women produced and marketed their surpluses primarily to Africans living in the townships and at the mines but also to the growing number of settler families in the Salisbury suburbs. In order to satisfy demand, African women developed two strategies: they established commercial relations with white traders from whom they "ordered" crops they did not grow themselves, or they began growing crops desired by white families.

As the demand for African labor increased and as depleted soils produced even less in the reserves, wives began to join their spouses. Seeking their own means to become economically self-sufficient and to escape the traditional constraints of patriarchy, single women also migrated. In town, women sought means to provision their families in a severely constrained financial environment.

Adapting their knowledge of horticultural crops to the urban environment, many women followed the pattern already established: ordering commodities from African growers or white traders at a central urban location, and then reselling what they had ordered in their neighborhoods. These strategies were challenged in 1965 with the Unilateral Declaration of Independence (UDI) and the global imposition of trading sanctions. White farmers began growing horticultural crops commercially in order to supply indigenous demand. Instead of selling crops grown in South Africa, greengrocers began selling what was grown by local white farmers. Linking producer to consumer were the white traders cum wholesalers who expanded their operations to satisfy local demand. Customers included greengrocers and general dealers, hospitals, schools, the armed services, and others who demanded top quality commodities.

White producers needed an outlet for their harvests of lower quality commodities. To take entrepreneurial advantage of this opportunity, African males developed wholesale businesses to meet the food demands of an ever growing African township population. The needed link in the distributive chain was the urban women vendors who came first to Highfield and then to Mbare to order and then purchase stocks to be resold in the high density areas. This pattern prevailed throughout the liberation war and is the pattern that remains today.

▲ Formal/Informal Market Distinctions

Commodity marketing has developed in two streams. Maize, other grains, and cash crops such as tobacco and cotton have been marketed by a parastatal marketing board. This "formal" market documents production and sales and contributes to state revenue. Fresh produce has always been privately traded in an "informal" market (with the exception, most recently, of horticultural crops grown for export). Transactions in this sector are largely undocumented and do not contribute directly to state revenue.

In this context, women's vending microenterprises suffer from a triple burden of invisibility: one based in the commodities they sell; one based on the unrecorded and undocumented nature of their trade; and one based on their gender. The effect of this invisibility is that women fresh produce vendors are never considered as an integral end point in the production-marketing chain of horticultural crops; their efforts are not viewed in terms of the contributions they are making to family maintenance and community provisioning because they are not consulted for official data collection; and they are not considered—in the literature or by the state—as committed businesspeople driven by the ethic of self-reliance. Consequently, vendors (and other microentrepreneurs) are not considered as contributors to development.

▲ Market Women as Businesswomen

Women fresh produce vendors see themselves as businesswomen, equipped to trade in a certain range of commodities that provision a large, urban-based population. Their trade, however, has been analyzed in the literature as marginal because it has been characterized as "income-generating activities." This term connotes the "pocket" or "pin" money women derived from selling eggs or butter in early America: it was once assumed this income was for frivolous items women "needed." More recent analyses have found, however, that this income was critical to the survival of the farm household because it was generated with regularity and could be depended on throughout the year. Research conducted on incomes generated by women in developing countries similarly illustrates the integral nature of this cash flow to family survival.

Assumptions about women's marginal contribution to the economy are strongly rejected in this writing. Data collected support the assertion that what women earn in establishing microenterprises is used to provision their families, educate the next generation, conduct business from which they gain status, and provision an entire city with its fresh produce needs. Hence, the women I will present to you do generate income, but the way they accomplish this goal is by establishing their own businesses or microenterprises. The women see themselves as business operators; we have a responsibility to do likewise.

But are these vendors business operators in the classical sense? Is profit their end goal? In this writing, I will argue that, yes, the women are business operators. I will also argue, however, that business goals and objectives incorporate cultural parameters that are enmeshed in an historical adaptation to a labor reserve political economy; an urban environment; a sociological milieu of disadvantageous gender biases; an economic arena uncaptured by the state; and an overall context of rapid social and political change brought about by world economic imbalances. Within this contextual vortex, women vendors have established a constant that serves as the end distribution point for perishable commodities and provides for family survival.

This constant, however, is itself dynamic. Women's trade takes place in times of glut and scarcity; it adapts to changing demands and changes in the allocation of family resources. As risk-taking ventures, vendor microenterprises epitomize the self-sufficiency ideal of development.

The contextual vortex has had and continues to have an impact on the parameters of women's businesses. Just as these same contextual parameters have put their unique stamp on the way Japanese, Saudis, or U.S. citizens conduct business, so too have they given rise to a profile of the way women in Zimbabwe conduct their trade in fresh produce.

▲ Obtaining the Data

Economic activities in African society cannot be separated from the social context within which they take place (Bell 1986:170).

Culture and context have shaped a gender-based urban economic behavior in Zimbabwe and many other developing countries. Guiding the data collection in this instance was the challenge advanced by Polly Hill in 1970:

> If the investigator is an economist, he should usually discard his tradition-al procedure of collecting most of his material through field assistants using questionnaires in favor of a method learned from anthropologists which mainly relies on questioning and observing individuals while they are at work. Marketwomen should be interviewed in the market. . . . The procedure should be semi-statistical, in the sense that similar, even identical, questions should be put to many informants independently, with a view to comparing, even totalling, their results (Hill 1970:11–12).

As an anthropologist identifying the culture and context that produced a particular urban economic adaptation, I was interested in telling a story from its rural origins, through changes brought about by colonial manipula-tion, to events since Zimbabwe's independence—April 18, 1980—especial-ly the most recent imposition of the Economic Structural Adjustment Program (ESAP). While I explored an economic activity, I did so in the soci-ological context of the city, the economic context of the informal market, and the cultural context, primarily, of the rural-based belief systems and patterns of behavior of Shona-speaking people.

One of the first tasks of this research was to identify the distribution of the population delineated for research. Colonially-imposed African urban influx legislation created a city segregated according to color. Since inde-pendence, the population has shifted, and more middle class Africans now live in the low density suburbs. Accordingly, women vendors could be found preponderantly in the high density suburbs (formerly called town-ships), but also at bus stations and shopping centers in low density suburbs (formerly called suburbs). To identify the potential clientele pool, I needed to know Harare's population.

According to the 1982 census, Harare's population was 658,364, of which 582,427 were African and 62,138 were of European descent (Zimbabwe, CSO, Table 20, January 3, 1984). By 1992 the population had grown to 1,478,810 (Zimbabwe, CSO, 1992:123).[2] Droughts, rural landless-ness and unemployment, and spin-off effects of ESAP are cited as the main reasons for this urban population expansion. Africans live primarily in the sixteen or more high density suburbs, while whites live in the seventy-plus low density suburbs.[3] The 1992 census indicated geographical shifts in the urban population brought about largely by housing accessibility to Africans in the low density suburbs (see Table 1.1). The distribution of the African population and the markets in Harare presented methodological problems in determining a sample.

Table 1.1 Suburban Distribution of Harare Population, 1982 and 1992

Suburb	Number of Households 1982	1992	Population 1982	1992	Average Household Size[a] 1982	1992
Low Density						
Adylinn	459		1,291		2.8	
Alexandra Park	1,499		3,673		2.5	
Amby/Beverly/ Bingley[b]	955		2,965		3.1	
Arcadia[b]	524		2,138		4.1	
Aspindale		3,276		14,217		4.3
Avenues[c]	7,347	6,803	17,128	21,387	2.3	3.1
Avondale[c]	3,949	6,752	9,019	26,776	2.3	4.0
Avondale West	929		2,326		2.5	
Belgravia/ Milton Park	1,495		3,669		2.5	
Belvedere	2,739	5,414	7,976	18,534	2.9	3.4
Bluff Hill	651		1,954		3.0	
Borrowdale	1,979	8,179	5,698	24,071	2.9	2.9
Braeside[b]	1,493		5,292		3.5	
Chadcombe/ Meadowlands	1,157		3,984		3.4	
Chisipite/ Lewisham	701		1,858		2.7	
City Center	1,747		4,192		2.4	
Colne Valley	1,547		3,794		2.5	
Crowborough	159		703		4.4	
Eastlea	2,518	8,266	6,268	34,243	2.5	4.1
Glen Lorne	1,154		3,485		3.0	
Greencroft	1,072		2,883		2.7	
Greendale	3,198	9,557	8,243	36,769	2.6	3.8
Greengrove	1,110		3,725		3.4	
Greystone	1,276		3,388		2.7	
Gun Hill	488		1,178		2.4	
Hatfield	2,903	6,132	10,236	26,109	3.5	4.3
Helensvale/ Luna/Carrick Creigh	659		2,129		3.2	
Highlands	3,406	7,314	8,448	19,820	2.5	2.7
Hillside	876		2,404		2.7	
Horley	181		774		4.3	
Houghton Park	442		1,854		4.2	
Industrial Area	911		2,247		2.5	
Kopje	878		2,646		3.0	
Lochinvar	472		2,000		4.2	
Mabelreign/Hazel Park/Meyrick Park	5,232	8,217	17,397	33,916	3.3	4.1
Mandara	1,054		3,030		2.9	
Marlborough	2,220	5,593	6,954	20,788	3.1	3.7
Mt. Pleasant/ Groombridge	2,923	5,658	7,649	20,796	2.6	3.7
Northwood	1,231		3,243		2.6	
Parktown	671		2,708		4.0	

continues

Table 1.1 continued

Pomona	390		1,033		2.6	
Prospect Hill	1,049		3,929		3.7	
Queensdale	406		1,567		3.9	
Rietfontein	383		1,148		3.0	
Ridgeview	792		2,995		3.8	
Rolf Valley	435		1,238		2.8	
Southerton[b]	918		4,132		4.5	
St. Martin's[b]	225		995		4.4	
Sunningdale[b]	278	4,922	1,485	18,833	5.3	3.8
Strathaven/						
Monovale	867		2,137		2.5	
The Grange	467		1,333		2.9	
Tynwald	580		2,504		4.3	
University	54		179		3.3	
Uplands	156		754		4.8	
Vainona	769		2,186		2.8	
Waterfalls	1,768	6,120	7,186	28,952	4.1	4.7
Westwood[d]	247		874		3.5	
Willowvale	239		1,030		4.3	
Wilmington Park	227		782		3.4	
Workington	1,131		5,514		4.9	
Low Density Totals	74,455	93,334	218,036	350,725	2.9	3.6
High Density						
Ardbennie	470		2,052		4.4	
Budiriro		9,039		34,542		3.8
Chikurubi	1,347		5,131		3.8	
Cranbourne	1,322		5,479		4.1	
Dzivarisekwa	4,818	10,461	22,718	44,946	4.7	4.3
Epworth[e]		17,282		62,701		3.6
Glen Norah	11,265	15,062	45,668	66,867	4.1	4.4
Glen View	15,960	27,623	59,775	109,704	3.7	4.0
Hatcliffe	2,096		8,161		3.9	
Highfield	19,201	26,007	73,501	101,134	3.8	3.9
Kambuzuma	6,607	9,630	25,521	40,558	3.6	4.2
Kuwadzana		19,074		75,080		3.9
Mabvuku	9,151	10,741	38,958	47,471	4.3	4.4
Marimba Park	813		3,342		4.1	
Mbare	14,211	23,888	59,366	97,078	4.2	4.1
Mufakose	9,291	13,031	44,703	61,846	4.8	4.7
Rugare	1,475		8,362		5.7	
Tafara	4,602	7,336	21,069	30,693	4.6	4.2
Warren Park	3,301	11,874	13,672	52,663	4.1	4.4
High Density Totals	103,834	203,144	429,317	833,444	4.1	4.1
Harare Totals	178,289	296,478	647,353	1,184,169[f]	3.6	4.0

Source: Zimbabwe, Central Statistical Office, Table 41, January 16, 1984, and Table 3, 1992:127–128.

Notes: a. Averaging the columns does not yield the same number as dividing the total number of households into the total population. The difference is due to individual rounding.

b. Suburbs formerly reserved for "colored" people.

c. Apartment dwellings dominate these suburbs.

d. This suburb was racially mixed from the time of its establishment.

e. Although in existence at the time of the 1982 census, Epworth was not considered part of Greater Harare.

f. Does not include "Rural" Harare or Chitungwiza.

Phase One (October 1985–February 1986)

The hypothesis posited in my proposal for the Fulbright-Hayes and National Science Foundation grants sought to identify how rural/urban family ties would be strengthened by rural female producers sending their surplus garden production to their urban male husbands who sold the produce in Harare. A dual economic dependency would have been created as rural female producers would be dependent upon their husbands for cash remittances, but male migrant vendors would be dependent on their rural wives to supply them with crops.

My initial forays into the field indicated my total misconception of the enterprise. Marketing fresh produce in Harare did not rest upon a rural wife to urban husband produce-for-cash exchange, but upon commercial transactions between African female retail vendors and African and/or white farmers and predominantly male wholesalers.

In mapping the location of vendors in Harare, I noted their relatively sparse distribution in predominantly white neighborhoods. In conducting background research at Michigan State University, at the Zimbabwe National Archives and at the University of Zimbabwe, I learned that the city had been divided along racial lines and that certain regulations prevented the spontaneous establishment of small scale enterprises in predominantly white neighborhoods (see Table 1.2).

Where I found market stalls, streetside tables, or makeshift stands, I stopped and interviewed vendors in a focal group format.[4] The responses I received from these reconnaissance interviews led me to investigate the actual incomes women generate. If returns are so limited, as many vendors indicated, why are so many women engaged in the enterprise? This question, along with many others, led me to design the next research phase.

Phase Two (March–August 1986)

The need to discern anthropological, economic, and sociological information, as well as to identify variables affecting women's marketing enterprises in particular, led me to create a lengthy interview schedule and a pricing data sheet (see Horn 1988). The methodological problem was identifying a relevant sample of the 3,426 vendors. To meet the time criteria inherent in participant observation, I had to stay at a vending location longer than the time it took us to interview. To understand the internal dynamics of each market site, it was necessary to interview every vendor at each selected site. How to incorporate these two necessities of anthropological research in a survey that would produce statistically reliable results was the challenge. With the assistance of Dr. James Rosenberger, then statistician in the Department of Land Management at the University of Zimbabwe, I developed a sampling strategy that brought these divergent research methodologies together: a directed random cluster sample. For the high density

Table 1.2 Suburban Distribution of Stall and Table Vendors, 1986–1987

Suburb	Table Sites	Number of Vendors	Stall Sites	Number of Vendors
High Density Suburbs				
Ardbennie/				
Mbare	8	30	3	60
Dzivarisekwa	9	59	3	51
Glen Norah	1	8	5	137
Glen View	8	157	4	108
Hatcliffe			1	8
Highfield	14	117	5	245
Kambuzuma	4	35	4	60
Mabvuku	4	108	3	86
Mbare/				
Pedzanhamo			3	1,209
Mufakose	6	138	5	106
Kuwadzana			4	88
Rugare			1	7
Tafara	1	8	3	101
Warren Park	1	4	3	54
Subtotal	56	664	47	2,320
Low Density Suburbs[a]				
Arcadia			1	10
Braeside			1	10
Downtown and				
Southerton	4	52	3	106
Kilwinning/				
Hatfield			1	16
Other Suburbs	40	248		
Subtotal	44	300	6	142
Total	100	964	53	2,462
Total Number of Vendors Enumerated				3,426

Source: Horn 1986.

Note: a. Identifying vending sites in the low density suburbs is such that by enumerating them I would be revealing their location. Since these vendors are not registered nor do they own valid licenses, the presentation of their locations might possibly subject them to harassment. Such presentation is not restrictive in each of the high density suburbs as vendors are located in many different sites.

suburbs, this term translated into choosing one vending site per suburb on a random basis. For the low density suburbs, it meant grouping all vending sites and randomly choosing eight. At all selected sample sites, all vendors conducting business were defined as the "cluster" and all were interviewed. A total of 325 vendors conducting their trade at 24 market sites were selected.

Intensive interviewing was conducted at one site two days per week, while participant observation, informal conversations, and information gathering on wholesale and retail pricing were conducted the remaining days of the week. In most cases, we spent one full week at each site, but in four cases we spent two weeks because of the large number of vendors to be interviewed.

At interviewing day's end, a Polaroid picture was taken and given to each respondent as a way of expressing my thanks for their help. As an additional indication of my gratitude, I baked cakes and cookies with the produce vendors were selling—bananas, carrots, zucchini, mangoes, apples—and distributed some to each vendor during morning tea break. These small tokens of thanks had a profound effect on the relationship I was able to establish with many of the vendors. As I subsequently learned, only a very few white people in Zimbabwe have ever learned how to speak any of the Shona or Ndebele languages. My facility in Shona and my casual chats with vendors over tea made them feel more at ease and more interested in my work and hence more responsive in interviews.

I had found during Phase One that questions posed would often elicit expansive responses. In training my research assistants, I instructed them to mark direct responses to questions on the interview schedule; expanded responses were to be recorded in a notebook kept open during the course of the interview. This very rich data source provided me with information the interview schedules could not—and also clearly illustrated to me my shortcomings in questionnaire design.

Phase Three (September–November 1986)

The objective of the final phase of research was to ascertain the institutional context in which the women operate. To determine the parameters of wholesaling and the degree of market control exercised, I undertook an informal survey of some 50 wholesalers conducting their trade in both the informal and formal markets of Harare. To understand more about production/marketing problems, I interviewed approximately 175 farmers at their farms, at the farmers' market at Mbare, or at the ad hoc farmers' market held every weekend at Mabvuku. Conversations with leaders of the farmers' unions, agricultural extension (AGRITEX) personnel, the marketing manager of the horticultural export crop marketing agency, and officers of the municipality rounded out my knowledge of the institutional context of the women's activities.

Follow-up Research

During a revisit to Zimbabwe in July 1993, I conducted informal questioning at four marketing sites where vendors had been interviewed in 1985–1986. In the interim years, a major drought had occurred and ESAP had been implemented to stimulate the economy. Data analysis indicates that changes in the economic context in which vendors operate have had an extremely negative impact, owing in large part to the devaluation of the Zimbabwe dollar and the relaxation of urban vending regulations. Changes in the value of the dollar have impoverished urban workers and increased the prices of all foodstuffs, while the relaxation of vending regulations has produced an explosion in the number of ad hoc streetside vendors throughout the city, each trying to earn any income possible to meet basic needs.

▲ Research Assistants

Eddie, Elijah, and Taka were all fresh produce street hawkers who had been in the business between four and eighteen years. In transactions with them, I informally interviewed them about their trade, and at one point asked if they would escort me around the city to have conversations with other vendors similar to the ones I had had with them. The three were so helpful and insightful that I asked if they would be willing to enter into a more formal contractual arrangement for employment. All three enthusiastically accepted.

I was somewhat hesitant to hire three male research assistants since the methodological training I had received on conducting research on women stressed that women might feel more comfortable being interviewed by women. I shared this concern with my assistants, the reply to which offered me the first cultural insight of my field research. They argued that Shona-speaking women are trained "from small up" to talk to men. Enmeshed in patriarchal hierarchies in a patrilineal cultural environment that included patrilocal postmarriage residence patterns, women acquire the rules of male/female interaction as a part of the socialization process. Interactions between women oftentimes, I was informed, led to jealousy, misunderstanding, and witchcraft accusations. The men's warnings implied that friendship in the marketplace among vendors was not automatic but had to be negotiated due to the divergent background of each vendor. While I did not necessarily agree with what they said, their desire to have paid employment and the insights into the vending business I believed I would receive from them led me to hire all three.

I also hired two women to help in the interviews. Florence was a personal acquaintance whom I had met at Michigan State when her husband was working on his graduate degree. Her knowledge of the informal market in fresh produce stemmed from having relatives in the trade. Junior worked for a number of other foreigners in Zimbabwe in various capacities; she also grew an urban garden and sold her produce door-to-door.

The data gathering techniques utilized reflect a personal ideological orientation that permeates this work: women are full economic actors in their families and their communities, and hence have a critical role to play in government development efforts. Their invisibility to the state and to development programs in the past has led to neglect in the present. This has been the pattern of the past; it will not be the pattern of the future.

▲ Unfolding the Story

I have chosen to tell the story of the women fresh produce vendors of Harare through the analytical lenses mentioned above. Chapter 2 presents the historical context of the development of women's urban economic niche, including the impact of the development of the labor reserve economy on women's ability to maintain their economic roles in a relatively hostile urban environment. Chapter 3 discusses the theoretical aspects of the informal economy, microenterprise development, and women's economic roles that provide the framework for the presentation of the empirical data appearing in subsequent chapters. Chapter 4 analyzes the bifurcated marketing structure in which women act as the final distributors in a horticultural crop production-marketing chain. Chapter 5 tells the story of the women vendors: the many experiences that brought vendors to their economic world—rural origins, migration push and pull factors, how family life adapted to an urban milieu, the ties vendors maintain to rural kin, how vendors established their fresh produce marketing enterprises, and the problems of doing business. Chapter 6 analyzes the women as business operators of trading microenterprises. It considers gross margins and the variables that contribute to generating this income; net financial returns; household expenditures; additional incomes from spouses, kin, and other sources; additional expenditures; and the portion of household expenditures met by women's income. At the conclusion of this chapter, a question is posed: Are these operations indeed businesses in a classical, profit-making sense, or are other motivations being implemented? Chapter 7 answers this question by looking at the range of goals and objectives these businesses satisfy and by arguing a hierarchy of needs met as the true rationale for establishing marketing microenterprises. Chapter 8, the conclusion, summarizes the major points made throughout the book and argues for an alternative methodological rigor in considering the contributions women make to the economy by establishing and maintaining microenterprises.

▲ Notes

1. During settler and colonial years, Harare was known as Salisbury; Zimbabwe was first named Southern Rhodesia, and during UDI—Unilateral Declaration of Independence (1965–1980)—was called Rhodesia.

2. At the time I conducted my research in 1985–1986, the population of Harare was estimated at one million, although annual increase estimations ranged between 4.8 and 10.5 percent. The 1982 census enumerated 7,501,470 people in the

country (Zimbabwe, CSO 1985:8), and the 1992 census identified a population of 10,401,767 (Zimbabwe, CSO 1992:15).

3. In 1982, there were 70 or more low density suburbs. In 1992, many of these suburbs were consolidated, although it is not clear which suburbs were collapsed into which enumerated suburb.

4. The results of this initial mapping and fact-finding research appear in a working paper written for my host institution—the Land Management Department of the University of Zimbabwe (now known as the Agricultural Economics and Extension Department) (Horn 1986).

▲ 2

Agricultural and Urban Development: Historical Background to Fresh Produce Vending

The historical as well as the contemporary context in which women conduct their trade in perishable commodities is ultimately based in policy. Prior to colonial contact, "policy" regarding women was rooted in patriarchal cultural belief systems and practices. During colonialism, a blend of ethnic patriarchies (both African and colonial) directed policies concerning women, but the prevailing policy climate was one of colonial aggrandizement at the expense of Africans. Following independence, the Ministry of Community Development and Women's Affairs[1] was established to provide needed assistance to both urban and rural women in their struggles for self-sufficiency, all within a policy context favoring broader capitalist expansion and further integration into the world market. In very recent years, women have been negatively affected by structural adjustment policies that place onerous burdens on their ability to provision their families and generate incomes. Indeed, the informal sector—once dominated by female activity—has grown considerably, challenging the well-established fresh produce distribution system women developed during a century of activity.

▲ The Rural Division of Labor and Precolonial Trading Practices

Women in Zimbabwe are now and always have been active participants in household economies. The contributions they made in precolonial times were circumscribed by patriarchal cultural systems evidenced in the rural division of labor.

Precolonial Shona-speaking farmers grew a wide variety of both grain and horticultural crops. Crop diversification derived from several aspects of rural adaptation: individual taste, ritual and life cycles, trade with neighboring groups, coastal Swahilis, and with the Portugùese; and periodic drought (*shangwa*) that made for a precarious existence (Beach 1977:43; see also

15

Bhila 1982:62). The basic staples grown included finger millet (*rapoko* or *rukweza*), bullrush millet (*mhunga*), sorghum (*mapfunde*), maize (*chibage*), and rice (*mupunga*). Horticultural crops included pineapples, pumpkins, lemons, zucchini, papaya, cucumbers, melons, groundnuts, peas, yams, beans, cassava, and sweet potatoes (Palmer 1977a).

Cultivation of these crops was divided spatially according to land allocation practices among Shona-speaking groups. Married men were allocated homestead land by the headman (*sadunhu*) (Holleman 1951:362), which included a plot each for the construction of a dwelling, a kitchen, and a granary; the cultivation of rain-fed field crops; the grazing of cattle (in common with others); and a *vlei* (wetland) area on a riverbank or like area for vegetable and fruit cultivation (Truscott 1986:30; du Toit 1981). In turn, men allocated to each of their wives their own fields—*tseu*—over which they exercised domain. Wives cultivated crops to feed their families and could dispose of any surplus in trade (Holleman 1951). Traditional law ascribed to women domain over the garden plots (Holleman 1952) and over any harvests ensuing therefrom as part of *mawoko* (labor of the hands) property (May 1983; Schmidt 1992:44–45).[2]

> A woman is dependent on her husband for the allocation of land and will be given a plot for a garden. She has control here of the produce over and above the needs of her family, and property gained through outside transactions belongs to her alone. She must also till her husband's fields and, although she does not own the produce, she has control of the granary where the family staple food is stored. Women are responsible for the production of food for the family and their control over this represents an important status source. . . . She has, as the producer of food for her family from cultivation through the stages of preparation to the final serving, considerable autonomy in its production (May 1983:26–27).

Autonomy, however, was limited. Domain was given to women by men—either husbands or fathers; it was not women's right to access land in the same way it was men's right (Cheater 1986; Auret 1990). Within this patriarchal system, however, women were provided the wherewithal to fulfill their culturally prescribed roles, i.e., to provision their families and to exchange any surplus grown for other commodities needed by the family.

Agricultural tasks during the precontact period were delineated according to gender. Men were concerned periodically with land clearing, tree felling, and soil preparation, while women were ever occupied with planting, weeding, harvesting, shelling, and winnowing (Weinrich 1979:13; England 1982:58). As early as 1903, native commissioners in Mt. Darwin, Mutare, and Mtoko discerned that women were the tillers of the soil and that it was due to their efforts that family food consumption was ensured (England 1982:5).

Documentation from the 16th century indicates Shona-speaking cultivators traded with other Shona-speaking groups, with the Matebele, and with the Portuguese, who established trading *feiras,* at which both gold and crops were exchanged (Bhila 1982:74–75):

> The bazaars were operated on a weekly basis and it is not unlikely that where the African peasant producers took gold dust to the bazaar they also brought with them some agricultural produce. One can only guess that this must have stimulated production of surplus grain, meat and vegetables (Bhila 1982:253).

African women also figured in these exchanges:

> There was perhaps, as in the markets in West Africa, a segregation of merchants according to the products they sold and also according to sex; that is, some women traders probably sold different articles from those sold by men (Bhila 1982:77; see also Schmidt 1992:55).

Women, therefore, have a long history in agricultural commodity trade made possible by their own surplus production. It is these efforts that allowed African families to challenge the colonial hierarchy's belief that a hut tax payable in coin would force Africans to labor in white fields, mines, and industries.

▲ Land Alienation and the Labor Reserve Economy

The dream of building a Cape-to-Cairo railway linking all the British colonies in eastern and southern Africa motivated Cecil Rhodes, then governor of the Cape Colony in South Africa, to expand territorial domain. Intent on finding a second golden rand, in 1890 Rhodes and the British South Africa Company (BSAC) organized a group of men, the Pioneer Column, to undertake a mining expedition north of the Limpopo. As a result, the Union Jack was hoisted over the area known today as Harare on September 12, 1890 (Salisbury, Municipal Council 1932:1). Shona-speaking Africans living on and/or near the Kopje and Mt. Pleasant areas of Salisbury settlement came to the fort/town to market or barter their crops to whites (Tanser 1965:14–16; Riddell 1978a; Beach 1977:55; England 1982:24). Women figured prominently in this food trade and were described in Baines's diaries (an early settler): women would gather around the wagons with "eggs, corn, honey, mealie-meal more or less finely pounded, white, dull grey or pink in colour according to the quality of the corn" (Baines, quoted in Bhila 1982:208). This trade was critical to the survival of the pioneers because the BSAC, more often than not, failed to transport sufficient food staples to the fort and hunger was a common problem to the settlers in the early years.[3] African surplus production thus provided a buffer against white starvation (Tanser 1965:50).[4]

Policies favoring settler aggrandizement at the expense of Africans were implemented in Rhodesia very shortly after the arrival of the Pioneer Column. Although Africans claimed ownership via their ancestors to land, white settlers—ostensibly to protect Africans "from competition with Europeans on land" (Kay 1970:50)—created the first African reserves in 1892. It was anticipated that African labor would be obtained from these reserves to work at the mines from which the pioneers sought to extract great riches. An attempt was made to co-opt African labor by imposing a hut tax of 10 shillings payable in coin (Ordinance No. 5 of 1894) (Johnson 1968:79).[5] Instead of producing a labor force to serve the needs of white enterprises, however, the ordinance stimulated an increase in African agricultural production and trade.[6] African ability "to relate to the new economy as peasants rather than as workers" (Ranger 1985:25) frustrated settlers who were in need of African labor. "The sale of labor was attractive only when it increased the total real income, i.e., when it added more than it subtracted from the income achieved through agricultural production" (Jambwa and Simmons 1980:2).

To entice African labor, mining companies steadily increased wages between 1899 and 1902 (Phimister 1977:258–259; Arrighi 1973). The necessity for the rising supply price of labor was based on the ability of African peasants to generate incomes without selling their labor.

Thus, despite the imposition of regulations to reduce Africans to units of labor, the general response was to dodge them by increasing agricultural output for sale. Due to market demand, production was expanded to include a variety of crops that appealed to the European palate—potatoes, cabbage, cauliflowers, onions, cucumbers, beans, etc. (Native Commissioner, Umtali 1898).[7] African attempts to be provisioners rather than subservient to settlers, however, were relatively short-lived.

Unusual to the literature on traders and marketing is the interest taken in these enterprises by settlers. Those with little ability or desire to farm took advantage of the increased and expanded agricultural production by Africans: "Most 'farmers' were primarily transport riders, storekeepers or traders, who bought—and sometimes stole—food from their African neighbours" (Palmer 1977a:228). It was common for white traders to receive five times the amount they paid to African producers for grains and other produce (Phimister 1977:261). Though aware of being exploited by the traders, Africans grew even more to sell to reduce their risk of having to become wage labor (Ranger 1985:22–28). The traders' ploy, in response to increased African production, was to offer goods—not cash—in return for produce (Schmidt 1987:22).

Separating Africans from their means of production was a systematic policy of the Rhodesian government and its forerunner, the BSAC:

One of the main strategies pursued by the colonial administration was to embark on a deliberate policy of dispossessing Africans of their land, and also moving them to marginal and poor lands, culminating in the creation of Reserves. This was for two notable reasons: to force them into the labour market and more significantly to undermine their economic power and potential thus ensuring that they did not compete with the emerging white farmers (Shava 1986:6).

If white farmer goals were to be realized, African competition had to be stifled (Riddell 1978b:6). In 1925, as a result of the recommendations of the Morris Carter Commission, access to all land was divided along racial lines. Under the Land Apportionment Act of 1930, some 48 million acres were made available for the habitation of 250,000 non-Africans, while only 39 million acres were set aside as reserves for some 2.5 million Africans (Brown 1959:5). Africans were removed from their high potential arable lands and resettled on to much less productive reserves.

Between 1931 and 1941, long after the 1920 government reports indicated the reserves were full, some 50,000 more families were resettled; these were followed between 1945 and 1959 with another 85,000 families; and from 1964 to 1977, another 88,000 families (Riddell 1978b:8–9). Increasing the African population inhabiting the reserves by such inflated numbers translated into the sought after landless unemployed. Contrary to the popular perception that urban Africans maintained their ties to the land, by the late 1950s approximately 30 percent of the African population were landless, and by 1978 this had increased to almost 50 percent (Phimister 1988:9).

Africans lucky enough to gain usufruct rights over land had to transform their farming system from slash and burn to intensive. If farmers were able to harvest sufficiently to market a surplus, they were still saddled with a regulatory environment designed to stifle competition. The Maize Control Amendment Act of 1934 sought to finish off any competition in maize sales remaining. The *Report of Native Production and Trade* in 1944 found that white farmers were paid proportionately for their maize, i.e., the more individual farmers had to sell, the more per kilo they would receive, while Africans were paid at set prices less the trader's fee for the "identical product" (Johnson 1968:48). Moreover, farmers living in the reserves had to travel long distances to market their commodities. Their only other option was to barter with local traders who would not pay cash for deliveries. With one marketing opportunity effectively limited in staving off male labor migration, another was stimulated: that in fresh produce. Women's horticultural crop cultivating activities in nearby tribal trust lands expanded even more to meet an ever-growing urban market demand (Schmidt 1992:77–78).

Women's efforts to increase incomes through marketing garden surpluses notwithstanding, the Native Land Husbandry Act of 1951 was the final stroke to force Africans into becoming full-time labor. Ostensibly passed to provide for a reasonable standard of good husbandry and for the protection of natural resources in the reserves, the law effectively gave license to government to force the destocking of family herds (Pendered and von Memerty 1955:103–105). Harassed by these new promulgations that cut into their income generating abilities, farmers, especially males, sought livelihoods elsewhere. Once a farmer became an urban laborer, however, the act provided that such a worker could not own land, that is, no split vocations: *either* the farm, *or* the job. In effect, the act created an urban landless proletariat (Bush and Cliffe 1982:2; Rifkind 1968:97).

Africans maintained a toehold in the rural areas through kinship linkages while, at the same time, government found it too difficult to enforce the provisions of the 1951 act. It was so problematic to implement that it was ultimately abandoned in 1962 (Weinrich 1975:29).

The effects of these agricultural and labor policies on women's rural economic roles were significant. The combination of land alienation and male labor migration meant that many women were left behind in the tribal trust lands to cultivate patches of land that were decreasingly fertile. Where labor was sufficient, an attempt was made to expand grain crop production for the market. This expansion took place at the expense of women's food crop production: "The introduction of cash crops and general land shortage in the peasant sector contributed to the disappearance in many areas and reduction in a few others of the women-designated pieces of land and their crops" (Zimbabwe, Ministry of Community Development and Women's Affairs 1982:5).

The onerous nature of cultivation, the low economic returns to their labor, the limited cash remittances they received from their salaried husbands, plus the difficulties of managing a geographically split household precipitated women's movement into cities. The difficulties in fulfilling their economic roles as food provisioners women encountered in the cities, however, were as cumbersome as those in the rural areas.

▲ Migration, Urbanization, and Housing

As a consequence of the need for African labor in Harare, the Municipal and Town Management Ordinance was passed in 1894 to empower local authorities to set aside land for African occupation (Gargett 1977). The Registration of Natives Act of 1896, however, sought to curtail movement in the municipalities in order that "malingering" would not become a problem (Mitchell 1969:162).

By 1899 the first African township—Harari—was created for African workers (Christopher 1977:18).[8] The township was situated some four kilometers from the then town center and was composed of some 50 huts and a brick barracks said to be suitable to house 328 Africans in dormitories (Patel and Adams 1981:5; Barnes and Win 1992). While legislation requiring passes and/or registration certificates largely curtailed male movement,[9] females were not as stringently controlled:

> In Salisbury municipal authorities only minimally enforced legislation that was passed to help African women out of town, and this was coupled with a persistent refusal on the part of the colonial state to require African women to carry the registration certificates with which African men were burdened (Barnes 1987:10–11).[10]

In the 1950s, legislation was passed making it necessary for wives to carry certificates indicating their spouse's workplace and residence. This was also not enforced: "In no single area were the provisions relating to an 'approved wife' being enforced strictly, if at all" (Southern Rhodesia 1958:112). Since urban influx and registration ordinances were not enforced against African women, those who grew foodstuffs in the nearby reserves were able to come to Harare to sell their surplus harvests.

The demand for permanent male labor in town entailed a demand for family housing; without one, the other was not possible, and vice versa: "We have had ample evidence to show that many more families would in fact come into Salisbury if accommodation was available for them and thus the existing structure of the population is conditioned by the type of accommodation available" (Southern Rhodesia 1958:18).

The Legislative Assembly debated the need for more African housing in 1935 on the basis that "the native is a visitor in our white towns for the purpose of assisting the people who live in towns and that no other natives should be present in the towns unless he is of some assistance to the white people inhabiting them" (Southern Rhodesia, Legislative Assembly *Debates* 1935: cols. 583–584).[11]

The combination of low wages and lack of family housing, as well as a prejudicial gender orientation designed to keep women in the rural areas,[12] effectively prevented large-scale migration of females to Harare. However, the overriding demand for long-term, stabilized African labor made necessary the presence of African families. The passage of the African (Urban Areas) Accommodation and Registration Act (No. 6) of 1946 attested, finally, to the official recognition of this fact. The act compelled local authorities to (1) set aside lands for urban "native areas," as provided in the 1930 Land Apportionment Act; (2) provide adequate housing for all Africans in urban areas; and (3) equalize rental payments made by employers regardless of whether housing was for married or single employees (Cormack 1983:79).

Prior to the 1946 act only two townships were available for African habitation: Harari (Mbari), established in 1899; and Highfield, established in 1934. It was not until 1952, a full six years after the 1946 act was passed, that Mabvuku was established, some 17 kilometers from the city center—and jobs (Moller 1978:83–84). In this township, Africans, for the first time in an urban area, could acquire freehold title to land in the city (Moller 1978; Barber 1967:101).[13] What did not occur, however, were significant salary increases to reflect the financial needs of an urban family.

Although habitation for Africans continued to expand over the succeeding decades,[14] the only acknowledgment that employment opportunities were not keeping pace with increased urban migration was the opening in 1961 of all African township centers to African trading (Rifkind 1968). This led to the establishment of African-owned grocery stores, clothing stores, and the like. African shop proprietorship rose proportionately with demand, but continued to be limited by the policy climate of the city, whose leaders informally still sought to curtail permanent African habitation.

With independence in 1980, all restrictions on African movement into the city were removed, with the resultant "Explosion in the Cities." The capital had an enormous inherited housing backlog: "It was deliberate past policy to encourage lodging rather than build more homes—the new freedom of families to join their menfolk working in the city, and the number of people too poor to afford even the cheapest rents, the growth of squatting must follow" ("Explosion in the Cities," *Moto,* Sept. 1982:6).

Rising unemployment, in combination with salary levels that did not meet urban household budgets, precipitated further creation of small scale enterprises on the part of both men and women.

▲ Formal and Informal Sector Fresh Produce Marketing Systems

The fresh produce provisioning system was shared in the early settler years between African female farmers and white traders. The development of a dual, color-based provisioning system into a formal and informal sector has its origins in 1893 when the Market Hall was constructed in Salisbury to provide a permanent, central location at which agricultural commodities could be traded (Howland 1963:40). Africans appear not to have been allowed to trade in this formal market, perhaps because their earnings would have prevented them from becoming labor in white enterprises. The following quote might support such an argument:

> In the early years, the market was well supported by growers and buyers. It was a weekly event to look forward to. The drawback, however, was

that everything was sold by auction and larger buyers, such as hotels and retailers, monopolised the proceedings, and it was very difficult for the ordinary person to obtain his small requirements. The small customer, therefore, transferred his custom to hawkers who had gardens outside the municipal boundary. Hawkers became more numerous, and by about 1918 no further supplies of vegetables were brought to the Market Hall and sales came to an end (Howland 1963:40).

Hawkers—informal market entrepreneurs—were largely African women, while the structured market, conducted inside the Market Hall, was composed largely of white producers and traders.

Subsequent to the close of the Market Hall, white traders sought to control the provisioning of white inhabitants (see Christopher 1977; Smith n.d.). Those taking greatest interest were Greeks who had migrated into the area via Egypt, Mozambique, Tanzania, and South Africa (Kosmin 1974:69). Many settlers of Greek origin did not have a very high regard for farming and manual work, both of which were associated with low-level peasant status in their homelands.[15] It is this nonfarming, nonmining population who became the traders, and later, wholesalers, of fresh produce and other commodities (Kosmin 1974:109).

Formal retail trade in foodstuffs officially began in 1936 when 26 ethnic Greeks were granted bakery licenses in Harare. Bakeries were transformed into general provisioning dealerships and, subsequently, greengrocers that sold top grades of fresh produce at premium prices to white customers (Kosmin 1974:108). Produce distribution in the informal market was shared between Greek hawkers and African women who came from nearby reserves to sell their surpluses. Growing such commodities as peas, cabbage, beetroot, and green, leafy vegetables, African women developed retail trade with both Africans in Harari and Highfield Townships and with white families living in the more northern parts of Salisbury. By 1927 women were regularly found hawking in Salisbury Commons (Barnes 1987:33).

By 1930, an African spokesman registered his concern at the lengths African women were going to sell produce. He requested that "native" markets be established officially "so girls don't have to wander around hawking" (Barnes 1987:33). During the 1930s, especially, a marked increase in the number of women selling fresh produce was observed throughout the city (England 1982:55).[16] As more women settled in town, the economic niche first established by the women farmers was expanded. At first, to provision their families, women began cultivating rice and maize on the open plain between Harari and Highfield, and vegetables (e.g., tomatoes, cabbage, and peas) along the Mukuvisi River (Barnes and Win 1992:108). Thereafter, women in town created supply linkages with the women farmers: they ordered certain commodities from the farm women when they came to town, and then resold what they had ordered throughout the townships. Opportunities for selling were not limited to townships: more courageous women would go to the homes of white families and sell their commodities door to door. Although harassed by police from time to time, the profit women could make was sufficient to motivate them to take the risk (Barnes and Win 1992:111).

The Native Land Board in 1931, reversing policy against issuing trading licenses to Africans, argued that they should receive preferential consideration to trade within the African townships and tribal trust lands (Holleman 1969:143; Wild 1992:32–33). It was not until 1942, however, that market stalls for women vendors were established in the township of Highfield (Kosmin 1974:260).

As more townships were created at a greater distance from Harari, a demand arose for the sale of foodstuffs in each township neighborhood. Female vendor ability to meet these needs became problematic: distances to be travelled to order from a centrally-designated location were too great, and distances to be covered on foot by producers were also great. Regulations curtailing male movement in the towns notwithstanding, it was most likely during this period that African men with access to transport became wholesalers. The *Native Trade and Production Report* of 1944 supports this contention: African farmers sold their crops to African middlemen who in turn resold them to female vendors.[17] The locus of wholesale transactions at first was Highfield but then moved to Mbari. Eventually, African wholesalers were joined by white growers who also had an interest in centralizing operations.

Greek traders who established exchange linkages with their fresh produce growing kinfolk in South Africa expanded their efforts after the collapse of the market hall. The firm of Maltas and Divaris, Ltd., was a very active importer of fruits from South Africa in the decades prior to UDI (Salisbury Municipal Council 1932).[18] After UDI in 1965, however, sanctions effectively stopped this trade, and Greek marketeers were instrumental in developing further the local production of these once-imported commodities. Fresh produce importing companies were transformed into the distribution link between local production and local consumption.

Today ethnic Greeks maintain their wholesaling and retailing businesses under general dealership licenses that allow them to trade throughout the country and to gain access to hard currency to import commodities for resale.[19] Wholesalers, who either purchase their commodities outright from farmers or, as agencies, act on behalf of farmers in importing, exporting, or internally distributing their crops, are subject to government income taxes. In contrast, African wholesalers and retailers who sell from Mbare Musika or other market sites throughout the city are not subject to taxation and thus do not fall under the purview of national statistics. They also cannot own import/export licenses that would allow them access to hard currency.

Their nonexistence to any officially recorded government documentation is the factor that characterizes these enterprises as informal.

▲ Women's Retail Vending Niche

While it can be argued that women have been selling/trading fresh produce in Harare since the arrival of the Pioneer Column in 1890, the increasing number of vendors has presented problems at various times. For instance, once family housing was made available to Africans in the 1960s, women found the sales they conducted in their neighborhoods were limited because too many other women were doing the same thing. Despite earlier freedom of movement, by the 1960s if the women vendors crossed the railway line into the city center or the northern white suburbs to sell, they were fined (see *Herald,* January 14, 1964).

From the mid-1970s on, the population of Africans in Harare grew considerably as a consequence of the liberation struggle being waged in the rural areas. By 1977, the police were unable to deal with the number of informal sector activities that had been established in the city (see *Herald,* May 13, 1977; see also Wild 1992:43). Pressure to find suitable outlets for the overwhelming numbers of these spontaneously-established businesses resulted in the designation of 10 sites at which informal trading could take place (see *Herald,* June 20, 1978). City councillors who sought to provide a voice for Africans argued that these sites were too far from pedestrian thoroughfares, and pointed out that regardless of whether spaces had been designated, Africans would sell where customers were. As one alderman argued, "Do you really think that you are going to direct these Africans to go to these out-of-the-way sites?" (*Herald,* June 24, 1978). An editorial four days later reported the following: "To set aside only 10 sites for the whole of Salisbury is quite inadequate and when people are struggling to make a living it seems pointless to introduce new laws which, if they *could* be enforced, would restrict their activities" (*Herald,* June 28, 1977). These 10 sites were to be distributed among vegetable vendors, women who make and sell crochet items, and men who sell fresh flowers.

To avoid conflict over designated selling sites, as new townships were planned, market sites were included. Moreover, in 1981, Eddison Zvogbo, then minister of home affairs, advocated the construction of "people's markets" in preexisting townships. Later in the same year the Harare City Council elicited suggestions for the location of 25 new market stalls in the high density suburbs to meet the demand of some 1,300 women. At that time, there were 2,300 stalls at 28 markets throughout the city, but there were an additional 1,300 women selling at 40 other streetside sites without the approval of the council.

Throughout the period from 1977 to the present, many incidents of police intervention into vending were reported. To protect themselves from police harassment, in 1982 many women were enticed into joining the Fruit and Vegetable Vendors' Co-operative by a certain "Mr. M," who guaranteed he would personally stop the harassment. Newspaper articles highlighted Mr. M's attempts to negotiate with police and city officials to allow the women to sell their produce. Mr. M also spoke with vendors about conforming with municipal sanitary regulations. Vendors paid a joining fee of Z$10, plus a monthly fee to maintain their membership. In 1984, however, when the harassment didn't stop, and membership records mysteriously disappeared, as did membership fees, the cooperative disintegrated.

In August 1982 an attempt was made by the municipality to take a census of all vendors. At Mbare, 1,035 were identified; and 1,344 were counted at 26 markets located in Dzivarisekwa (1), Glen Norah (5), Glen View (2), Mbare (2), Kambuzuma (3), Mabvuku (5), Highfield (7), and Warren Park (1) (*Herald,* August 20, 1982). With pressures for more stalls continuing to mount, by the time I conducted my research in 1985–1986, I found 110 market and table vending sites throughout the high density suburbs, with 1,209 vendors at Mbare, 1,695 in other high density suburbs, and 479 in the low density suburbs.

▲ Droughts and Structural Adjustment

The outset of the 1990s brought many changes to the Zimbabwean economy. One of the worst droughts in memorable history destroyed potential harvests, and food commodities were in short supply throughout the country. Structural adjustment measures were implemented to stimulate a more export-oriented economy. Both of these events precipitated broad-reaching changes felt hardest by women and other vulnerable groups.

In the absence of urban kin to provide them accommodation, many drought-induced migrants to Harare became squatters who were periodically chased by police and moved out of the city to rural locations (see Bourdillon 1991). While in Harare, squatters tried to earn an income in any way possible, e.g., buying and reselling old newspapers to vendors to use as wrapping paper, growing vegetables at squatter settlements, selling used clothing, "protecting" cars downtown, and selling fruits and vegetables at bus stations. If situated in a prime selling location, squatters could meet their cash needs through vending.

The sheer numbers of street vendors throughout the city—in low and high density suburbs as well as downtown—induced a change in accessibility to wholesale markets. Whereas prior to the 1990s vendors could access both formal and informal wholesale markets, during the early years of this decade formal establishments catered only to those retailers with licenses.

This means that legitimate, long-term women vendors can now buy their stock only at Mbare Musika. If farmers do not sell their commodities at Mbare, then women cannot access these items. In times of scarcity, such as the drought and the annual rainy season, women are not able to offer the range of commodities they had in the past. Ultimately, this means a reduction in profits.

ESAP was fully implemented in 1990 ostensibly to alleviate an economic crisis brought about by a shortage of foreign exchange, growing unemployment, low levels of investment, high levels of inflation, escalating debt, and infrastructural decay (Kadenge 1992:1). However, the goals of this International Monetary Fund (IMF)/World Bank plan were to restructure "the economies of indebted Third World countries into export economies so that they may pay off the debt" (Balleis 1993:37). Intent on decreasing external debt, the reform package included three key areas of adjustment: (1) fiscal and monetary policies, (2) trade liberalization to move from a foreign exchange allocation system to a market based system, and (3) deregulation (Zimbabwe 1991a:4–15).

The effective result of the imposition of ESAP has been to impoverish Zimbabweans by reducing their incomes and increasing the cost of basic necessities:

> Inflation, the increase in the cost of living, the fall of "real wages," and increased unemployment through retrenchment are making the majority of people in Zimbabwe poorer. . . . In 1991, the real value of minimum wages decreased in all sectors in relationship to minimum wages in 1980 (for domestic workers by 14.8 per cent, in agriculture by 9.1 per cent, in manufacturing by 24.3 per cent and in mining by 10.1 per cent). An even sharper decline occurred from '91 to '92. In manufacturing the minimum wage was 36.9 per cent less in 1992 than it was in '80. In mining it was 26.6 per cent less. . . . In October 1992, the Consumer Council of Zimbabwe set the value of a basic food basket for an urban household of four (2 adults and 2 children) at Z\$380 a month, more than double the de facto minimum wage of Z\$161 for domestic workers (Balleis 1993:25–26).

The overall effect of ESAP on the informal economy, women and vendors, in particular, has been and will continue to be severe: "As a result of ESAP, business in the informal sector was no longer viable as prices of essential commodities had gone up" (*Business Herald,* July 22, 1993). On the basis of women's economic roles in the urban environment, several consequences have already been measured: (1) family provisioning has been made more difficult owing to the increased cost of the basic food basket; (2) educating the next generation and maintaining one's health have become more costly owing to cost recovery programs; (3) generating an income through formal employment has been made more difficult owing to retrenchment and mechanization of industry; and (4) generating an income through informal sector activities has been made more difficult through increased competition prompted by the relaxation of regulations preventing ad hoc development of enterprises (see Brand et al. 1992, and Kanji and Jazdowska 1993 for a detailed analysis of these and related points).

Specific effects of ESAP on women fresh produce vendors in Harare were related to me in interviews: (1) currency devaluation has increased the wholesale cost of commodities at Mbare Musika, thus necessitating an increase in retail prices; (2) relaxation of hawking and vending restrictions has given rise to the development of markets everywhere by both men and women in order to generate cash income for survival; (3) increased costs in stall rental and transport have decreased profit margins or necessitated further price increases, thus sending customers to the street vendors since they pay no rent and hence can charge less; (4) many stall vendors have gone out of business owing to high costs and low profits; and (5) vendor health is deteriorating owing to extremely stressful economic conditions and the need to pay for health care.

At one high density suburb stall site, out of 40 vendors interviewed in 1985–1986, 15 had remained, 8 had passed away, and 17 had quit business or went outside on the street to sell where greater profits could be obtained. All had increased their base prices, and only one newcomer had the broad range of commodities for sale in evidence during my earlier research.

▲ Conclusion

I have discussed how the many historical aspects of agricultural and urban development shaped the parameters of fresh produce marketing in Harare, and how African women, in particular, came to occupy their retail niches. In summary, operating in a cultural system based in patriarchy, women were deeply affected by the development of the labor reserve economy imposed by white settler colonialists. Owing to the provisioning demands created by this system, and the misperception of African women's economic roles by settler males, women were able to establish and expand an urban economic niche they maintain today.

While women have steadily sought other means of earning an income, salaried jobs in the formal economy of Harare were not generally open to unskilled and uneducated females. The reasons included: (1) men, not women, were perceived by white employers as the breadwinners of their families (Muchena 1982; England 1982); (2) women still in the childbearing years were considered high risks since pregnancy prompted dismissal; and (3) medical examinations required for domestic work acted as a disincentive to many women to seek such employment.

As a result of formal employment not being an option for women,[20] many sought to generate an income in the informal sector:

Women workers regard informal sector trading as a substitute for unobtainable wage employment, or see it as more compatible with household responsibilities, as it may largely be carried out in or near the home, or the children may accompany the mother to the trading place. It is often seen as an extension of domestic work and the accepted sex-role, the using of normal "women's work" to exploit the urban situation (May 1979:48).

What many women traded was premised on what they knew best: fresh produce. Beset with financial problems in the city brought about by the policies of the labor reserve economy, and, in more recent history, ESAP, women were faced with a dual economic problem: how to generate an income and how to provision their families. For many, selling fresh produce helped resolve this problem.

▲ Notes

1. Most recently, Women's Affairs was incorporated by the political party, ZANU PF.

2. *Mawoko* property included anything a woman acquired via craft production, acting as a midwife, or in her activities as a *nganga* (traditional healer/herbalist) or a spirit medium (see May 1983:65).

3. Parsons argues this was due mainly to problems with rinderpest and other cattle diseases in Botswana that prevented wagon trains moving north: "'hundreds' of wagons were abandoned with oxen rotting in their yokes—the value of goods abandoned between Mafeking and Phalapye (a distance less than 400 km) was estimated at £25,000 in April 1896" (Parsons 1977:126).

4. Much like early United States history in which Native Americans provisioned the colonials and helped provide the meat and crops for the first Thanksgiving, so too did Africans assist in the first festival in Zimbabwe held on St. Patrick's Day, March 17, 1891. "The menu included Mashona fowls, roan antelope and sable cutlets, pumpkins, sweet potatoes, green mealies and Mashona rice" (Tanser 1965:33).

5. The continued attempts to induce African labor via taxation led to subsequent increases in levies. In 1904 the tax was expanded to include all males over 18, and every additional wife over the first. Amounts demanded were also increased from ten shillings to one pound each (Johnson 1968:79).

6. It is highly likely, because women constituted the bulk of agricultural labor, that their burdens increased to meet the demands of the market (Schmidt 1987).

7. African farmers did not grow these crops solely to trade with the colonials; by 1921 these same crops were being consumed by Africans (Ranger 1985:37).

8. The urban location was so named after a Shona-speaking chief—Mharawa—who had once occupied the area, but who was, just subsequent to the arrival of the Pioneer Column, forced to leave as the result of a battle waged with another chief, Gutsa (Tanser 1965:14–16).

9. See especially Ordinance 16 of 1901, the 1901 and 1913 Registration and Pass ordinances, and the 1906 Native Urban Locations Ordinance (No. 4) (Devittie 1974; Gargett 1977).

10. A similar situation prevailed in South Africa shortly after formation of the Union in 1910. Although passes were required of women in the Orange Free State for a brief period, their defiance led to the law's subsequent repeal. A governmental committee to investigate the pass laws delineated the reasons why passes were not required of women: harassment, interference, and control to which police subjected women (Wells 1982).

11. Beliefs held by many white settlers in Rhodesia followed those of their counterparts in South Africa. For instance, the Stallard Commission of 1921, reported in the 1921 Transvaal Commissioner's Report, declared that Africans should only enter the white urban domain to satisfy their needs, and then depart.

12. For a detailed discussion of the collusion between rural African male elders and white settlers concerning rural controls exerted on women, see Schmidt 1992:98–121.

13. The date for urban freehold is disputed in the literature (see Kay 1970).

14. Rugare, 7 kilometers from the city, was developed by the railroad in the mid-1950s for its African employees; Mufakose was settled in 1959 some 14 kilometers from the city; Dzivarisekwa township was established in 1961 some 13 kilometers from the city; Kambuzuma was opened in 1964, 9 kilometers from town; and Tafara was constructed as a township of the Greendale council some 18 kilometers from the city in 1967 (see Kay and Smout 1977).

All told, during the 1960s some 16,462 new housing units for Africans were added to the already existing 18,217 units, plus 51 hostels (with an addition of 2,846 at St. Mary's, a township incorporated only in the 1992 census as part of Greater Harare), for a total of 37,525 dwelling units and 51 hostels available for an African population in 1969 of about 280,000 (Moller 1978:83–85). On a per housing basis, each dwelling unit, composed largely of one or two rooms, housed 7.5 Africans (slightly less when the hostel population is deducted from the total).

Census results and population estimates for the 1961–1962 and 1969 surveys have been challenged on the basis that data were collected "during the harvesting period when it is known that a significant number of Africans return to the tribal areas to help with the harvest" (Rhodesia, Ministry of Finance 1979). The population of Highfield is cited as an example. In 1969, 52,560 Africans were enumerated and 7,424 dwelling units were counted. Because the African population was under-reported, an unofficial estimate of the real population of the township was 72,280 (Stopforth 1977). This would bring the housing density for Highfield Township to 9.7 individuals per dwelling unit.

In 1971 Glen Norah was established 12 kilometers from the city, providing 6,444 more housing units; subsequently, Glen View was established in 1979. Warren Park opened in 1981, Kuwadzana in 1984, Hatcliffe in 1984, and Budiriro in 1988 (Zinyama 1993:23).

15. The exception to this dislike of farming was in tobacco growing. Greeks excelled in the cultivation of this crop, which is still today one of the most profitable crops earning foreign exchange in the country.

16. It appears the flight of so many women to town was objectionable to traditional leaders in the rural areas. The "chiefs wanted a pass system for women introduced to restrict the number of women who 'escaped' by taking trains" (England 1982:53).

17. While I am unable to provide an analysis of when and how African men developed the wholesale trade in fresh produce, I might speculate that this occurred as more African men became unemployed, as the population in the townships grew, and as the source of African-demanded fresh produce became more distant owing to land alienation by white farmers. African male fear of what might happen to their

women while travelling far distances and while remaining in the cities overnight in order to sell their surpluses might have guided males into assuming the wholesaler role. Others might argue that males perceived a means by which they could generate an income from the surpluses their wives produced, thereby usurping the female income-generating role. A further argument might be the mobility of males in being able to leave the rural homestead for longer periods than, say, a woman who had responsibility for small children. Also, male knowledge of the city might have made them more perceptive in trading at the wholesale level, since male information networks were more constant owing to the pattern of employment in cities biased in favor of males. Women, at the early stages, moved in and out of the cities; they were not necessarily permanent city dwellers able to develop strong communication and support networks that would provide certain economic information to them. Men, on the other hand, while at first oscillating migrants, became permanently ensconced in the city and could develop ties on the basis of work or residence.

A very different argument might entail identifying who the producers were. Where consistent wholesale supply necessitated making an agreement with a white producer, husbands of vendors might not have consented to an African female negotiating with a white male producer. These agreements could be entered into between African male wholesalers and white male producers with little or no hidden agendas.

18. The Babliokos brothers, whose parents came to Zimbabwe via Mozambique at the turn of the century, were involved in the produce trade beginning in 1953. At that time they established Wholesale Fruiterers, an outright purchase wholesaling business, and imported many fresh produce commodities from their kin in South Africa. In 1970, they established the Independent Market as an agency acting on behalf of producers.

19. Four out of six of the wholesaling enterprises are either owned or managed by ethnic Greeks, while the greengrocers and small grocery shops throughout the low density suburbs are owned almost exclusively by members of this ethnic community.

20. Even where formal sector employment was open to women, they consistently received lower wages for the same work performed by men (England 1982:115).

▲ 3

The Informal Economy, Microenterprises, Women, and Business

Women's trading enterprises in Africa are not generally viewed as commodity-linked to appropriate economic subsectors. Neither are these enterprises viewed as economically significant, mainly because they are located in the informal sector. This triple invisibility, based in the commodities traded, the locus of trade in the informal economy, and the gender of the trader, are all biases inherent in economic research in developing countries. It is important, then, that we rigorously examine these biases and deconstruct some of the myths about women's economic activities. With a more accurate perception of women's contributions and the actions they undertake to attain the ideal of development—self-sufficiency—we may be able to reorient socioeconomic theory to reflect the primacy of a range of women's economic behaviors. I begin this deconstruction with an analysis of the locus of their activity: the informal sector.

▲ The Informal Economy

Since its conceptualization by the International Labour Organisation (ILO) on the basis of research in Kenya (1972) and Hart's research in Ghana (1973), the "informal sector" has incorporated those economic activities not a part of the "modern" sector, i.e., that "in which production and distribution units could be characterized in terms of Western modes of production, organization and management" (United Nations 1989:215):

> Since most of the developing countries considered development to be synonymous with the promotion of the "modern" sector, in which production and distribution units could be characterized in terms of Western modes of production, organization and management, the so-called informal sector, consisting of small-scale units using indigenous modes of organization and technology, was given little or no attention at all (United Nations 1989:214–215).

33

Details of the theoretical formal/informal economy split have been identified by McGee (1973) (adapting the characterization of the urban economy generated by Santos 1972), who explains what he terms the "two-circuit" urban economy (summarized in Table 3.1) (see also Sethuraman 1981; Portes 1983). In addition, the formal sector is characterized largely as protected by legalized barriers to entry, relying upon both indigenous and imported resources, oligopolistic or monopolistic, and subject to taxation (ILO 1972; Moser 1978; and Peattie 1980). In contrast, the informal sector consists of "small-scale units using indigenous modes of organization and technology" (United Nations 1989:215). Economists labelled the informal sector as a "residual" of capitalist development (Sethuraman 1976), and characterized it by ease of entry, self or family ownership, reliance on indigenous resources, a high degree of competition, and a laissez faire attitude on the part of government. Incomes generated are normally compared to the lowest obtainable salaries for unskilled workers in the formal sector (Davies 1974).

Table 3.1 Characteristics of Informal/Formal or Two-Circuit Economies

Characteristics	Formal/Upper Circuit	Informal/Lower Circuit
Scale	Large	Small
Organization	Bureaucratic	Family organized
Technology	Capital intensive	Labor intensive
Capital	Abundant	Scarce
Training	Formal education	On-the-job or informal
Earnings	High	Limited
Inventories	Large	Small
Government	Regulation	No regulation
Financial resources	Banks	Personal
Hours of work	Regular	Irregular
Pricing	Fixed	Variable
Reporting	In government statistics	Not reported

Source: Adapted from McGee (1973), Sethuraman (1981), and Portes (1983).

These structural characteristics defining the informal sector set parameters for investigating its participants. In Latin America "women, rural migrants, the young and the old" were identified as preponderant (Roberts 1990:25). Reasons are very clear. Structural imbalances in the economy have not kept apace of employment demand (Tinker 1981:54), resulting in the necessity for those who have not received adequate or appropriate education, those who are discriminated against, and those who have not yet established urban networks to gain knowledge of employment opportunities, to establish their own means of generating an income (Roberts 1990:23–24). Comparable studies in Africa and Asia have yielded similar results.[1]

In Zimbabwe, the most significant factor differentiating the two sectors is that the formal is government regulated via registration, licensing, and the imposition of taxes, while the informal is not. Most other characteristics are variable. For instance, one formal fresh produce wholesaling enterprise is run by a family that utilizes its members as workers, calls upon family members for loans, varies prices in accordance with the relationship of the family with the customer, does not require formal educational qualifications to conduct business, and works irregular hours.

If this classification system is applied to the Zimbabwe data, then formal sector enterprise characteristics include government registration, dealers' licenses to trade and/or export, taxes on recorded profits, and subjection to government pricing regulations. Marketing enterprises classified as informal are subject to minimal government intervention (in the form of stall or table rent paid to the municipality), have no licenses to trade, pay no taxes (incomes are not recorded) and do not fall under the purview of government pricing regulations. The enterprises in this sector are not officially acknowledged in government documentation and not included in national income statistics. Moreover, there is no government protection from market abuse, no security of tenure, and no means of ensuring an income (Davies 1979).

Incomes generated in the informal sector have not been captured by many national bureaus of statistics, which often do not consider the category "self-employed." Zimbabwe census takers in 1982 did identify such a category of employment for enumeration—paid or self-employed—but data collection was fraught with difficulties:

> The designation "informal sector" is based essentially on the legal status of the activity. All enterprises in Zimbabwe must be registered (by a prescribed statutory authority) or licensed (by a government authority). The distinction between formal and informal hinges, therefore, on whether the respondent to the Labour Force Survey is employed in a registered or licensed enterprise or an activity outside these categories. However, a complication arises with licensing, since many informal sector activities—hawkers, tuck-shops, for example—require a license to operate (Saito 1990:2).

Neglect and oversight in data collection most critically affects our understanding of women's urban economic activities. Why women comprise the majority of microentrepreneurs is the result of a combination of patriarchal cultural norms, disadvantageous laws that do not take women's productive roles into account, historical biases of westerners, and a complete misunderstanding by the state of women's economic needs, including those of education. Women's marginal presence in the considerations of the state translates into performance of their economic activities in the equally marginal area of the informal economy, where they structurally cannot gain access to inputs for growth and development.

This is the critical reason why I have included a discussion on the informal sector in this writing. Because researchers have dichotomized the economy, because governments collect data on the basis of this differentiation, and because national planners and donor agencies are biased by these analyses, the informal sector and women's entrepreneurship have not been accorded adequate recognition. To relegate these microenterprises to a category of "residual in capitalist development" is to disregard the meaning of the self-sufficiency model of development—for both women and men (see Smith 1990:1–22 for a similar argument).

A more appropriate and incorporating definition of this sector is found in Portes and Sassen-Koob (1987:31): "the sum total of all income-generating activities with the exclusion of those that involve contractual and legally regulated employment." Such a definition does not rest on government-generated strategies for development and incorporates individual efforts to become self-sufficient. This definition at least allows scope for us to consider both gender and agency in the development of microenterprises.[2]

Using this definition, the breadth of the informal/microenterprise sector in Zimbabwe in 1991 was estimated at one quarter of the adult population, or 1.6 million (including proprietors and workers) with 67 percent run by women (McPherson 1991:iv and 7).

▲ Marketing Perishables and Urban Food Security

How food commodities are channelled from rural producers to urban consumers has generally fallen under the research purview of agricultural economists. Their primary focus, however, has been on grain staples (with the notable exception of Harrison et al. 1974). Analyses have considered the structure, conduct, and performance of the market, government policy, pricing, supply and demand, transport, competitive conditions, and the political desire on the part of government to "capture" the peasantry. Social scientists and historians have considered social and political organization facilitating or impeding urban food distribution, as well as urban effective demand in the context of welfare needs (see Guyer 1987:8–19).

I can see primacy in no one variable among those previously explored in analyzing urban accessibility to foodstuffs. Under the conceptual umbrella of food security, defined as "access by all people at all times to sufficient food for a healthy and productive life" (Saito 1991:1), both production and distribution processes are taken into account. What is glaringly absent from food security research, however, is a consideration of nongrain foodstuffs and the markets people themselves—as opposed to government—have developed to distribute food. Redefining urban food security to include perishables, production, and access cannot be facilitated without the presence of markets which, in turn, in the Zimbabwe case, relies upon the individual and collective action of women vendors.

Analysis of this final retailing node in the distribution of perishable commodities has generally been limited to more formal, wholesale outlets. Informal markets, the locus of a very large percentage of this trade in Africa, have not been so analyzed mainly due to the unwieldy nature of data collection. Additionally, women's roles in food distribution are often overlooked because of a gender bias of many food security researchers. This means that vendor efforts have not been analyzed for their economic significance in linking rural producers to urban consumers and to urban food security.

Women vendors have had and continue to have an impact on rural-urban food distribution systems throughout the developing world. For instance, in her discussion of women vegetable vendors and male and female farmers coming to town to sell their surpluses, Jules-Rosette asserts that in Zambia, "the Zambian marketeers who come to town to sell vegetables linked the rural and urban economies and represented a point of interaction between the formal and subsistence sectors" (Jules-Rosette 1981:93). The rural-urban system in Zimbabwe links rural subsistence and commercial producers (both African and white), transporters, urban African and white wholesalers, formal greengrocer retailers, and informal fresh produce vendors in bifurcated production and marketing channels. The marketing activities of urban vendors, therefore, provide direct financial returns to horticultural production.

As direct purchase marketeers, women redistribute commodities to consumers throughout the city. White wholesalers and retailers serve a similar function. On a retail level, however, African women sell to a significantly larger population and thus distribute greater quantities than do white retailers.

The microenterprises African women have established are integral to the national food distribution system. Because they are located in the informal sector, however, they have not been analyzed as contributing to development: "A significant part of women's actual economic contributions goes unrecorded in national statistics and it is on the basis of these statistics that development plans are devised" (Gill 1984:9). Market women's activities must be analyzed economically for their contributions to urban food security and the further development of horticultural crop production. From a marketing standpoint, they should be analyzed as the end transactors in a production-marketing chain within the agricultural subsector. I believe these types of analyses—more appropriately integrated in economic subsectors than in informal economy research—will enrich national statistics and broaden the range of development initiatives available to be explored.

The vendors in Harare view their roles as provisioners to the wider community. Because of this view, and because women see themselves as business operators, they conduct their trade in characteristic fashion: vendors maintain a pricing and availability intelligence system so they can replenish stocks and meet customer demand; they sell commodities at prices underpaid African urban dwellers can afford; they absorb the costs of doing business, e.g., transportation, rent; they endure very long workdays; and they withstand harassment by police and wholesalers (see Horn 1991a).

Supermarkets and shops in the high density African suburbs of Harare do not sell fresh produce because, as one supermarket owner commented, "these women have to be given a chance." Supermarkets and greengrocers in the low density suburbs do carry perishables, but prices are generally higher and often stocks do not appear very fresh. White clientele normally frequent these shops, while Africans who have recently moved into these areas often buy what they need from the vendors (normally situated adjacent to or, in the case of hawkers, within a shopping center).

The system for marketing perishables is not the deliberate construction of the state for its own benefit (as was grain marketing); it is the result of a tradition of individual producers and marketers creating opportunities for themselves to stave off oppression. The most recent policies of the World Bank and IMF implemented in developing countries promote privatization as a cornerstone to structural adjustment. The case of fresh produce marketing in Zimbabwe stands as a model for the implementation of these policies. What is lacking, however, is a clear understanding of how this model is based in individual innovation and the desire of individuals to be self-sufficient. This writing should provide a significant portion of that needed insight.

▲ Women, Work, Self-Sufficiency, and Development

As an economy develops, it is presumed, all members of society should be able to enhance their quality of life. Concepts guiding women in development (WID) analysis, however, reveal that women's activities are often overlooked in formulating national development plans and in designing development projects (see, especially, Safilos-Rothschild 1985; Moran 1988). Conceptually, two approaches have been used in analyzing WID efforts: the reformist and the redistributive. The former "affirms that established institutions, although currently not working in the best interests of women, can be modified to do so"; the latter "believes that women are disadvantaged not by 'malfunctions' in the system but by the structural features of the global economic order" (Gallin and Ferguson 1989:6–7).

I find these concepts useful in analyzing the behaviors of fresh produce

Vendor selling fresh produce to a customer in the high density suburbs.

Hawkers awaiting customers in a low density suburb shopping center.

market women in Harare. On the one hand, the policy of neglect on the part of government and assistance agencies provides the vendors an opportunity to pattern their economic activities in ways that suit them. Constraints for so doing are laid down by the municipality through its legal ability to extract rent and to harass "illegal" vendors (i.e., those who do not pay rent), and by the structure of the market itself. In effect, by the women's very own actions, they have made the system work in their favor. On the other hand, the vendors operate within a maladjusted economic system that has created imbalances effectively denying women formal sector employment and necessitating private actions on their own behalf (see *Business Herald,* July 22, 1993).

These two macrolevel approaches are blurred by policies and strategies to promote development. Programs oriented toward women generally fall into two categories, poverty alleviation or growth. The former, in the Zimbabwe case, would consider the work of vendors as income-generating activities, while the latter looks at them as small business entrepreneurs:

> WID researchers warn of the dangers of growth-oriented strategies, because of the concentration of women in low-growth, low-return microenterprises. They fear that assistance schemes based solely on growth objectives will at best ignore women's needs, if not harm their economic interests (Downing 1990:v).

Others have argued similarly that "abandonment of the poverty focus in programming for the informal sector would translate, among other things, into diminishing the possibility of incorporating initiatives for women" (Berger 1989:11). Berger's observation is well taken and is a concern of the Agency for International Development (AID) in implementing its gender strategies. In their "stocktaking" report on projects to enhance women's income generation, AID found "there is often a tradeoff between concentrating on generating successful and sustainable businesses and the goal of targeting special disadvantaged groups (i.e., women)" (AID 1989:1). AID reported that many women benefited from the application of the "enterprise formation approach"—community development programs designed to overcome constraints the poor face in becoming microentrepreneurs (e.g., not reinvesting earnings because incomes were needed to meet household consumption needs). Women also benefited when the "enterprise expansion approach" was utilized as small loans and minimal technical assistance was made available to them. Where women did not benefit was in the application of the "enterprise transformation approach" designed to "graduate larger clients up and out of the microenterprise sector" (AID 1989:2), because not very many women were found in this relatively successful targeted audience.

Because of the differential impact of AID's prior programs, the Growth and Equity through Microenterprise Investments and Institutions (GEMINI) project was developed; this, in turn, gave rise to Downing's suggestions for projects that focus on women as profit makers (growth-oriented projects) rather than implementing projects for women that do not view them as legitimate business entrepreneurs (or welfare-oriented projects) (1990:15–22). What concerns me about these strategies for poverty alleviation or growth is that the former takes the view that women doing business in the informal sector are all poor and that to view these women as microentrepreneurs somehow diminishes their work in the eyes of development planners; that is, a profit-making woman microentrepreneur is a contradiction in terms.

At the basis of this confusion, I believe, is an attitude or belief about women's economic roles that relegates them to poverty—or inability to transform their enterprises into more productive, profitable businesses. This "blaming the victim" mentality is highly suspect because it indicates that a proper assessment of policy constraints to women's advancement has not taken place (see, e.g., Blumberg 1989:53–56).

Downing has taken us several steps in the right direction by positing that women's (and men's) establishment of microenterprises exhibits entrepreneurial behavior. Initially, the motivation to establish a microenterprise may be based in survival needs that cannot be satisfied through formal sector employment. Once these are satisfied, and security has been obtained, entrepreneurs can adopt more growth-oriented behaviors, which include diversification and specialization. What differentiates women from men in these enterprises is the rate of change, with men advancing more quickly than women (Downing 1991:4–6).

All too consistently, however, microenterprises are viewed as monolithic and undifferentiated. Little attention is paid to their growth and development because they are not viewed by the preponderance of researchers as legitimate businesses worthy of access to resources. As a result, a Band-Aid approach is utilized in assisting these businesses and their individual proprietors. What is needed is a policy transformation and implementation approach that views microenterprises—whether female- or male-owned—as businesses in their own right, as integrally connected to formal sector businesses, and as contributors to the development process. Like other economic activities, microenterprises suffer the pains of growth—which comes in stages—and require different supports at different stages, all within a policy context valuing the contributions they make (see, e.g., Eigen 1992:7).

In this context, structural adjustment policies may play a critical role in rethinking policy directed toward the informal sector. Targeting this sector as that in which individual initiative is now valued to reduce dependence on the state, the World Bank and IMF are faced with the need to make recommendations on how institutions can support the development of this sector.

A major factor complicating these efforts are the individual and institutional beliefs about women's economic roles and responsibilities, since the overwhelming majority of business operators in this sector are women (see Milimo and Fisseha 1986). For instance, myths of male dominance over every aspect of women's lives completely disregard the separate purse analyses of women worldwide (see Blumberg 1989:15; Palmer 1991:20–21; and World Bank 1989). These analyses (and that presented in subsequent chapters here) reveal very specific ways in which women's income is utilized to meet certain financial obligations while men's income is utilized to satisfy other needs. These domains of responsibility are overlooked in quantitative data collection because it is assumed that households pool income to meet all needs, and that women's only work is that of nurturer, which, it is believed by many, has no economic consequence (see Mazur and Mhloyi 1988; Fapohunda 1988; Folbre 1988; Omari 1989:15–20; and Feldman 1991, for extensive discussions on this subject).

If we look at "work" as a concept illuminating women's economic productivity, we run into similar difficulties. The way work is defined is an aspect of an androcentric model that guides data collection. Within a female paradigm, however, work is anything a person does in or outside the household that another person can do for hire. The international economic system is identified as being at fault for defining work in such a way as to exclude most of women's productivity:

> The international economic system constructs reality in a way that excludes the great bulk of women's work—reproduction (in all its forms), raising children, domestic work, and subsistence production. Cooking, according to economists, is "active labor" when cooked food is sold and "economically inactive labor" when it is not. Housework is "productive" when performed by a paid domestic servant and "nonproductive" when no payment is involved. Those who care for children in an orphanage are "occupied"; mothers who care for their children at home are "unoccupied" (Waring 1988:30–31).

Waring takes to task Jaffe's definition of the "Labour Force" found in the *International Encyclopedia of the Social Sciences* and argues that including such productive work in the labor force would direct policymakers to an understanding of why females around the world are the poorer sex.

The male paradigm of work reflects a gender bias that centerstages what traditionally are considered men's roles—formal employment and market productivity—"those activities that produce surplus value (that is, profit in the marketplace)" (Waring 1988:27). By extension, the work that is involved in producing surplus value is accorded recognition and visibility to the state in the form of national statistical representation, and of course becomes the basis for educational policy and training.

The definition of work as well as of the division of labor require rethinking. Waring clearly sums up the literature when she states that when work is performed to enable members of the household, it is not economic, while when these same tasks are performed in the marketplace, they are. In other words, when traditionally female tasks are performed in what is traditionally understood as the domain of men, that is, the market, they are economic activities.

Our understanding of women, work, self-sufficiency, and development is premised upon many theoretical frameworks that, in the past, have viewed women's economic activities as marginal. These views emanate from patriarchal beliefs about women and their ability to make a significant economic impact. The evidence challenging these beliefs has been presented by feminist researchers who have altered theory and shifted the household economy paradigm to demonstrate women's partnership, if not primacy, in economic sustainability. We must shift this paradigm further to include women's contribution to the broader economy. The case of Zimbabwe vegetable vendors stands as an excellent base for our broader understanding.

As traditional growers of horticultural crops, and as traditional family food provisioners, women were required to make adaptations to a changing environment. They were able to do so because of their ability to innovate and take risks. While males are able to perform similarly, they have generally had access to new inputs, that is, education, to innovate; women in developing countries, generally, have not.

What this "model" of self-sufficiency suggests is that individual innovation, the ethic of work, the ability to take risks, and a sense of personal pride—all characterizing women's informal market behavior—are cornerstones of development (see Meredith et al. 1982:3). The World Bank, the IMF, and a very large number of public and private donor agencies have, at long last, recognized the potential not only of the sector, but also of the individuals within it. This recognition, however, is short-sighted. Rather than focusing on individual qualities to be enhanced and supported through policy changes and education, the focus in narrowly on increasing incomes. While this is needed, without first understanding the nature of entrepreneurs—especially women—their strategy to provide more credit is viewed as a panacea to alleviate growth and development problems. This might help a few, but does it address fundamental problems? I think not. Addressing the policy context as well as prevailing attitudes about gender and the informal sector might prove more productive.

Women who migrate to urban areas, or female urban dwellers seeking means to earn an income, are generally constrained from doing so due to a deficiency in education or lack of job opportunities. Confronted with the need for cash on a daily basis, women establish their own businesses (see AID 1991:37–38). Ostensibly, women create their own ventures to ensure their ability to provision their families, but several other factors are important: (1) the flèxibility of self-employment (Otero 1987:6), (2) its compatibility with child care (Palmer 1991:51), and (3) a rejection of subordination that other forms of employment entail (Reddock 1990:54). Additionally, women establish microenterprises that will ensure them an income over the long term since their cash flow needs do not diminish over time.

The steady growth of women-owned enterprises has led to a number of studies and a number of interventions on the part of development assistance organizations (see Hodder and Ukwu 1969; Johnson 1973; Wood 1974; Obbo 1980; Jules-Rosette 1981; Kaba 1982; African Training & Research Centre for Women 1984; Robertson 1984; and Clark 1986). The fresh produce vendors of Harare as well as women operating microenterprises throughout the country have also gained recognition (see Brand 1982, 1992; Horn 1986, 1988; Osirim 1990; Saito 1990; Downing 1990, 1991; and McPherson 1991). These studies clearly document the significance of women's activities in the urban economy. Findings from this research have led to the development of worldwide intervention strategies aimed at enhancing the ability of microentrepreneurs to be successful (see Downing 1990). The rationale for designing and implementing these strategies is to attempt to bridge the growth/gender schism in the microenterprise development literature:

> The strategy includes the (1) support, but not subsidization, for women's enterprises in subsectors that have few prospects for growth—in light of the importance of women's income to family welfare; (2) identification of interventions associated with viable subsectors in which women predominate—to unleash their income-generating and growth potential; and (3) promotion of policies, projects, and other interventions that facilitate the transition of female entrepreneurs out of low-return, low-potential subsectors into higher-return and higher-potential subsectors (Downing 1990:v).

In essence, while project focus is to work within the system to make it better for women, the result is policy transformation and implementation to move women from economic marginality to more mainstream, growing enterprises. Hence, while focusing on the reformist perspective, the ultimate goal is the redistributive one in which women do not occupy the lowest economic level within an international capitalist system.

Research and intervention on specific activities within the microenterprise sector has delineated a gender-based division of labor according to materials, implements, and conformity to culturally-based perceptions as to what constitutes women's work and what constitutes men's work. This body of literature asserts that the origin of the gender-based division of labor is the household (Feldman 1991). For instance, men, on the one hand, generally use wood, metal, rubber, and spun thread (carpenters, furniture makers, shoemakers, weavers and tailors) (Howard 1987). They are also involved in electrical repair, tinsmithing, building, and upholstery (Moyo et al. 1984). Women, on the other hand, use straw, fibers, and clay (baskets, mats, and pottery). They also brew beer, make confectionery items, knit, and crochet (Milimo and Fisseha 1986).

Marketing activities are not as easily divided, although it appears that volume of trade, and thus financial returns, play a role in whether women operate these enterprises. Within the fresh produce trade in Zimbabwe, there is a distinct division in accordance with volume traded and financial returns: women are generally the retail traders, while men operate on the wholesale level. In West Africa, a different ethos prevails: the market is a woman's domain (Sudarkasa 1973; Frolich 1940/1982; Johnson 1973; Gore 1978; Trager 1979; Obbo 1980; Kaba 1982; the African Training and Research Centre for Women 1984; Robertson 1984; Clark 1986; Turrittin 1988; and Osirim forthcoming). Countries of West Africa, however, have experienced a radically different history and perceive women differently according to cultural beliefs. Many societies in West Africa are matrilineal, providing women access to resources and power. Traditionally, women were responsible for short-distance trade, while men travelled widely in trans-Saharan trade routes. Also, West African countries were colonized under different geographically-influenced modes of governing. White populations did not settle in these colonies primarily because of climate. Outgrower schemes prevailed in generating income for the colonies. Provisioning activities were left directly to the women who managed a majority portion of the system locally.

In southern Africa, white settlers alienated and exploited lands formerly under the domain of Africans. Settler colonials derived direct benefit from an African labor force, integral to the evolving agricultural and mining economy. Colonial perceptions of patrilineage and patriarchy fed into settler beliefs that African women would stay at home and tend to the farm while their spouses went to earn a wage. Because women were not counted as laborers, they became invisible to the colonial state.

While the historical development of the marketing systems in both regions differs, research comparisons can be made on several points.

Locus and Focus of Research

Data were collected in this study from the market women solely in the marketplace, similar to the approach utilized by Johnson (1973), Trager (1976), Kaba (1982), and Clark (1986), each of whom followed the suggestions of Hill (1970:11–12) that "market women should be interviewed in the market." The rational for following this advice for the current study is based on the question of profitability.

Other researchers, however, sought to answer different questions: how market women in Nigeria employ various tactics to meet the objective of acquisition, accumulation, and manipulation of capital to enhance their positions within the marketing structure (Johnson 1973); how place and spatial structure affect social organization in Yoruba markets in Nigeria (Trager 1976); what the range of women's economic activities is in Liberia (Kaba 1982); and how Asante women's position in Kumasi Central Market in Ghana helps determine their capacity for autonomous social action (Clark 1986).

Studies that seek to contextualize women's marketing activities or to measure their effect upon social relations both within and outside the marketplace include interviewing market women in the markets and in their homes (Sudarkasa 1973; Obbo 1980; Robertson 1984). By so doing, Sudarkasa could ascertain "the effect of trade by women on the structure of, and the behavioral patterns within, the kin and residential units to which women belong" (Sudarkasa 1973:2). Obbo determined how and why women in Uganda migrate. In identifying their "struggle for economic independence," she found many women become self-employed in marketing activities so as to reduce their dependence on men (Obbo 1980:125). Robertson set out to analyze social change among Ga women in Accra, Ghana, "but by the time I had tried an initial pre-survey in 1971–72, the overweening importance of trading activities in pervading every aspect of the women's lives made a consideration of economics imperative. . . . I started out to work with women; I ended by working with traders" (Robertson 1984:25).

Interviewing women in the marketplace has provided definition to many of their urban economic activities. Each research endeavor has contributed to our understanding of why women are economically important.

Trade in Food Commodities

The cultural and historical circumstances forging the link between women and fresh produce, and the sociohistorical account of how women during the colonial era in Zimbabwe sold these commodities constitute aspects of uniqueness in the exploration of market women in this country. The market women of specific ethnic groups in Nigeria are linked to yams and kola nuts (Trager 1976), and in Ghana to various fresh food crops (Gore 1978; Robertson 1984; Clark 1986). In Zimbabwe, the link between women and specific food commodities is rooted in traditional beliefs about the nature of women and their roles as family food provisioners. Similar arguments have been posited for market women worldwide. Kaba (1982) and Moran (1988) in Liberia, and Gore (1978), the African Training and Research Centre for Women (1984) and Robertson (1984) in Ghana, and Schildkrout (1979) in Nigeria have all linked women to food marketing via their roles as rural food producers and family food provisioners. In particular, Schildkrout demonstrates how the cultural values of Hausa society validate this category of work for women. She argues that the cultural expectations of Muslim women's behavior in Kano determine what women can do to generate income. These expectations or boundaries require an intermediary for exchange to take place: the women's children. In Papua New Guinea, women are said to be involved in the food trade because of their rural link to food cultivation and distribution (Epstein 1982). In Jamaica, women are said to supply at least 80 percent of fresh produce needs because they are traditionally the gardeners of the society (Durant-Gonzalez 1976). In Costa Rica, women enter these businesses because the rhythm of buying and selling is compatible with women's domestic chores (Ashe 1985).

The link between women and food provisioning is one way to analyze women's fresh produce marketing activities in Zimbabwe; sociological and political variables related to education and constraints to obtaining formal employment are other constituents of this analysis. This study adds to these conceptual positions by analyzing an ideological link between women and horticultural crops. In so establishing this link, the argument can be made that women who continue to be involved in food provisioning in the city are performing in culturally-accepted patterns. Guyer's statement seems to apply to this situation: "new tasks [are] subsumed under existing cultural categories" (Guyer 1978:6). That is, when a change occurs in the social context out of which women's economic activities have been derived, the expertise they have acquired is carried with them to their new environments. The ideological link is rooted in the rural belief system of the Shona-speaking people.

Pricing

The dynamics involved in price determination of any given commodity rest upon the elements of supply and demand. In Zimbabwe, an aspect of this dynamic concerns the expectation a customer has of what payment will be required for a given quantity of a commodity. Clark (1986) found in Ghana that women vendors and customers engage in a type of quantity bargaining. For example, a heap of tomatoes might be offered at a certain price. A customer will agree to the price with the expectation that she will be "dashed" (given) an added amount. If the addition is not sufficient in the eyes of the customer, bargaining will ensue over the "dash," not over the price.

The Zimbabwe case offers little evidence of this dynamic. In my research, I found the price of a given heap of tomatoes does not change, regardless of who the customer is, and is not subject to bargaining. While certain vendors include a free tomato when a heap is purchased, the added quantity generally comes from a pile that is "going off" (spoiling) that the vendor keeps under her stall. In only two instances did I observe vendors giving fresh tomatoes to entice the customer's return. While pricing is not absolute, there is less variability in Zimbabwe than in West Africa.

Visibility and Women's Businesses

Making market women visible to policy makers and development planners is a challenge:

> The result of women's invisibility in informal work has been that the way gender relations structure informal activity was ignored. . . . given the extant gender division of labor, women's contribution to and demand for more informal work are likely to go unnoticed—unless one initially recognizes that the gender division of labor within the household shapes employment demand and provides the context for social reproduction (Feldman 1991:74–75; see also Lewis 1981).

In other words, the division of labor in the household is reproduced in income generating activities within and outside of the household. Following this line of reasoning, if a women is a food provisioner in the household, then she can extend that role to the broader community. The role will not be interfered with by husbands or other kin members of the patriarchy unless the enterprise generates a sizeable income. If, on the one hand, the enterprise is construed as a provisioning mechanism and as a limited income generation operation, then a woman can continue; if, on the other hand, the enterprise is profitable, then it is construed as a business worthy of male intervention and recognition. What constitutes "profitable" is very subjective. My data indicate, however, that the women who are very successful (generating Z$100, net, or more per week) are not married.

Gender blindness has been a characteristic of development programs in Zimbabwe designed to enhance the production and marketing of horticultural crops (see ARDA 1985; especially, pp. 97–98): "Produce marketed from Chinamora is mostly sold at Mbare Musika. It is seldom graded and *most producers are represented by their wives*" (emphasis added). The continued misperception of women's roles in both production and marketing has been perpetuated and reasserted in projects that seek to correct past inaccuracies. An EEC-funded project was to modernize the African fresh produce wholesale market and its adjacent retail market at Mbare Musika, occupied largely by women vendors. No mention of training to enhance the efficiency of women's marketing operations was included in the proposal.

Government failure to consider women's contributions to urban food provisioning and family maintenance perpetuates women's invisibility in the development process. Making the consequences of women's marketing activities more visible is one of the goals of this study.

Income

Theoretically significant are the incomes generated by the vendors. Significance derives from the need to challenge the assumptions posited in the literature about women's earnings and their relative insignificance to the national economy. These data are not easily accessible. The methodological difficulties collecting data on income in Zimbabwe are related to those described by Hill for any research on markets:

> An [African] market is one of the most uncomfortable and inconvenient places in the world in which to conduct respectable field work—the difficulties are the extreme fluidity and complexity of the undocumented situation and the need to trouble informants at their moment of maximum anxiety, when they are concluding transactions (Hill 1963:444).

These difficulties had to be overcome if anything approximating accurate income data could be collected. Unlike other studies that attempted to collect income data from recall, I conducted daily weighing, counting, and recording exercises with each of the vendors.

Having collected these data, I felt it was of theoretical importance to ascertain what women do with the incomes they generate. Since it is assumed, according to national statistics, women do not contribute economically to their family's welfare, it was critical to this study to document how much of this invisible income actually pays for aspects of family welfare. For instance, assumptions about males being responsible for provisioning, housing, and paying school fees were challenged in this research when women reported they paid for these items.

Additionally, an assertion made and attested to in this writing runs parallel to the findings of Blumberg (1987:2): that men and women in Africa have separate incomes and separate obligations for spending them; where women have resources under their independent control, they tend, more than men, to devote them to feeding their families and to their children's well-being; and given so many African women's needs for resources for family provisioning, they tend to allocate their labor toward activities that put income and/or food under their direct control. While Robertson relied mainly on reported household income, she found similarly that women's income was disposed of largely in meeting household expenditures and investing in the well-being of their children (Robertson 1984:216).

▲ Summary and Conclusion

In summary, this study both parallels and contrasts with other studies conducted on marketwomen. It diverges from other studies in the questions asked, methodologies employed, and many of the findings. It explains the historical and sociocultural development of women's economic niche, situates the women in the informal sector of the urban economy, analyzes market women's activities as businesses, and suggests reasons why women-operated businesses behave somewhat differently from those of men. Remarkably, however, it is similar to other studies in that most appear to draw the conclusion that the earnings women generate through marketing activities largely remain under their control, and that incomes are utilized both for family welfare and reinvestment. This writing builds on these findings and challenges the prevailing economic paradigm—based in patriarchal ideology—that designates women's activities as marginal to households, communities, and the state.

▲ Notes

1. For instance, in Zambia women own 60 percent of small scale enterprises, and constitute 54 percent of the employees. If only marketing enterprises are considered, then women own 75 percent of enterprises, and constitute 69 percent of the employees (Milimo and Fisseha 1986:52). In Zaire, "women, children, and retired/senior citizens" constitute the major proprietors in "sideline" income generating activities in urban areas (Tripp 1990:51).

2. Mezzera (1989:47) has put forward another workable definition more reflective of constraints: "a heterogeneous set of productive activities that share the common feature of employing a number of people who would be unable to find employment in the modern sector and must generate their own employment with relatively little access to the factors of production that complement the labor supply."

▲ 4
The Fresh Produce
Marketing System in Harare

The market structure facilitating the movement of fresh produce from the producer to the consumer, and the retail vendors' place within it, are the subjects of exploration in this chapter. Specifically, how does the marketing system limit or constrain women's ability to sell fresh produce throughout the city of Harare? The answer to this question begins with an analysis of the marketing system itself, and then explores the problems and constraints vendors must overcome to participate.

▲ The Fresh Produce Marketing System

A marketing system includes "exchange activities associated with the transfer of property rights to commodities, the physical handling of products and the institutional arrangements for facilitating these activities" (Harrison et al. 1974:4). Institutional arrangements are commonly referred to as marketing channels, "a series of stages, or activities, through which a product passes in going from producer to consumer" (Scott 1985:20).

The development of bifurcated marketing channels in Harare originated in the ideological context of racism operationalized in the geographic division of the city along racial lines. The dual channel system is characterized in the following manner: white, large scale commercial producers sell the bulk of their harvests to white formal sector wholesalers, who, in turn, sell to white formal sector retailers (supermarkets, greengrocers, and "cafes" [neighborhood grocery stores]), institutions, and individual consumers. African small scale commercial and communal farmers sell their commodities to food processors on contract, most recently to some white wholesaling agencies, and to African informal sector wholesalers, who, in turn, sell largely to informal sector retail market vendors and/or consumers. In the case of the African farmers' market at Mbare and Mabvuku, farmers also sell directly to retail vendors and consumers (see Figure 4.1).[1]

51

Figure 4.1 Formal and Informal Fresh Produce Marketing Channels

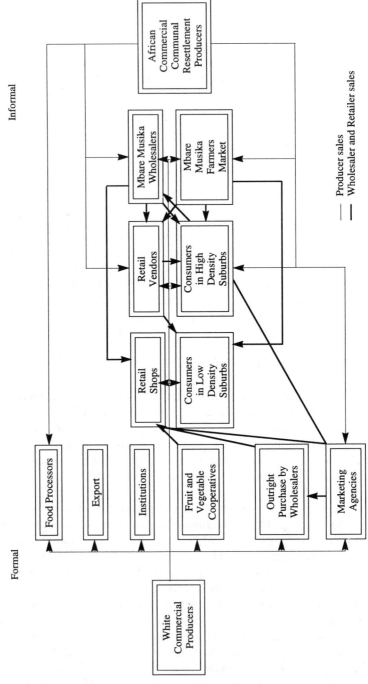

▲ Production and Marketing Systems Based on Race

The racial bifurcation of the marketing system has its roots in the labor reserve economy and farming systems practiced by Africans and whites. People of European descent established large scale commercial farms, gaining access to the most productive land, water, credit, improved seed, fertilizer, and other technological inputs. With virtually unlimited supplies of African labor, commercial farmers developed trading relationships with food crop exporters (generally wholesalers), food processors, institutions requiring steady supplies of fresh produce (e.g., the army, hospitals, boarding schools), retail shops and supermarkets, and, in some cases, with individual consumers (where producers opened a farm kiosk).

African farmers practice at least two types of farming system, neither of which, in general, produces the same quality and quantity of product as the white large scale commercial farm: small scale commercial and communal. The former entails cultivating both cash and subsistence crops on land that has been individually purchased. These lands are oftentimes situated in a buffer zone between white commercial and African communal farms (formerly known as tribal trust lands in the reserves). As buffers, small scale commercial farmers cultivate on soils that are not as good as those of large scale commercial farms but generally better than those of communal farms. Such farmers may or may not have access to permanent water sources, credit, improved seed, fertilizer, etc. With limited resources, small scale commercial farmers are not able to produce consistent yields. Limited amounts of labor and inaccessible paved roads prevent these farmers from gaining access to market outlets.

Communal farmers cultivate primarily for home consumption, but also sell some of their harvests commercially. Women have domain over garden crops, and it is they who market them on neighboring farms, in local markets and in towns. If a harvest is sufficient, it will be boxed and brought to the Harare farmers' market for sale. Harvests are limited, however, owing to the amount of land available for horticultural crop cultivation under communal tenure—between one-fourth and a whole acre. Seeds planted are generally those saved from previous harvests, and the only fertilizer that might be applied is manure. Technological inputs are almost nonexistent, and labor is that of women and their children. Harvests are not always dependable; neither are amounts available for sale. Transport is difficult since communal lands were historically situated in nonproductive areas many kilometers from roads and railways.

While the farming systems I describe appear to be based on class divisions, in fact they reflect an historical division of land based on race. Production systems differentiated by race gave rise to marketing systems based on the same principle.

▲ Formal Sector Wholesalers

Formal sector wholesalers generally fall into two categories: outright purchase wholesalers and marketing agencies. The former may make individual supply arrangements with producers and/or may fetch a crop, or a portion thereof, at the farm gate. The latter generally require farmer delivery to the marketing agency where commodities are sold on a commission basis.

Commercial farmer delivery at the Independent Market.

Regarding outright purchase wholesalers, transactions are based on a supply/demand price that is negotiated with the producer, generally at the time of delivery. Mutual agreements on price are arrived at with large scale commercial producers while purchases from others are normally on an ad hoc basis (PTA 1982:99). It is not uncommon for outright purchase wholesalers to obtain their commodities from the marketing agencies. One wholesaler indicated all the vegetables he supplies come from one agency, while another wholesaler reported that only 25 percent of his requirements comes from the agencies, while 50 percent comes from white commercial farmers and 25 percent from African small scale commercial producers.

Up until 1986, a 15 percent sales tax was levied against the sale of all food commodities. Payable at the wholesaler level, the amount of the tax was incorporated into retailer prices and passed on to the consumer (see Cheater 1979:12). The tax was done away with on vegetables when the budget was introduced in 1986; it remained, however, on fruits, although the rate was reduced to 12.5 percent. This tax is not payable in market agency transactions, as the agencies are not buying and selling per se; rather, they are selling on behalf of the farmers. A handling fee of 12.5 percent, however, is charged to the producer for all commodities sold. The tax is ultimately recovered by the retailers in consumer transactions.

When supplying supermarkets, wholesalers must weigh and package commodities purchased.[2] One wholesaler indicated that this extra task can be very problematic. He related that a bottleneck in operations had occurred one season when a permit to import the plastics necessary to produce the small trays used in packaging was not issued in time to meet marketing needs. Wholesalers, as a result of such tardiness, try to have at least a two-year supply of packaging materials on hand, thus tying up a portion of their capital.

Outright purchase wholesalers must also factor into their prices the cost of wastage, since the goods they sell have already been paid for. Although all these businesses have cold storage facilities, wholesalers assume a great deal of risk in purchasing commodities outright. As a result, their demand is for very high quality produce that has a greater likelihood of being sold than produce of a lower quality or grade.

If farmers are unable to produce top-quality commodities on a consistent basis, an alternative marketing outlet is chosen: the marketing agencies. Each of the two agencies in Harare acts as the farmer's agent, selling commodities brought in by the producer on a 12.5 percent commission basis.[3] Each agency has a cold storage facility so perishables can be stored. Commodities are sold on a supply/demand basis with prices changing as many as four times per day. A wholesaler that has the largest portion of stock at any one time might be deemed the market price leader, but pricing is very dynamic and market leadership shifts with the arrival of additional supplies of a given commodity—which can occur on an hourly basis. General practices at the Independent Market are as follows:

> Provided produce is accepted, it is then sold by one of four salesmen. They are controlled by a Market Master who, in consultation with his assistant and the owner, fix the prices for the range of fruit and vegetables they expect to sell each morning. This organisation owes much of its success to a very efficient market intelligence network which makes an accurate assessment of the volume of all fruit and vegetables likely to appear on the wholesale markets in Harare every day, before prices are decided (PTA 1982:96).

In conducting this portion of the research, I attempted to ascertain the volume of commodities sold through these formal Harare channels. I asked wholesalers, based on the records they kept on disbursements to producers, what market share they felt they had of a given commodity. This line of questioning produced the surprising response that they did not calculate volumes traded; they only calculated cash flow. One wholesaler, however, provided me with the company's records for one full year and I was able to calculate just how much of a given commodity they handle. Based on these records and wholesaler/agency perceptions of the percentage of their market share, the volumes in Table 4.1 were calculated.

Table 4.1 Volume of Crops Sold Through Formal Sector Marketing Channels in Harare, July 1985–June 1986[a]

Crop	Estimated Tons
Avocados	31.427
Baby marrows (zucchini)	35.547
Green beans	253.280
Beetroot	81.040
Brinjals (eggplant)	30.520
Broccoli	7.555
Butternut squash	66.073
Cabbage	
drum head (449,422 heads)	224.711
sweet (74,547 heads)	27.955
Carrots	540.476
Cauliflower	75.636
Celery (3,111 bunches)	.778
Cucumbers	279.503
Gem squash	167.970
Gooseberries	5.605
Grapefruits	302.818
Green peppers	64.504
Hubbard squash	25.745
Lemons	128.610
Lettuce (101,970 heads)	25.493
Mealies (maize) (507,670 cobs)	126.918
Onions	
dry	1,406.943
spring (16,612 bunches)	4.153
Oranges	3,716.500
Peas	106.574
Potatoes	83,174.523
Pumpkins	112.708
Spinach (32,482 bunches)	8.121
Sweet potatoes	735.340
Tomatoes (gem/jam)	102.345
Tomatoes	1,484.070
Turnips	223.12

Source: Field notes.

Note: a. These figures represent only an estimation of goods that move through the *formal* wholesale markets of Harare. They do not take into account the commodities that never reach these markets because they are marketed elsewhere; nor do they consider direct retail shop, consumer, food processing, and export sales.

Although these estimates are very crude, I rationalize presenting them on two counts: no production records exist anywhere for these commodities and thus their presentation can be interpreted as one set of working figures to be utilized in ascertaining production figures; and information on crop deliveries and prices is shared among wholesalers several times during the day so that each wholesaler/agency is aware of which producer's crops are being delivered where, and at what price they are being purchased/sold for.

To entice customers, or perhaps merely to provide a base line wholesale price for fruit and vegetable crops sold, the Independent Market publishes its prices in the *Herald* once or twice a week. A figure is also published in the weekly *Financial Gazette*. How these prices fluctuated over the year December 1985 through November 1986 for selected commodities is presented in Table 4.2.[4]

For comparative formal/informal sector purposes, Table 4.3 illustrates the formal sector wholesale prices per kilogram published in the *Herald* on various dates, as well as the actual prices I obtained when informal sector retail vendors reported what they had paid for a particular wholesale quantity of a commodity. This record covers the period of my intensive research, March through July 1986.

Despite my attempts to ascertain price changes in 1993, both the *Herald* and the *Financial Gazette* had discontinued regular publication of prices. Alternatively, I obtained current prices for wholesale commodities available at Mbare Musika; these are presented in Table 4.4. Owing to currency devaluation and the implementation of other structural adjustment policies, 1993 prices are much higher.

The produce sold by most formal sector wholesalers in large part meets the demands of the supermarkets, greengrocers, cafes (grocery stores), and other shops in the white-dominated low density suburbs. While one wholesaler made a concentrated effort to have African farmers bring in a variety of crops, not just those in demand by people of European descent, difficulty in selling the crop ensued since a sufficient number of retailers had not yet begun to sell such crops in large quantities.

Producers have many options for selling their commodities other than to formal and informal sector wholesalers. These include export markets, food processors, the Fruit and Vegetable Growers' Co-operative, institutions, and directly to retailers or consumers. Since this study concerns the effect of the marketing system upon the African retail vendors, I will simply summarize these different marketing options, pointing out how vendors are affected by producers exercising a particular choice. Additionally, I will indicate where farmer choices reflect participation in either the formal or informal sector.

Table 4.2 Average Wholesale Prices for Selected Commodities, December 1985–November 1986[a]

Commodity	Dec.	Jan.	Feb.	Mar.	Apr.	May	Jun.	Jul.	Aug.	Sep.	Oct.	Nov.
Apples												
case (18 kg)[b]		19.88	17.63	18.00	18.30	18.75	19.00	17.50				
tray (6 kg)[b]		4.25	3.44	2.44	2.25	2.25						
Avocados												
tray (5 kg)												
large	4.00	4.19	4.25	3.25	1.75	1.94						
small				2.22	.69	.88						
pocket (12 kg)							2.00	2.20	2.69	2.75	2.90	3.25
Cabbage (head)												
small	.04	.05	.07	.06	.07	.07	.08	.08	.08	.06	.05	.04
medium	.08	.10	.13	.12	.13	.14	.18	.17	.12	.11	.10	.05
large	.13	.18	.25	.22	.22	.24	.29	.27	.19	.21	.14	.09
Lemons (pocket [10 kg])												
grade 1 (smooth skin)	4.38	4.46	4.16	3.81	3.50	3.31	3.44	4.30	4.50	4.50	5.88	5.50
grade 2 (rough skin)	1.31	1.38	1.31	1.25	1.25	1.25	.88	1.00	1.13	.88	3.13	3.75
Onions (pocket [10 kg])												
grade 1	3.25	4.50	5.38	6.38	8.55	9.50	9.00	9.30	8.50	5.00	3.25	2.50
grade 2	2.38	3.81	4.53	5.41	7.30	7.25	7.25	6.90	6.00	4.25	2.63	1.88
Oranges (pocket [10 kg])												
Valencia			2.25	2.25	2.50	2.50	2.63	2.75	2.75	3.53		
navel					3.50	3.72	4.00	3.69				
Potatoes (pocket [15 kg])												
grade 1	4.00	4.53	3.39	2.84	4.16	4.92	4.25	4.35	5.25	5.42	6.63	6.56
grade 2	2.25	2.69	1.97	1.53	2.19	2.38		3.75	3.42	3.79	4.75	4.75
grade 3	1.75	1.94	1.50	1.63	1.75	1.75				3.00	3.70	3.50
Sweet potatoes (pocket [10 kg])												
grade 1				2.29	1.73	1.78	1.75	2.03	2.08	2.25	2.75	3.50
grade 2				1.25	.88							
Tomatoes												
tray (6 kg)[b]	1.75	2.50	4.75	4.50	3.05	4.13	4.00	4.23	2.83	3.38	3.94	2.13
box (10 kg)[c]	.75	2.56	5.06	5.88	4.31	5.44	5.13	6.25	4.75	4.25	3.63	1.25

Source: Compiled from twice-weekly published prices in the *Herald.*

Note: a. While 16 crops have been selected for further analysis in Chapter 6 on the basis of the main income generating crops women sell retail, only seven of these are sold at the Independent Market. That not all crops in demand by African retailers are sold by formal sector wholesalers is an indication of the bifurcation of cropping and marketing outlets, and a compelling feature directing retailers to make their purchases elsewhere. These figures, however, will be compared with prices women reported paying for the same commodities, at the informal market at Mbare Musika.

b. First grade only.

c. Second grade only.

Table 4.3 Wholesale Prices per Kilogram of Selected Fresh Produce at Independent Market (IM) and Mbare Musika Farmers' Market (MM), March–July 1986 (in Z$)

	March		April		May		June		July	
Commodity	IM	MM	IM	MM	IM	MM	IM	MM	IM	MM
Apples	1.00	.53	1.02	.64	1.04	.77	1.10	1.10	.97	1.32
Avocados	.46	.53	.20	.56	.24	.43	.20	.79	.22	.47
Cabbage	.13	.20	.14	.21	.15	.21	.18	.26	.17	.22
Lemons	.13	.26	.13	.25	.13	.26	.09	.22	.10	.27
Onions	.54	.82	.73	1.30	.73	.93	.73	.90	.73	.65
Oranges	.23	.72	.23	.50	.30	.48	.31	.43	.33	.45
Potatoes	.13	.25	.18	.25	.20	.26	.28	.28	.27	.32
Sweet potatoes	.18	n/a	.13	.22	.18	.21	.18	.29	.21	.21
Tomatoes	.51	.70	.59	.67	.43	.86	.59	.85	.51	.61

Source: Compiled from twice-weekly published prices in the *Herald* and from field notes and pricing questionnaires administered to vendors.

Table 4.4 Wholesale Prices of Selected Commodities at Mbare Musika, July 1993

Commodity	Quantity	Price (Z$)
Apples	10 kg	15.00
	15 kg	22.00
Avocados	n/a	n/a
Cabbage	small head	.50
	large head	1.00
Lemons	each	.20
Onions	each	.50
	10 kg	35.00
Oranges	10 kg	10.00
Potatoes	1 kg	2.00
	2 kg	4.00
	5 kg	5.00
	12 kg	15.00
	15 kg	20.00
Sweet potatoes	heap (9 count)	4.00
Tomatoes	10 kg	10.00

Source: Field notes.

▲ Informal Sector Wholesalers

Historically, conducting the wholesale trade in fresh produce shifted geographically for the African community between Mbare (Harari) and Highfield. Ultimately, in 1979, Mbare Musika was built to provide African informal wholesale marketeers a more permanent site (*Herald,* February 19, 1979). Each of the 157 spaces in the open-air market is rented on a daily basis to semipermanent wholesalers. Wholesalers indicated that slots are rented on a first-come, first-served basis, with 1993 rents averaging Z$205 per month. Prior to the internal changes at Mbare in 1991 (permanent roofs were constructed), gaining access to a space required that the entrepreneurs construct a trading shed, using their own capital. Most stalls at the market place were on open ground with no shelter from the rains and the blazing heat. All the vendors said they had no means to preserve their wares (*Herald,* November 20, 1980). Those who constructed sheds received priority treatment for rental by the municipality. If rents were in arrears, however, the municipality would knock down the shed and reallocate the space. Since the permanent roofs were constructed, it has become much easier for the municipality to deny access to a wholesaler on the basis of rental arrears.

Since there is no water in this market and no adequate means of overnight storage, one wholesaler reported: "Every day we throw away about a third of the commodities because they will have gone bad. We also have to reduce the prices at times because people become reluctant to buy as days go by and customers who usually buy in bulk start reducing their orders" (*Herald,* November 20, 1980).

African wholesalers purchase their commodities either at the farm gate (from white or African farmers) or await producer delivery at the wholesale market at Mbare Musika. At the farm gate, a wholesaler may arrive with his own transport, may be willing to pick the portion of the crop to be purchased, and may have his own packaging materials. The prices of commodities at the farm gate are generally lower than those paid to the producer at the Harare markets because wholesalers absorb the costs of packaging and transportation. Table 4.5 illustrates some typical prices paid in 1985–1986 to transport commodities from given destinations by wholesalers who purchase at the farm gate. The type of vehicle hired is generally a seven-ton truck, although larger vehicles are sometimes used to make purchases at farms a greater distance away, e.g., at Chimanimani, Chipinge, Nyanyadze.[5]

Wholesalers take enormous risks in using relatively scarce capital to make farm gate purchases since it is unknown, at the time of purchase, whether commodities purchased will be sold and whether the resale price will cover transport costs. Wholesalers, either having hired transport or paid for the fuel for their own transport, are at a disadvantageous bargaining position. It is highly likely, so it was reported, that once a wholesaler goes to the farm he will come to some sort of agreement on price for the commodities offered.

Wholesalers can avoid incurring the expenses of transport by awaiting the arrival of producers at Mbare Musika. An accurate count of farmers coming into Mbare Musika on a daily basis could not be ascertained because those coming to sell at the farmer's market are not identified as

Table 4.5 Typical Wholesaler Transport Costs to Selected Areas[a]

Destination	Approximate Km from Harare	Commodities	Transport Cost (Z$)
Mutare	265	tomatoes	400
Bindura	88	tomatoes, carrots	300
Shamva	90	tomatoes, carrots, cabbage	350
Borrowdale	15	cabbages, carrots	45
Mutoko	143	tomatoes, onions, guavas	150
Chimanimani	523	bananas	750
Nyanyadzi	350	tomatoes	500
Mazoe	40	tomatoes	60
Rusape	180	sweet potatoes	112

Source: Field notes.

Note: a. Information for this table was provided in 1986 by semipermanent wholesalers selling from Mbare Musika who go to the farms to make their purchases anywhere from one to four times per week, depending on sales, distance, availability of capital, etc. The cost of transporting commodities from the farm gate depends on whether or not the wholesaler owns or rents his/her vehicle, the size of the vehicle, and the distance to be travelled. Not all vehicle rentals are reckoned in kilometers; an owner may charge a flat fee for vehicle rental, or vehicle rental plus driver expenses. Rental transactions are generally undertaken with individual owners, as opposed to transport companies. Thus, with rental fees not reckoned on standard charges per kilometer, wholesalers may pay above what rental agencies would charge if vehicles were available for such transport.

Display of commodities at Mbare Musika.

either producers or wholesalers. Between 65 and 232 farmers/wholesalers per day were recorded during the latter months of 1986.[6] The 157 or more semipermanent wholesalers, however, are extremely competitive in bidding for a truckload of commodities. To bring some order to the chaos, producers (or, in the case of white commercial farmers, their drivers or farm managers) make agreements with different wholesalers to supply them on a continual basis throughout the season. Problems arise, however, when there is a glut and contracted wholesalers cannot handle what a producer delivers. While there are no written agreements, the verbal agreement reached between producer and wholesaler normally suffices. However, in this sector, if this understanding is breached, there is no real recourse for either party.

How a producer determines which wholesale outlet he will use is largely based on the quality of the product. After sorting, top grades are delivered to the white wholesalers to obtain top prices. Lower grades are marketed at Mbare Musika or at individual retail markets throughout the city. While the incidence of African producers delivering a portion of their harvests to formal sector wholesalers is increasing, the color bias still plays a role in setting the parameters of operation.

▲ The Production/Marketing System and Retail Vendors in Harare

Fresh produce vendors are dependent upon both the production and marketing systems that determine which crop is sold by which producer to which wholesaler. Considering that the production and marketing systems have both been bifurcated in their development, selected commodities never reach certain markets. For instance, in times of scarcity, high-quality tomatoes do not appear on the informal market because they are either exported or sold directly to formal sector wholesalers who resell them to preferred customers. In other instances, many formal sector wholesalers do not sell the green, leafy vegetables eaten daily in African households because most white commercial farmers do not grow them.

The problems market women selling fresh produce encounter relate both to the bifurcated structure of the marketing system and the perishable nature of the commodities they sell.

Seasonality. It is clear, from the constraints experienced by several types of producers, that only those farmers who have irrigation or permanent water sources can bring their commodities to market when there is a high demand and low supply. This means the prices market women must pay during seasons of scarcity are very high. In certain instances (e.g., onions during the winter months), a commodity is not purchased wholesale as it is simply too expensive. This was especially true during the 1992 drought when the price of 10 kilograms of onions went to Z$40.00. Retail prices simply could not cover the wholesale purchase price.

Quality. It has already been stated that high quality produce is sold to formal sector wholesalers who export or supply greengrocers, cafes, supermarkets, and institutions. However, during glut periods, formal sector wholesalers may be unable to move all the high quality stock at their disposal. At this juncture, a producer may attempt to sell his/her fruits and vegetables at the Mbare Musika farmers' market, and female retail vendors might take advantage of the opportunity to purchase first quality produce at lower prices.

Commodity access. Vendors travel many kilometers from their homes to the wholesale market to purchase their daily needs. Mbare Musika is located south of the city center several kilometers distant from the market agencies and outright purchase wholesalers. In 1985–1986 vendors occasionally purchased stocks at the Independent Market in order to satisfy a particular customer demand. This option is no longer available since the implementation of ESAP as the Independent Market could not accommodate all the vendors, and so closed its operation to all but licensed retailers.

Market access. In 1985/86 retail vendors paid a mean of Z$1.30 per day to transport themselves to and from the wholesaler, and anywhere between Z$.20 and Z$2.00 to transport their purchases from Mbare to the retail site.[7] Transport can entail taking one or two buses from home to Mbare, and the same for the return to the retail site, or taking an "emergency taxi" (a Peugeot 404 station wagon), along with neighbor vendors, from Mbare to the retail vending site.

The way in which the urban transportation system was devised also reflects the racial divisions of the city. The depot for buses traveling throughout the low density suburbs is located in one section of the city, while the depots for those traveling throughout the high density suburbs are located in others. Buses going to the high density suburbs do not originate at or pass by the formal sector wholesalers.

Reliability of published prices. Wholesale prices quoted by the Independent Market in the newspapers do not necessarily reflect wholesale prices throughout the city. Retailers reported the following:

- Day-to-day commodity price fluctuation may be the result of the commodity "going off" overnight at the wholesaler if it had not been properly stored.
- On-the-spot price reductions might be granted to those who wish to purchase an entire lot of a commodity.
- Prices may vary from hour to hour of business operation, depending

on what time and how much of a commodity is brought into the market.

- Certain customers may receive preferential pricing, thus reducing the average reported in the newspaper.

Competition. The physical location of marketplaces, the consumer need to purchase fresh produce provisions daily, and the urban contextual need for women to generate income all contribute to the proliferation of vendors throughout the high density suburbs. Although new market sites were constructed over the past decade, and more will be built in the low density areas in the near future, problems have arisen with the market stall design.

On the one hand, the municipality has responded, in part, to the expressed need of many women for stalls. In some cases, as many as 105 stalls were constructed at one site. On the other hand, it is extremely difficult for that many vendors to generate an adequate income when each sells similar commodities. Desire on the part of municipal planners to design and construct markets adjacent to shopping centers (see Mpofu 1979) has prevented them from seeing how uneconomic such designs are for the women who operate their businesses from them. While it may be economic to construct one centralized marketplace, it is very inefficient from the perspective of the vendor.

Ever since ESAP and the relaxation of regulations limiting street vendors, competition has led to declines in income and the decision by many businesswomen to quit their stalls and go to the streets or quit vending altogether. As an example, in conducting follow-on research, I found that at one low density site only two of 10 vendors remained; at a high density site, only 15 of 40 remained. Many of the others had taken to ad hoc streetside tables or door-to-door sales in order to avoid weekly rental fees.

▲ Conclusion

Both the production that feeds the marketing channels and the bifurcation of the marketing system itself impose limitations on the incomes that can be generated by African retail vendors. As discussed above, for top-quality tomatoes and green, leafy vegetables, the dual system brings certain commodities into one sector, with the remainder entering the other. The urban transportation system also impinges upon the accessibility of commodities. When women go to Mbare Musika, they must overcome the problem of *makoronyera* (hoodlums) who harass and cheat them. Vendors who wish to enter into or continue these businesses must therefore cope with a number of structural obstacles inherent in the system itself.

Vendors must also cope with the barriers to entry imposed upon them by virtue of the limited number of "legal" spaces available from which to sell.

An overabundance of market stalls in high density suburbs has caused women to abandon the site in favor of selling at the bus station down the street.

Women must create their own market environment in the low density suburbs where the municipality has not constructed stalls.

Women themselves set up barriers to entry for other women. At one market site in the low density suburbs I asked the women what they would do if others came along and wanted to join them. I was frankly told: "We would chase them away. We are already too many here." This complaint echoed throughout the conduct of this study. It echoes even louder now that the policy environment has changed and vendor activities are viewed as even more trivial: With the floodgates open to more informal sector traders, women no longer have the collective strength to chase other vendors away.

▲ Notes

1. I found little evidence of shops in the high density African suburbs selling fresh produce. Up until the last few years, supermarkets established in the low density suburbs had no direct equivalent in the high density areas. Supermarket chains established in the low density suburbs sell a range of commodities, including fresh produce. As these chains extended their services into the high density areas, they offered the same array of choices. Prior to this recent expansion, however, African-developed supermarkets did not sell fresh produce because it was assumed women would continue in their sales of these commodities, especially in light of the construction of market stalls by the municipality.

2. Up to this point very little, if any, weighing of commodities is conducted—it is assumed that a box of tomatoes weighs 10 kilograms, a pocket of peas weights 6 kilograms, etc. Farmers are responsible for purchasing relevant sacks, pockets (mesh bags), boxes, and other packaging materials, and then filling them accordingly. Major problems in filling containers with an appropriate number of kilograms have arisen owing to the fact that few farmers own scales. The same can be argued for the Mazoe citrus syndicate: when weighing small pockets of oranges (purchased directly from the distributor who had not repackaged them) at one retail vending site, I found each weighed anywhere between 3.5 and 5.0 kilograms, yet each was priced the same.

3. The operator of one marketing agency informed me that they are attempting to attract more African producers by reducing their commission.

4. A price analysis for tomatoes, onions, cabbages, and mangoes was performed as part of the EEC proposal for the years 1979–1984 (ARDA 1985:75–76). These prices correlate directly with the seasonal variation in harvesting noted in PTA 1982:30.

5. Research conducted in northeast Brazil showed that peasant producers preferred selling their harvests to wholesalers who came to their farms to purchase. This was apparently because middlemen paid cash for their purchases, albeit at lower rates, while middlemen in urban areas only offered credit (Forman and Riegelhaupt 1970:205).

6. This information was available beginning only April 1986 when a change occurred in the administration of the Department of Housing and Social Services, a division of the Harare municipality in charge of collecting rent at Mbare Musika. In order that appropriate rentals could be levied against farmers for their daily 5:00–10:00 A.M. sales, farmer names, origins, and commodities to be sold were recorded. Since the system was a new one, there were some gaps; therefore, numbers of farmers selling a given commodity should be taken as an indicator rather than an actual fact.

7. Since ESAP, bus fares have increased by 60 percent.

▲ 5

A Profile of Harare's Female Microentrepreneurs

This chapter presents the demographic characteristics of market women found selling fresh produce throughout greater Harare and discusses some of the cultural and urban contextual variables explaining women's establishment of microenterprises. The data are presented along with data on like entrepreneurs collected by other researchers. These include: Brand (1982 and 1992), who conducted research on microenterprises in selected locations in Harare; Drakakis-Smith and Kivell (n.d.), who report on food production and purchasing in two low density suburbs of Harare and one high density suburb on the fringes of the city; Saito (1991), who reports on a study undertaken by World Bank consultants in Harare, Masvingo, and Murewha; and McPherson (1991), who conducted a country-wide study under the auspices of Michigan State University's GEMINI project (Growth and Equity through Microenterprise Investments and Institutions—an AID-funded project).

A problem in data collection and analysis exists, however, in the research of Drakakis-Smith and Kivell, and McPherson: neither study disaggregates data by gender. McPherson does provide us with the frequency of female-operated microenterprises (66.6 percent for all of Zimbabwe, and 76.5 percent for Harare [McPherson 1991:19]), but fails to disaggregate the entire data set. The studies undertaken by Saito and Brand are thus relied upon more heavily as a basis for comparison or contrast. Where gross differences in the data exist, I render a brief analysis as to why. Comments made by vendors in this chapter are taken from my field notes.

▲ Language, Birthplace, and Ethnicity

Shona speakers can be found throughout Zimbabwe, but they reside primarily in the northern two-thirds of the country. For the 325 women interviewed, 82 birth places were identified. While most vendors were born in Zimbabwe, 6.2 percent (20) came from Malawi, 5.2 percent (17) from

Mozambique, and 1.2 percent (4) from Zambia. Of the remaining 87.4 percent, 14.15 percent (46) were born in Harare. Thus, almost 74 percent of the population surveyed originated in rural Zimbabwe. Brand's study of 184 microenterprises in Harare found that 77.2 percent of proprietors were Zimbabweans by birth, with 13 percent from Mozambique, 8.7 percent from Malawi, and 1.1 percent from Zambia (Brand 1982:6).

Ethnicity and language are strongly related to the area in which one is born. For instance, those who speak Chi-Toko/Chi-Budya are found in the Mutoko environs and are culturally distinct from those who speak Chi-Manyika in the Eastern Highlands and those who speak Chi-Ndau in the Sabi Valley region. Sindebele speakers are found largely in the Bulawayo region and in the southwest quadrant of the country. Each of these groups has a different history of occupying Zimbabwe, and different cultural traditions.[1] Table 5.1 sets forth the percentage and number of vendors who reported their native language as either a variant of Shona or Ndebele. The remaining 58 respondents indicated their mother tongue is a language spoken in Malawi (Chi-Nyanja or Chi-Chewa), Zambia, or Mozambique.

Table 5.1 Distribution of Zimbabwean Languages Spoken by Vendors

Language	Percent	Number
Chi-Zezeru	45.8	147
Chi-Ndau	3.1	10
Chi-Karanga	10.3	33
Chi-Manyika	8.1	26
Chi-Ungwe	3.4	11
Chi-Toko/Chi-Budya	5.9	19
Chi-Korekore	4.0	13
Sindebele	1.2	4

Source: Interview schedule.

The language bringing these culture groups together in the marketplace is that spoken in the Harare environs, Chi-Zezeru. Until a customer establishes his/her origin through language in a purchasing transaction, the vendors use Chi-Zezeru. If a customer is known as coming from the same home area as the vendor, then the mother tongue is used.

▲ Growing Up in Zimbabwe

Education

As vendors were growing up, going to school was an important way in which parents invested in the future. Where possible, girls as well as boys were sent to school, but, in one vendor's estimation, educating boys seemed more important:

> Long back, only boys went to school. If a woman was educated it was only to teach her how to write. Boys are more educated. Only men were working long back, so the boys were sent to school so they could get work. Girls didn't know they could also benefit from going to school. It was always thought that only boys could take care of their parents. The girls were sent to herd cattle so the boys could go to school.

Family finances seemed to be the overriding problem in sending children to school. As one vendor, whose parents had been working on a tea estate, reported: "None of us went to school because there was no money. My parents were farmers at Chipinge on the Jersey Tea Estate past Mount Selinda. They just weren't paid enough to send us to school."

Although some 18.8 percent (60) of vendors never went to school, 63.4 percent had achieved between grade one and grade seven, while almost 18 percent had had some secondary education. The preponderance of vendors without education are either older (over 40) or come from Mozambique or Malawi where fewer educational opportunities existed.

Many women born in rural areas received some formal schooling, but not as much as males. Of the 238 vendor spouses, 18.9 percent had not been to school, 48.7 percent had received between grade one and grade seven education, and 32.4 percent had achieved some secondary education. In comparing percentages, there is a parallel between men and women who did not attend school, but differences emerge in the number of years they attended: men attended school for several years more than women.

This assertion about vendors is not paralleled in Brand's study. Of both men and women microentrepreneurs, 23.5 percent of females and 19.5 percent of males had never attended school; 70.6 percent of females and 73 percent of males had between one and seven years of education; and 5.9 percent of females and 6.8 percent of males had received some secondary education (Brand 1982:10). I believe these percentages vary because in my study vendors reported the educational levels of their spouses, who may have been employed in the formal sector, while Brand's study reports educational levels for men in the informal sector.

Saito's data (1991:25) indicate that in Harare, 4 percent of women interviewed had achieved education below grade seven; 51 percent achieved grade seven; 34 percent had attained a Junior Certificate; and 11 percent had attained an "O" Level Certificate. The variance in these findings may be attributed to increased urban migration by women, the greater availability of education for women after independence, and the broader spectrum of informal sector occupations women had obtained since independence.

Socialization and Acquisition of Skills

Vendors were socialized into the world of women's work. They learned from their mothers not only their domestic chores, but also how to grow garden and field crops. They learned, in helping their mothers to produce food crops, that their responsibilities in their families of creation would be similar. Moreover, the women learned that their acceptance into their husbands' patrilineages is measured in terms of their own ability to grow food to provision their families. In the rural areas, when women marry they are allocated a well-watered plot on which to grow vegetables, the abundant harvests of which would stand as a measure of ancestral acceptance into their husbands' patrilineages. If such harvests were not forthcoming, then divination by a *nganga* (traditional healer or diviner) might occur with subsequent gifts being offered to the *vadzimu* (family ancestors) to pray for a second chance (see Lan 1985 for a more detailed discussion of this subject).

Another skill women acquire as they grow up is how to brew beer, which serves both an economic and a ritual function. At peak agricultural times, e.g., harvests, a farmer makes it known in the community that a work party—*kushandira pamwe*—is needed. As a cultural norm, neighbors willingly participate, but the promise of good beer and/or a good meal as payment for the day's labor acts as a further incentive to come and work. Hence, the woman who brews the best beer is most likely to have the most assistance in meeting farm labor demands.

Women are also required to brew beer for many ritual celebrations, including the *kurova guva* (bringing the spirit home) ceremony about a year after the death of a family member. The aroma of the beer, the active gathering of people, and the rituals performed collectively woo the spirit home to care for the living members of the family.

▲ Marriage

Marriage, as a social institution, is highly regarded for cultural, economic, and sociological reasons. As Robertson posits for Ghana, "marriage is not a choice but a social necessity" (Robertson 1984:177). Similarly, in Zimbabwe:

> Since the traditional family had to be large in order to guarantee the material well-being of all its members, of children, of the sick, the disabled and the old, and since this required continuity over time, every person had

a moral obligation to marry and to contribute to the social reproduction of his kinship group. This most basic value, to beget or bear children, was instilled in all members of the society from early childhood onwards. Nobody was allowed to shirk this duty and social pressures ensured compliance. Even today a single life is still regarded as abnormal (Weinrich 1982:34–35).

These assertions are borne out by the data on the vendors. Table 5.2 presents the marital status they reported. Table 5.3 presents comparative data on the marital status of other microentrepreneurs in Harare. My survey results on marriage contrast with those of Brand and Saito. Brand's explanation for the high number of widowed entrepreneurs is attributable to the impact of the liberation war (won just a year prior to her study). The higher incidence of married women in my study may reflect marital adjustments in years subsequent to the war.

Table 5.2 Marital Status of Female Fresh Produce Vendors in Harare

Status	Percent	Number
Married	61.0	192
Married, polygynous (one other wife)	5.7	18
Married, polygynous (more than one other wife)	0.3	1
Divorced and remarried	4.4	14
Widowed and remarried	1.9	6
Total married	73.3	231
Divorced	14.0	44
Widowed	11.7	37
Single (never married)	1.0	3
Total not married	26.7	84

Source: Interview schedule.

Table 5.3 Marital Status of Female Microentrepreneurs

Marital Status	Brand Data[a] (percent)	Saito Data Harare[b] (percent)
Married	33.3	62
Monogamous	—	54
Polygamous	—	8
Widowed	51.0	6
Divorced	11.8	12
Single	3.9	20

Sources: a. Brand (1982:7).
b. Saito (1991:107).

The findings presented above can be compared and contrasted with national data sets. The percentage of women who are married is reportedly lower for the entire country (64.6 percent), and for urban areas in general (62.3 percent) than it is for women in Highfield (84.9 percent) and for vendors in Harare (73.3 percent). Both the Highfield and national census data reported in Tables 5.4 and 5.5, respectively, were collected just prior to or just after independence in 1980, while the data on vendors were recorded in 1986. A shift in urban marital status seems to have occurred. These figures might be explained in several ways.

Table 5.4 Marital Status of Women in Highfield Township

Status	Percent	Number
Single	5.9	22
Divorced or separated	5.7	21
Widowed	3.0	11
Married		
Customary registered	30.3	112
Customary unregistered	31.6	117
Church or civil	19.7	73
No response/other	3.8	14

Source: Adapted from Muchena (1980:23).

Table 5.5 Marital Status of Women in Zimbabwe According to 1982 Census[a]

Status[b]	Nationally[c]	Percent of Population	Urban[d]	Percent of Population
Never married	453,512	22.4	46,671	25.2
Divorced or separated	91,391	4.5	13,185	7.1
Widowed	171,736	8.5	9,702	5.3
Married	1,307,821	64.6	115,403	62.3
Not stated			188	0.1
Total	2,024,460	100.0	185,149	100.0

Notes: a. Statistics on marital status based on data collected for the 1992 census were not yet available by the time we went to press.

    b. Does not include women under the age of 15.

    c. From Zimbabwe, CSO (1985:38).

    d. From Zimbabwe, CSO (Table 19, October 3, 1983).

How such unions come about is challenged in the city, and this could be one of the reasons for the variance in marital status statistics. The prestations leading up to marriage between two corporate kin groups are many and varied. Among urban dwellers these practices continue, although many well-educated young people feel the processes involved are anachronistic. Most emphatically, these women object to husbands paying *lobola* in return for exercising their rights over women's labor, the children that ensue from the marriage, and over any income women generate (see May 1979:48).

Women's socialization into the culture of Shona-speaking people entails learning about marriage customs. As vendors grew up, they learned that when they married, they would have to move from their parents' homes to those of their husbands. The groom's *tete* (father's sister) was especially important, as it was her task to familiarize the new bride with the particular practices and beliefs of the groom's patrilineage and to escort the bride to her new husband on their wedding night.

Marrying under customary law used to require the payment of *lobola* or *roora*[2]—bridewealth (Stewart et al. 1990:171). Amounts varied according to whether the young woman had been educated and for how many years, and/or whether the woman came from a "good" family in which people were known to be honest, hardworking, and not tainted by any spirit possession.

Lobola is being contested rigorously by many women in Harare: of the 281 vendors who reported once having been married, only 28 percent indicated that their husbands had finished paying lobola. This means, technically, that any children ensuing from the remaining 72 percent of the marriages "belong" to the wife. Husbands/fathers have full rights over their children only once lobola payments have been completed. One vendor argued very strongly that lobola is good: "When a woman gives birth it will be her husband who pays for school. Lobola is the first indication of responsibility. Lobola is responsibility and authority over the rights of the child."

Lobola cash agreements for the 28 percent of husbands who paid ranged between under Z$50 and Z$770. Requirements in cattle ranged between none and 10, and a combination of cash and cattle ranged between one beast and Z$30, and 10 cattle and Z$200. Bridewealth requirements, as reported by vendors, appear in Table 5.6.

Marriages take different forms, among which are *chipare* and *kutiza*. Chipare is the practice of two sisters marrying the same man. Such a marriage might take place if the sisters' parents are financially unable to support them, a younger sister is desired when the elder has not yet been married, or two wives are desired to help with the farm.

> I was married together with my elder sister and I had problems with her. My parents forced me to go and stay with my sister because her husband was helping my father with everything. My husband thanked my father a lot and gave him Z$30 more, not a part of lobola, but thanks only. My sister was told to go home and plow, but she started screaming, saying "I can't leave you staying with my husband; better you go home and plow because you are young."

Table 5.6 *Lobola/Roora* **Required for Vendor Marriages**

Type of Payment (in Z$)	Percent	Number
None	10.4	29
Less than 50	10.8	30
50–100	15.1	42
101–150	5.0	14
151–200	7.5	21
201–250	3.9	11
251–300	6.5	18
301–350	2.5	7
351–400	5.0	14
401–450	.7	2
451–500	2.9	8
More than 501	1.8	5
Cattle and cash combination	27.9	78

Source: Interview schedule.

Evidenced in the elder sister's behavior is her belief that she would be forgotten by the husband if she were to "go home and plow," while the younger would become the husband's favorite.

Among the vendors the incidence of kutiza marriages (the groom "kidnaps" the bride and pays "damages" to the bride's parents afterwards) is relatively high, especially among the younger, more educated women. Men pay "damages," in lieu of lobola, which are invariably lower than the amounts required in marital prestations. However, sometimes not even kutiza payment is required:

> I can't get money to educate my children. If I get someone to marry me and help me with the children, I could like it. This time, my young sisters are helping me with school fees and all other things I need. This time I don't want to have a child—only a boyfriend. Finally, I have someone to give my problems to. I don't want to be given laws by someone. I have one looking after me now. He gives me Z$10 after two or three weeks. He comes home every day, so we nearly stay together. This man is known by my brothers and they give me permission to sleep with him.

In this instance, the vendor had already been divorced from the father of her children. Believing that she was unlikely to find a man who would take on the financial responsibility of her children, or someone who would actually pay lobola to her father, she accepted the next best thing—someone who will live with her, listen to her problems, and help her solve them, and who will also give her some financial support.

Vendors who spoke about polygamy did not favor the institution, perhaps because of the complicated economics of running two households in the city. Others related their fears ensuing from such marriages:

> This other wife uses a lot of magic. She once wanted to kill me. After I left home being sick, I had three operations. We never stayed properly with that lady. I also left my property there. I am ever scared to go and take my things. My husband knows that his second wife uses magic. My husband was also given medicines so he really doesn't know what to do.

The "medicines" to which this vendor referred are powerful herbs, or "magic," put into the husband's food to make sure he thinks only of the woman who gave him the "teaspoonful."

Housing also acts as a deterrent to polygamy: "My husband is trying to chase me as he took another wife, but we got the house together and government won't let them chase me."

When a man applies for housing from the Harare City Council, his wife's name must appear on the application. If the couple subsequently divorces, the woman is entitled to remain living in the house as much as her husband. Who ultimately remains in the house is then a matter for the courts to decide.

▲ Divorce, Widowhood, and Remarriage

Despite the "necessity" for marriage and the social and economic ties produced in the process, divorce is a growing phenomenon ("When 'Till Death Do Us Part'" 1986:22). Refusal of conjugal rights, the inability of a woman to have children, and female infidelity are all reasons why divorce occurs. A double standard exists in which men perceive their rights as being relatively unlimited because they have paid lobola. "I don't think she has a right to divorce me. After all I paid lobola for her and in any case, traditionally a man could marry many wives and a girlfriend or mistress could be seen in the same light" ("Marriage Under Fire" 1985:5).

Even in cases where bridewealth payments have not been made (*mapoto* marriages—see Muchena 1982:26), a man can discontinue his commitment on the grounds of "the irretrievable breakdown of marriage," which may be the result of either spouse's activities (Stewart et al. 1990:174). The 58 (17.9 percent) vendors who reported they were divorced cited the following reasons: 34.7 percent, male infidelity; 16.3 percent, wife beating; 12.2 percent, inability to bear children. The remaining said divorce occurred due to the women not bearing sons, desertion, and abandonment. The women's comments indicate certain cultural norms: "I could not have any children"; "I gave birth to girls only"; "He had too many girlfriends"; "I was accused of being possessed by vadzimu" (i.e., spirits); and "He got drunk and beat me so my parents took me away."

Of those divorced, 61.4 percent reported their children stayed with them, and 18.2 percent said the children went with their fathers (in the remaining cases, children went to relatives). This finding runs counter to the traditional claim that men "own" their children as a result of having paid lobola (see May 1979:41). Relating this finding with that on the percentage of husbands having finished paying lobola (only 28 percent), it would appear that many men are unwilling both to fulfill their financial obligations to their spouse's families and to raise their children from one marriage, especially when they intend to start another.

Responsibility for children in the city means increased expenses a woman must bear. Oftentimes a woman who does not have financial resources will send her children home to her parents in the rural areas, and send a cash remittance on a regular basis to maintain them (May 1979:42). I surmised this was the case with many vendors who reported their children were living away from them and who were sending remittances on a regular basis to their rural kin.

It is common practice, I was informed, that when a man divorces his wife he takes with him many of the household assets. If the couple were living in Harare, a man might bring his new wife to the household, essentially forcing out the first wife. If a husband demanded that his children remain with him, the new wife might make life very miserable for the youngsters:

> When I went to look for my father in Harare, I found him living with a new wife. My mother didn't even know he had taken another wife. I told him I wanted to stay with him so I could continue my secondary schooling. He agreed. But after a few months, I started getting very bad stomach pains. I had to go back to Masvingo to my mother. While there, the pains stopped, so I went back to Harare. The pains started again. After some time I realized my father's new wife was trying to poison me because she didn't want me around. She wanted everything for her children.

Similar to information reported on the disposition of lobola after being widowed, 83.7 percent of divorced women said nothing happened, and 8.2 percent said the in-laws asked for it back. Of the majority, women said since many of their husbands had not finished paying, they really did not have a right to ask for the portion that had been paid to be returned.

Widowhood also produces problems. Since all African marriages come under the domain of customary law, if a husband dies, all the assets of the family can revert to the man's kin. These belongings might include a house in the city, its furnishings, an automobile, and other movable property. Repeatedly related to me was the practice of a dead husband's kin coming to claim the family assets after the funeral, leaving the widow destitute. In earlier times, I was told, the woman's in-laws would also take the children, if the lobola had been paid. Nowadays, however, assets may be taken, but children are not. Women said the high cost of sending children to school was the main reason children were left with their mothers; the in-laws did not want the additional financial responsibility:

> They [in-laws] told me to go back to my parents, and they gave me money equal to the bus fare only. They even took the bank book. The one who conducted the funeral wanted to take over [*kugarwa nhaka*], but his wife refused. She shouted very strong. But I really wanted to stay there because they told me that I was going to leave my child with them.

Fortunately, since the passage of the Deceased Persons and Family Maintenance Act as amended in 1987, all women—including those who were in a polygamous marriage—can obtain maintenance from the estate of a deceased husband (Stewart et al. 1990:187–188). Although maintenance is legally possible, "A widow is often not aware of her rights, nor, even if she knows of them, is she in a fit condition emotionally to deal with the grasping relatives" (Stewart et al. 1990:186).

Families of deceased husbands may attempt to impose the levirate—kugarwa nhaka—upon widows. It was common practice in the rural areas for a widow to be taken, as either a second or third wife, by one of her dead husband's brothers. I was informed that such a practice prevented embarrassment on the part of the widow's parents because, technically, the lobola would have to be returned if the husband died. This was especially the case if the woman was still relatively young at the time of her husband's death. Since marriage was a preferred state of being, such a woman could marry again and command another lobola. Thus, the first one had either to be returned or used in the marriage of the widow to her husband's brother. Vendors reported how this practice has given rise to a number of problems:

> I am staying with my dead husband's younger brother, but he is also married. He is a painter. My "brother" is very economic—he doesn't want to pump out money. Since my husband died, my husband's relatives couldn't even come to look for me and couldn't buy these children some clothes. Within some days of his death, they brewed beer for the funeral. After that they wanted to take over and they all wanted me to be their wife. And they started to fight. My husband's brother is the one who was serious about taking over. The elder one said "you can't because you didn't do anything during brother's illness." My

father said "you did not pay lobola and you want to take over. Who is going to pay the lobola?" Nobody answered. Then my father said "I am taking my child home. She can't suffer in my presence." I was given two acres to plow by my husband's father, but I refused because the soil was very bad. The main problem now is my husband's wife. She is now refusing to keep my children, saying she has plenty of relations who are suffering and nobody is looking after them. I can't kill myself, but I'm not supposed to be here on earth. I've been treated like a small mad boy.

A vendor on whom kugarwa nhaka was imposed reported as follows: "I refused to be married by my husband's young brother, so he just moved into our house for free. Instead of taking me, he tried to take over the house."

Another vendor linked nhaka with economics: "After my husband died and I refused nhaka, my husband's brothers took all the furniture and cattle saying that they wanted to keep the cattle for his sons when they grow up. They did not take the sons. They didn't even give my children the cattle when they grew up."

This practice was once valued more in the rural areas than it is now in the city. A period when women were pressured into complying with this practice, according to the vendors, was during the liberation war when many men died: "After my husband died, his brothers wanted kugarwa nhaka, but I refused. That's when my troubles started. They reported me to the freedom fighters saying that I was having affairs with the Rhodesian soldiers. That's when I ran away."

As women create the means to be self-supporting, they refuse nhaka on the basis that they will be discriminated against in the husband's brother's household, especially if he already has a wife. Rather than put up with the difficulties of two wives in one household, widows opt to remain alone and struggle along as best they can.

The proportion of vendors who had been widowed is 13.4 percent, with women having been in this state for up to 35 years. I asked the women what kind of help they received after their husbands passed away. Of those widowed, 35 percent reported that nothing was done to help them. Some (17.5 percent) were given money, but many indicated that in-laws seized furniture, cattle, and children. Interestingly, 83.3 percent reported that the lobola was not asked to be returned. Perhaps this is linked to two factors: that lobola payments had never been completed; or that the children of the marriage were not taken by the in-laws.

Since so many women are left destitute from widowhood or divorce, I asked these women whether they tried to go back to their families in the rural areas to get assistance. Of a total population of 88, 67 percent reported they did. The 33 percent who did not reported some 43 reasons why they did not want to return. Some of these include: "I had nowhere to live; my parents were dead"; "nobody in the rural areas could support me and my children"; "I wanted to keep my children, which I couldn't do if I went home because my husband would have taken them"; "my husband wouldn't have supported me if I went home; besides the kids are used to living in the city"; and "my parents were going to force me to go as a second wife to my sister's husband, and I didn't want that."

The upset caused by death and divorce left women with few choices. For the most part, either they did not want to/could not return to their parents' rural homes or they went there and ultimately returned to Harare.[3] In the city, they had to learn to cope as single parents with the problems of finances, housing, schooling, and provisioning for their families. As reported above, several women sought another husband and remarried. Remarriage, however, did not necessarily resolve their financial burdens.

When ascertaining family expenditure information, one woman who was divorced and remarried explained to me why her position with her new husband was not economically secure:

> After I divorced my first husband, I stayed with my children at my parents' home here in Harare. After some time, I met and married my husband. He took me to his parents' home, also in Harare, and we stay with them. Unfortunately, there was no room for my three children in my husband's house, so they stayed with my parents.
>
> I can't really tell you much about household expenses. Until this day I don't know how much my husband pays for rent, because he gives it to his mother every month. Also, since the birth of our daughter, he refuses to pay anything to support my other children. I have just received a letter saying that they are going to attach my first husband's salary so my children can have a better life. But until they start sending me the money, I have to keep selling vegetables so my children can go to school.

The complex problems of divorce and widowhood, linked to changes in lobola practices, have left children the real victims of social change. It is unclear to me whether the problems are the same in the rural areas, or whether they are exacerbated as a consequence of city life; further empirical research should enhance our understanding of this phenomenon.

▲ Housing and Marital Status

During the colonial period, urban accommodation was provided to single males only while they were working in the city. Subsequent to the Plewman Commission Report of the 1950s, freehold housing was made

available to men with families. Throughout the period of urban development, however, the number of dwelling units constructed has never kept
pace with actual demand. In 1986 there was a backlog of over 24,000 families on the municipal waiting list ("Housing: Keeping Pace with a Rising
Demand," in *Moto,* No. 45, 1986:7). Limited availability of accommodation means an employed person must live wherever housing is available.

Family housing in the townships of Harare in the two decades prior to
1980 was granted to male African migrant laborers who had resident wives.
Remnants of this policy existed in the years just after independence:

> Low income women have further problems in obtaining housing. When a
> couple who are tenants of the Municipality are divorced or separated, they
> must forfeit the house. The man may obtain "single" accommodation, but
> it is very difficult for a divorced woman with children to find accommo-
> dation. At the discretion of the township superintendent, and depending
> on demand in the housing area, widowed women may maintain the house
> providing that they can meet the rent; otherwise they have to find them-
> selves alternative accommodation (Patel and Adams 1981:22–26).

It is highly likely, therefore, that a woman would not have reported herself
as being divorced or widowed for fear of losing her accommodation. Since
the passage of the Legal Age of Majority Act in 1982 (enforceable beginning in 1984), women are no longer perpetual minors and can own or rent
their own housing in Harare (see Stewart et al. 1990:169–189 for the broad
implications of this act). If a woman has resources and can meet the monthly rental requirements, legally she can live wherever she likes. Moreover,
who resides in the former marital household is now a matter for the courts
to decide. Consequently, the vendors I interviewed might have felt more
free in reporting their divorced or widowed status than in studies conducted
prior to the passage of this law.

▲ Family Life and Children

Family size in relation to type of housing available has presented problems
of finding urban accommodation. Table 5.7 presents the number of children
vendors have. For comparison, the fertility levels for African women in
Harare are presented in Table 5.8. An approximate fertility figure for
African women in Harare is 2.78, while the national average is 5.62
(Zimbabwe, *First Five-Year National Development Plan 1986–1990*
1986:37). Comparing female vendors with these two figures, it would
appear average vendor fertility falls between the two at approximately 4.8.

When I asked vendors how many of their children were still living with
them, they reported a range between one and 10. Table 5.9 sets forth the
population of children in vendor households.

Table 5.7 Number of Surviving Children Born to Vendors

Number of Children	Percent of Vendors	Number of Vendors
0	3.1	10
1	8.8	28
2	10.3	33
3	14.7	47
4	14.1	45
5	9.1	29
6	16.3	52
7	13.4	43
8	5.3	17
9	3.4	11
10	.9	3
12	.3	1
14	.3	1

Source: Interview schedules.

Table 5.8 Fertility Levels of African Women in Harare and of Fresh Produce Vendors

Number of Children	Women in Harare	Percent[a]	Number of Vendors	Percent[b]
0	58,588	35.2	10	3.1
1	23,488	14.1	28	8.8
2	21,124	12.7	33	10.3
3	16,137	9.7	47	14.7
4	12,635	7.6	45	14.1
5	9,490	5.7	29	9.1
6	7,689	4.6	52	16.2
7	5,777	3.5	43	13.4
8	4,299	2.6	17	5.3
9	2,859	1.7	11	3.4
10	1,884	1.1	3	.9
11 and over	2,436	1.5	2	.6
Total	166,406	100.0	320	100.0

Notes: a. Statistics in the first three columns are from Zimbabwe, CSO (Table 30A, August 17, 1983).
    b. Statistics in the last two columns are from interview schedules.

Urban households are not composed solely of members of a nuclear family, however. When vendors were queried on whether other people lived in their households, 47.3 percent responded positively. When asked how many other people lived with vendors, the response ranged between one and twenty-three. Table 5.10 sets forth the distribution of other people in vendor households as a portion of the percentage of households with additional members. Summarizing this data, vendor households are occupied, generally speaking, by vendor, her spouse, a mean of 4.6 children, and a mean of 3.7 other people, for a total mean household size of 10.3.[4]

Table 5.9 Number of Children Living with Vendor Parents

Number of Children	Percent of Vendor Parents	Number of Vendor Parents
0	10.5	33
1	15.3	48
2	16.6	52
3	13.4	42
4	15.7	49
5	11.5	36
6	8.3	26
7	5.8	18
8	1.9	6
9	.6	2
10	.3	1

Source: Interview schedules.

Table 5.10 Distribution of Other Residents in Vendor Households

Number of Other Residents	Percentage of Households with Additional Members	Number of Vendor Households
1	19.4	62
2	11.6	37
3	5.9	19
4	3.8	12
5	2.5	8
6	1.3	4
7	.9	3
8	.9	3
9	.3	1
10	.3	1
11	.9	3
17	.3	1
23	.3	1

Source: Interview schedules.

When I asked who the additional residents in vendor households were, I was overwhelmed with the 71 different responses given. Some 23 categories of kin living with vendors are derived through the husband's kin, 35 through vendor's kin, and 11 through vendors and their spouses. Two others reported that lodgers and domestic workers are also included in this category.

The presence of so many kin living in the same urban household gives rise to a number of questions anomalous to several assertions in the Zimbabwean literature: that roots to the rural homeland are always maintained; and that urban households are proportionately smaller than those in the rural areas (due largely to economics and the size of housing available).

Urban household size may deliberately have been misreported if a landlord or the city council set limits to the number of people occupying a household.

▲ Migration to Harare

Most vendors (63 percent) reported having come to Harare after they were married, beginning as early as 1939. Of the 270 vendors who said they had been migrants, Table 5.11 presents a summary of when vendors left their rural homes for Harare.

Table 5.11 Vendor Migration to Harare

Time Period	Percentage	Number
1939	1.2	3
1940–1949	3.0	8
1950–1959	11.1	30
1960–1969	24.5	66
1970–1979	30.4	81
1980–1985	16.0	43
1986	14.1	38

Source: Interview schedules.

The preponderance of vendors (68.9 percent) reported having moved from their places of birth only once—after marriage—coming directly to Harare.[5] Another 23.9 percent said they had made a prior move, most of whom had gone to their husbands' rural homesteads at marriage. The remaining 7.2 percent have moved several times, for the following reasons: parents were moved from their homestead "during Hitler's war"; "the land was not fertile, so we had to find a place to plow"; "my father lost his job so we had to move"; "the white farmer sold the place my parents were working on"; "to run away from the war" (i.e., the liberation struggle); and to migrate to a number of other, smaller urban centers to look for work.

The women who came to Harare on their own looking for work (17.6 percent of 273) said they migrated for a number of reasons: "I ran away from the war"; "my husband died, so I came here with the children"; "I didn't like living in the rural areas any more, so I ran away"; and "I just knew there was a better life for me in the city."

Since finding accommodation has been and still is highly problematic, newly-arrived migrants usually resided with kin. A significant portion of vendor spouses (34 percent) who migrated first, however, resided in hostels or found some sort of lodging. Women, when they migrated, either joined their husbands at whatever accommodation they had found (55.3 percent), or stayed with relatives. Only 0.7 percent said they found lodging, and 1.7 percent said they had nobody to stay with.

Vendors reported having lived in the same place in Harare between 1 and 47 years, with a mean of 11.6. Interestingly, the mean falls directly on the year when guerrilla activities heightened in the rural areas during the liberation struggle.

Brand's findings (1982:9) are somewhat at variance to mine. She found that 39.1 percent of all vendors came to Harare more than 20 years prior to her study; 12 percent had arrived between 11 and 15 years prior; 14 percent came between 6 and 10 years prior; and 19 percent had arrived less than 5 years prior. I believe this variance is explained by Brand's inclusion in her statistics of both male and female vendors. Also, women dominate fresh produce retail microenterprises, and their pattern of migration to Harare has been affected by cultural norms, marriage, and economic opportunity in the city and the rural areas.

▲ Linkages to Rural Kin

A portion of vendors indicated that their families still lived in the rural areas. When I asked vendors whether either or both of their parents were still living, 72 percent responded that at least one parent was still alive. A similar question was asked about vendor spouses' parents, to which 45.2 percent responded either one or both parents were still living. When asked where parents resided, vendors indicated 19 percent of vendor parents and 12.5 percent of vendor spouse parents reside in one of the Harare suburbs. Of the remaining mothers and fathers, 6 percent live in Malawi, Mozambique, or Zambia, while 17.4 percent of spouse parents reside in these countries. Other parents reportedly reside in approximately 62 different rural Zimbabwean locations. The link between these rural families and vendors is maintained in several ways: visitation of rural family members to urban vendors, urban vendor family visitation to rural homesteads, remittances, fostering of children in female-headed households, and maintenance of rural land holdings.

One of the last questions I asked vendors was whether kin come from the rural areas to visit. In response, 74.8 percent indicated relatives come at least once a year, if not twice: on Christmas or on Easter. Again, the range of kin represented in responses was very broad, although visitation appeared to favor vendor parents or siblings. Some 34 responses said one or more of vendor parents visited, 18 said siblings and their offspring came, 18 said their spouse's relatives came, and the remainder were related through vendor parents of either side.

Believing that vendors might gain access to fresh produce grown in the rural areas to sell in their stalls via gifts from their kin, I asked whether relations brought food for vendors grown on the farm: 31.7 percent of vendors replied they did. I was informed, however, that food brought by relatives must be eaten in the home and not taken to the stall to sell. It would be in very poor taste to sell a gift, although in several instances the "gift" may be a payment in kind for agricultural work performed by the vendors during home visit. Green mealies (fresh maize cobs) and home-ground maize were the dominant gifts, with fresh-ground peanut butter, *nyimo,* groundnuts, and seasonal fruits almost as important. All together, relatives reportedly brought at least 25 different foods to vendor households.

Vendors and family members visit the rural areas to attend funerals and the like: 74.7 percent (n = 239) of vendors reported they go "home" between once a month and once every two years. Table 5.12 illustrates the frequency of vendor visitation.

Table 5.12 Frequency of Vendor Visitation to Rural Kin

Frequency of Visit	Percent of Vendors	Number of Vendors
None	25.3	81
Once a year	25.9	83
Twice a year	16.9	54
Three times a year	16.3	52
Four times a year	6.9	22
Once a month	7.8	25
Once every two years	.3	1
Once every four years	.3	1
Funerals only	.3	1

Source: Interview schedules.

Rural kin visitation is partially determined by the distance between Harare and the rural homestead and the cost of transport. The cost of transport, I was informed, is a limiting factor in determining who and how many of vendor's family accompany her on her journey. Table 5.13 illustrates the cost of transport to visit rural kin. While vendors reported going home mainly during the Christmas holidays, many women said they returned to their parents' rural homes at the time of plowing. Sometimes this coincides with Christmas break, if the rains are late, but usually occurs during October/November.

Another means vendors use to stay in touch with their rural kin is through cash remittances. Assertions concerning migrant male cash remittances to rural kin can also be made for female vendors who generate their own income. I asked vendors twice what amounts they remitted: once in the context of asking about family expenditures, and once in the context of "other" annual financial outlays. In response to the first inquiry, the mean

Table 5.13 Vendors' Costs for Transport to Visit Rural Kin

Amount (in Z$)	Percent of Vendors	Number of Vendors
Under $1	2.7	7
1–1.99	6.9	18
2–2.99	12.0	31
3–3.99	11.2	29
4–4.99	8.9	23
5–5.99	10.8	28
6–6.99	8.9	23
7–7.99	8.5	22
8–8.99	3.1	8
9–9.99	3.9	10
10–10.99	5.0	13
11–11.99	2.7	7
12–12.99	2.7	7
13–13.99	1.5	4
14–14.99	1.9	5
15–15.99	3.1	8
16–16.99	.8	2
18	.8	2
Above 20	4.6	12

Source: Interview schedules.

monthly remittance for 157 vendors was Z$21.52, with a range between Z$2 and Z$200. The second inquiry yielded a mean annual remittance for 149 vendors of Z$87.53, with a range between Z$4 and Z$600.[6] Rural families are said to use this financial input to maintain the farm and/or support schoolchildren.

While I have no hard evidence on this point, in informally interviewing vendors I found that the probability of remitting consistently is related to whether a vendor has sent a child to her relatives to be raised in the rural areas. This could be a consequence of being divorced, widowed, or simply not having enough money to raise children in the city.

It is a common assumption in the literature that men who migrate to urban areas for work simultaneously keep one foot in the rural areas. In Zimbabwe the passage of the 1951 Land Husbandry Act was designed to end the dual basis for economic livelihood. If men were registered as urban dwellers, they were not able to have land in the rural areas. While the Act was never fully implemented, I explored the issue of rural land ownership (or rights of usufruct under traditional tenure) with the vendors. Out of the 325 vendors interviewed, only 23 (7.1 percent) said their husbands had been allocated a plot. When I probed further, trying to determine whether what was grown on their own land at home ultimately was sold at their stalls and tables, I was informed by 20 of the vendors that the land no longer belonged to them because they do not cultivate it. Of the three remaining, problems of labor and water prevented them from using it effec-

tively. Thus, if women return periodically to cultivate, it is to their relatives' farms rather than to their own.

▲ Conclusion

Women in Zimbabwe are socialized into a cultural world in which norms
require that they marry, bear and raise children, and take on certain economic responsibilities. History has determined that these cultural norms
will be acted upon in a range of rural and urban environments, and within
the structures of state and traditional governments. Changes in the economy
and political independence have provided a greater range of adaptive
options to both men and women, but each entails a distinctive set of challenges.

What women in urban environments have had to adapt to are the
changes brought about by the interaction of all of the above. Marriages
have become more unstable, housing is scarce and costly, employment
opportunities are limited, and salaries are not adequate to meet financial
needs. With the incidence of marital dissolutions rising, women must
develop the means to support themselves and their children. A residual bias
against women in urban areas remains, however. Landlords take advantage
of women, who are not able to gain access to formal support systems, have
difficulty in obtaining business licenses and start-up capital, and, because
many have not received much education, cannot obtain reliable, long-term
employment.

Historical precedent, cultural norms, and the socioeconomic demands
of urban life require that women contribute economically to the maintenance of their families. Yet, the context set by these three parameters limits
women's chances for so doing. As McPherson's data (1991) indicate, most
women have made their way to the informal economy and established their
own microenterprises. Having arrived at a decision for self-sufficiency,
however, women find that they have not yet overcome their difficulties.
The problems of achieving financial security by trading in fresh produce
are many and varied. Strategies to surmount the problems are based in
women's business acumen and their ability to function in a patriarchal system. For some, the rewards and financial returns are substantial; for others,
hardships are multiplied. What behaviors differentiate these individuals?
How is it that some survive and others do not? And, for those who are not
achieving financially, what keeps them going?

The economic analysis on the conduct of the retail fresh produce trade
presented in Chapter Six will provide one-half the response to these questions. The other half will be explored in Chapter Seven, where I consider
the many reasons why women establish their businesses and endeavor to
maintain them.

▲ Notes

1. For an analysis of various cultural traditions represented in Zimbabwe, see Beach (1980); Bourdillon (1976); and Lan (1985) for cultural background of the VaKorekore people; and Ranger 1985 for an analysis of people who speak Chi-Ungwe in the Rusape area.

2. *Lobola* is the term for brideswealth in Sindebele, while *roora* is the term in Shona. For reasons I was unable to discern, *lobola* is the term generally used, even by Shona speakers.

3. A quote from Bourdillon (1991:312) is particularly relevant:

Many inhabitants of the towns have been born and brought up in an urban environment and many others have spent over half their lives in the towns. It is hard for these to give up the comforts of town life to revert to the more primitive rural life, and few have any intention of doing so if they can possibly avoid it. Some have no real ties with rural relations and would find it impossible to find a rural home even if they wished to. They are town or city people who would find themselves at a loss in the country: town is their home and they have no other.

4. This mean is much higher than that reported by the 1982 census. It is possible that vendors more freely reported the number of people living in their households to me than to the census takers. This, in turn, could be a reflection of certain lodging regulations that are supposed to limit the number of people who can inhabit a given housing unit.

5. Drakakis-Smith and Kivell (n.d.:21), in their study of Mabelreign, Glen View, and Epworth, reported that about half of their population interviewed had "moved in directly from village or rural settlement . . . , whilst another 40 percent moved directly to Harare form a small town, missing out the larger intermediary settlements, such as Mutare or Bulawayo."

6. Clearly, these figures do not concur. It is most likely that reporting error is in evidence here. It is probable that vendors could report a monthly figure for remittance but, owing to memory and inability to calculate, many misrepresented the amounts they remit annually.

▲ 6

The Business of
Generating Financial Returns

This chapter begins with a brief overview of the choices women in Harare have to earn an income. Ill-equipped educationally and facing a number of barriers to obtaining formal sector employment, women make the rational choice to earn an income by establishing a fresh produce microenterprise. Having done so, however, vendors assume a number of risks and must adopt specific business and maximizing behaviors if they wish to earn profits. The business activities of vendors are presented in an analysis of incomes and costs of doing business for all vendors, and in a more in-depth profile of six women (to illustrate individual variability). As will be demonstrated, incomes generated are not solely a function of pricing mechanisms, but are also attributable to variables related to the informal market context in which vendors operate.

▲ Choices and Limitations

For women, the urban workplace might be another person's home, an institutional or business setting, or an informal market. Depending on age, position in the life cycle, educational level, and employment opportunities, women make choices that must include balancing their domestic with their income generating activities. Historically, women were perceived by white settlers as being "home on the farm." If women came to town permanently and if they wanted to work, whites assumed African women would just hire themselves out as domestics.

This was the accepted practice for a large number of vendors when they first came to Harare and looked for work: 67.6 percent of 108 vendors initially sought employment as domestics. Some 17.6 percent, however, sought and found salaried employment in clothing factories, nursery schools, hospitals (cleaning and cooking), hotels (cleaning), and, for the few who had been educated, as teachers, receptionists, and shop girls. The formal economy has not been able to generate the number of jobs needed to satisfy demand. Hence, many women, especially, established their own businesses in the informal sector.

▲ Establishing the Fresh Produce Business

Whatever enterprise a woman establishes requires an initial capital investment. When I asked whether vendors had any financial assistance to establish their businesses, 74.8 percent said they did. Of these, 69.1 percent indicated their husbands had provided them funds to purchase initial stock. Of the remaining 30.9 percent, 8.2 percent had been helped by a sister or brother, another 7.8 percent had been helped by either one or both of their parents, while others reported receiving initial assistance from a variety of kin including husband's brother, mother's sister, father's sister, and the woman's children. Of those who did not receive any assistance, 23.4 percent said they relied upon their own resources—much of which came from former employment.

A vendor sets aside crochet work to wait on a customer in the high density suburbs.

To determine the importance of fresh produce vending as a category of work, I asked the women whether vending constituted their "main work." While 96 percent indicated it was, the remaining 4 percent (13) indicated they saw themselves primarily as domestics, clothes saleswomen, dressmakers, or crocheters. I then asked whether vendors had ever sold vegetables *and* simultaneously done something else to earn money; 16.3 percent indicated they had. Selling secondhand clothes and crocheting were enterprises in which 4.9 percent and 3.4 percent, respectively, of the vendors had engaged, while others knitted, made dresses or cushions, or operated a *shebeen* (house where homemade beer is sold).

I then asked whether vendors are currently earning incomes in other ways. Only 8.9 percent responded affirmatively, indicating they sell clothing (2.2 percent), crochet (1.2 percent), sew dresses, take in lodgers, and help their husbands run a tuck shop (a small kiosk selling manufactured goods or processed foods). In the past, 6.8 percent of vendors had earned income brewing beer, while currently only 1.8 percent said they did. Of these six women, only one indicated it was really profitable (she said she earned about Z$240 per month), while the others asserted brewing wasn't really worth their time. One was quick to recognize that she perhaps had revealed something of herself she ultimately did not want known and added, "of course, the beer I brew is for funerals."

Given that proportionately few vendors reported earning supplementary incomes, it is not a surprise that 73.6 percent of the population declared that selling vegetables is better than any other work; 26.4 percent said other work is better. Reasons for one preference over the other related to their inability to find work elsewhere, and both negative and positive aspects of the trade. Negative aspects included problems with wholesalers, low level of earnings, heavy loads that must be carried, and long hours.

In summary, women who sell fresh produce perceive a need to generate an income and have either tried to find salaried jobs in the formal economy or have been so employed and have left because the occupations conflicted with other demands on their time. At some point, women may have created other income generating opportunities—and might still be so engaged—but they ultimately settled upon fresh produce vending because it meets a number of needs: childcare compatibility; minimal initial investment; relatively consistent income; and less costly family food provisioning.

▲ Risk-Taking and Maximizing Behaviors

Once having established fresh produce microenterprises, women face a number of challenges to maintain them. The main problems cited by vendors are: (1) dealing with *makoronyera* at Mbare Musika; (2) developing strategies to ensure supply to meet demand; (3) transport; (4) to "cooperate" or not; (5) magic in the marketplace; and (6) coping with the long hours of trade.

Makoronyera

A particular bottleneck in the marketing system affecting vendor businesses is the "buyem-sellem" activities of the makoronyera—defined by the vendors as common thugs who steal crops from farmers and resell what they have stolen at inflated prices. A vendor's husband who had just transported his wife and her commodities from the wholesaler to her market site summarized the range of problems makoronyera create:

Many farmers come to sell at Mbare. The makoronyera take the things from the farmer—buy 30 cents, sell 60 cents. Makoronyera really set the prices at Mbare. I help my wife out. I go with her to buy at Mbare and argue with makoronyera.

When trucks come, one makoronyera jumps on the truck and says to the farmer "We want to buy." If women come and want to buy from the farmer, makoronyera chase them away saying the vegetables are his. The farmer wants 30 cents a bundle; makoronyera says 20 cents, and before the money is given to the farmers, makoronyera sells the bundle for 60 cents.

The city council police just stand around. Makoronyera swear and use bad language. They hit women if they try to persist. Makoronyera are a well organized group. They steal money also, and push women around to get money.

Makoronyera continually harass the vendors as they make their purchases.[1] The many complaints vendors had about these people include: being overcharged, 96 percent; being beaten when persisting in trying to buy a particular commodity, 75.7 percent; grass at the bottom of boxes of tomatoes to make them appear full, 95.4 percent; rotten commodities at the bottom of a box, 95.1 percent; and money taken without receiving the commodity purchased, 80.9 percent. Some 29 other problems were identified by vendors, the most significant of which is that vendors are prevented from buying directly from the farmers at the Mbare farmers' market (37.8 percent). Vendors also told me that if they wished to inspect a particular box of tomatoes, they would be forced to purchase them. The reason for such behavior became clear to me one day when I was interviewing producers at the farmers' market. I was observing a man packing tomatoes in a cardboard box. At one point, he looked up and saw me watching him. He began to unpack the tomatoes. And then he removed a rather large layer of grass. Once the grass had been tossed aside, he replaced the tomatoes, this time filling the box with more tomatoes than grass.

Makoronyera are extremely abusive "buyem-sellem" operators whom the municipal police cannot (or perhaps are not willing to) control. Their numbers vary at any one time between 6 and 14, and each is very active as farmers arrive at the adjacent bus stop or lorry park. On any number of occasions, I watched them jump atop an arriving bus and begin offloading before the bus had even come to a stop. They toss the pockets and boxes of fruits and vegetables to their colleagues, and then proceed to sell the commodities before the farmer has even alighted from the bus.

When I interviewed makoronyera at Mbare in between their selling activities, I asked them how they conducted their business. They replied they buy from the farmer, and turn around and resell the commodities to the women retailers, or anybody else who wanted to buy at their price. When I asked about the allegations of thievery, they were quick to change the subject or tell me they had to get back to their business. One respondent was interested in my questions and attempted to respond in a very straightforward manner. In very short order, several other makoronyera joined him and quickly cut off our conversation. In the entire interaction, with his friends and without, I was impressed with the polite demeanor with which I was addressed. I had conducted the interview in Shona, and this skill by a white person accorded me respect, even though it was clear that I was dealing with men who paid little heed to certain aspects of the law.

It was clear to me that if vendors wished to continue purchasing at Mbare they would have to either avoid these thugs or conform to their expectations. Most did the former, but at a cost because the thugs would sometimes monopolize the sale of certain commodities. If a vendor needed that particular item, she would have to take what she could get and bear any financial burdens the purchase required.

During my revisit in 1993, the changes that had taken place at Mbare had made it very difficult for makoronyera to operate within the market walls. The municipality had become very strict about the conduct of business between farmers and wholesalers and no longer allowed the behavior described above. As a result, the abuses suffered by vendors no longer occur within the market; a problem does arise, however, if the market cannot accommodate deliveries during a certain period in the morning due to congestion. Some farmers will then be accosted outside the gates where thuggery is not as carefully monitored.

Meeting Demand in Times of Scarcity

In times of citywide scarcity, vendors must identify alternative sources of supply. For instance, at the outset of this research, the wholesale cost of tomatoes exceeded Z$20 per 10 kilograms. Regardless of glut or scarcity, customers seem to have a fixed price in mind for a certain quantity of a given commodity. Thus, the smallest retail heap of tomatoes must cost 20 cents. This price, however, entailed a loss. Rather than raising the price and risking customer loss, vendors went out of their way to find a cheaper source of supply. They were willing to take a bus to a U-Pick farm some 20 kilometers from the city, pick quantities desired, and transport them back on the bus. Seeing their predicament, I volunteered to take four to the farm, help them pick, and pack as many boxes as we could into my trunk. They were very happy that they would not have to pay transport costs.

When we arrived, we found that only very green tomatoes remained on the vines. While I made it clear that the women were under no obligation whatsoever to purchase the 10 kilogram boxes for Z$12 (not a very good discount, according to the vendors), and that we could search for other farms in the area, the women decided they would pick what they could and set the very green ones aside to ripen. As an epilogue to the story, the following week, when the green tomatoes had ripened, the price of a 10 kilogram box of tomatoes had fallen to Z$8.

As we went from one vending site to another, I noticed certain wholesalers coming directly to the markets to sell. This occurred, I learned, when wholesalers had overages from their morning deliveries and wanted to sell what remained. At times women could buy onions, tomatoes, and cabbage at advantageous prices, but at other times wholesalers would increase their prices, arguing that women would not have to pay transport costs to have their purchases delivered.

Transport

Transport poses the biggest problem both financially and logistically. Bus and emergency taxi fares have increased over the years, impinging on amounts vendors have available for wholesale purchases. Logistically, buses travel along routes from high density suburbs to work sites downtown and the light industrial areas, not between African residential areas. Thus, some vendors find it necessary to take two buses to Mbare—one to the industrial area or city center, and another on to Mbare. Bus schedules are also a problem. Women feel it is necessary to be at the Mbare farmers' market when it opens at 5:00 A.M. Few buses are running at that time, and even fewer when it is time for them to return as rush hour bus routes bring people from the high density suburbs to town, and not vice versa.

Women must also pay to transport their commodities on whatever conveyance they use. Vendors reported difficulties with bus drivers who would either not accept vendor purchases or would charge vendors exorbitantly for their "packages."

When taking emergency taxis from Mbare, vendors reported being harassed by police, as many taxi drivers are not licensed: "When we get transport from Mbare, the police always stop us on the way so we might spend the whole day on the way. On another day, the policeman arrested our emergency taxi driver. They do this whilst there aren't enough buses."

In response to these problems, vendors have hired their own, cheaper transport. While the cost for delivery of people and goods is fixed, between 10 and 20 vendors must all be ready at the same time to board the vehicle with their purchases. This presents other problems of cooperation.

To "Cooperate" or Not?

Throughout the city, I observed evidence of cooperation among vendors. When they are short of cash, they will share the cost of a wholesale quantity with another vendor, and divide it up either at Mbare or at the market site. In no instance did we find cooperatives, which the government seeks

Several vendors hire transport to travel from Mbare Musika to their vending site in the high density suburbs.

to promote. Indeed, when I asked vendors whether they had a cooperative, 11.4 percent indicated they did. When probed for details, most could not even provide a name. A range of responses was recorded to the question, "Why/why not would you belong to a cooperative?" Most vendors were concerned with the disposition of their money. With daily wholesale purchases dependent upon daily intake, women were reluctant to part with any of their funds. "If the government tells us to form a cooperative, I will go home to plow because cooperatives don't pay you." Another vendor had a different view: "Having a cooperative is like having two wives: one is always lazy and not dependable."

The lack of enthusiasm in evidence may be the result of several experiences. Women feel the less they are "interfered with" by government, the greater incomes they can generate (cooperatives need to be registered, must keep accounts, and are subject to taxation). Also, many of the women had belonged to either one of two cooperatives formerly established for the vendors: M's (12 percent) and ZWB's (4.3 percent). Both dissolved when leadership proved irresponsible and untrustworthy:

> Near the independent market some women vendors told us there was a man who wanted to help us. We had trouble with the police so we needed some help. We asked around and were directed to Mr. M's office in Pioneer House. If we joined the cooperative, we were told, he

would help us—the police wouldn't trouble us any more. The women should contribute to the co-op so that they could buy a farm. From the Z$10 registration fee, a farm would be bought to grow tomatoes. M was then to transport the tomatoes to the women. The city council built this musika in November 1983 and we were told to pay them as M was a crook. But M came again for another Z$10 for a new card when the old one was filled. He came early in 1985 to collect more money. We didn't know he had taken all the money.

I did find evidence of financial cooperation in the form of revolving credit/savings societies. Two types of societies were identified: market-wide and small group. Of the former, 40.3 percent of vendors reported they belong, contributing a mean of Z$2.47 per day (with a range between 25 cents and Z$10.00). Of the latter, 56.9 percent of vendors indicated their participation, making a mean daily contribution of Z$2.67 (with a range of 10 cents to Z$10.00 per day). Membership in these smaller groups (which may spill over to other vendors in other marketplaces) ranged between 2 and 40, with a mean of 12.5. Participation in such a society, taking the mean daily contribution of Z$2.67, and a mean membership of 12.5, would yield to each vendor the sum of Z$33.38 every thirteenth day. Although vendors contributed daily, when it was their turn to receive the "pot," they viewed this income as extra to be used for special needs, e.g., school fees, extra stocking for the weekends, and remittances. By 1993, the strategy for contributing had changed: instead of paying so much per day, vendors con-tributed Z$20 once per week—every Tuesday—after greater weekend intakes (or Z$5 per day Friday through Monday).

Because the cost of living had risen so significantly since the imple-mentation of ESAP, vendors felt they needed to make some provision for the event of becoming a widow. Without access to formal insurance compa-nies, vendors joined a burial society that had a membership of 750. At the funeral of a member's spouse, a contribution of Z$3 plus vegetables and fruits was required. From the contributions the widow was paid Z$1000.

Cooperation was a difficult element to identify in each of the market sites. When a vendor had to be absent for a few hours, I observed that often a neighbor vendor sold her goods in her stead. But at other times, a vendor some three or four stalls down would take over. When I queried the women on this, I was told "that one cannot be trusted; she uses *mushonga* [magic]." For this reason, and probably for reasons of lack of trust, when I asked ven-dors who sells for them when they are away, 36.9 percent said "another vendor," while 34.2 percent said one of their children comes to watch the stall; 17.2 percent indicated no one sold for them. "I don't know whether they pitch my money when they sell for me during my absence. When they sell for you, the money is less than the heaps you have left over."

One elderly vendor's spouse spoke of absent ethics at his wife's mar-ketplace:

There is a lot of quarrelling here—a non-Christian spirit. They don't want to help each other; they are jealous. A person must have self control to be called a human being—*chimunhu*—to be trusted. The war spoiled people. People have not been raised well. People are suspicious—they think things will be taken away from them. If *ambuya* [his wife] stays to sell, then there is no fighting. If she goes home and leaves our granddaughter here, then we find out how badly people act toward each other.

"Magic" in the Marketplace

The issue of "magic" in the marketplace was encountered at almost every site. Vendors would make observations about other vendors who would do good business because they use magic: "Number Two doesn't have fresh things to sell, but people just buy from her whilst they do not buy from us. I don't even know the kind of magic she has."

Another comment:

We usually find magic on the tables and in front of the tuck shop. When they use magic, I usually fail to get customers, both for vegetables and the tuck shop. Sometimes I become sick. I really fail to get power—loose eyes, and shoulders being heavy as if I am carrying stones.

The perceptions of whose magic was stronger were interesting: for Shona women, the mushonga from Bulawayo was very strong; for Ndebele and Manyika women, that from Mozambique was more powerful; and for a variety of others, the mushonga ethnic Indians used in their shops was very effective.

I observed a vendor from Malawi who had been identified as one who uses very strong magic. I found that customers are attracted to this woman's stall for several reasons: it is always overflowing with very fresh produce; she is very cordial and has a happy demeanor in the way she treats her customers; and, most of all, to every customer's purchase she adds a fresh tomato or two to provide an incentive for them to return. Conducting an extremely lucrative trade, the vendor became the target of unfounded accusations.

Long Hours of Trade

Vendors spend very long hours occupied in their businesses. For many, the day begins at 4:00 A.M. when they wake up and prepare to get the bus to Mbare. Usually, they arrive at their retail market sites between 7:00 and 8:00 A.M., when they set out their new purchases. If commodities had been brought home the previous evening, then the vendor must go and fetch them to add to her display. At mid-morning, many women prepare tea and have their breakfast—normally tea, some bread, margarine, and/or jam. Shortly thereafter, customers come to purchase fresh greens to prepare for lunch. At 1:00 P.M. the primary school children are finished for the day, and many vendors must collect their sons and daughters and prepare lunch for them at home. Those without these responsibilities cook lunch at the marketplace. Those who go home to eat lunch return to the market by mid-afternoon when customers come to buy what they need for dinner. This evening "rush hour" extends through the time when people come home from work and ends between 7:00 and 8:00 P.M. The women then pack up what is left and carry it to their homes (as most markets do not have lockers for overnight storage). The long day continues as women attend to domestic matters before going to sleep.

There can be no doubt that the hours spent in this enterprise are not adequately compensated by the returns vendors experience from selling. While vendors would argue that this life is preferable to cultivating in the rural areas, or to many other forms of work, objectively speaking a 16-hour work day far transcends what would be required in many other types of employment. In a conversation I had with a woman who had recently established a "table," after having worked as a domestic for the same white family for 23 years, she reported that she was tired from her years in domestic employment. She added she wanted to "take it easy" and that is why she started selling vegetables!

The business environment with which vendors must cope has led them to developing maximizing strategies that aid them in maintaining their businesses. Women must utilize all the skills at their disposal, including traditional practices in the use of mushonga, in order that they might cultivate more customers to continue their trade. Because the women view their activities as businesses, they find the most economical means to access their supplies, and work extremely long hours to meet their customers' needs. For all of their efforts, do they experience the financial returns they need?

▲ Incomes and Gross Margins

While several questions on the survey attempted to ascertain daily and weekly cash intake, I found that most vendors were unable to report this information accurately. Reasons included inability to count very high, disinterestedness by some and inability by others to keep written records, use of incomes to purchase snacks and other items throughout the day causing confusion in remembering incomes, and an unwillingness to report financial information for fear that I would report their individual earnings to the government. Additionally, the women informed me, as did my male research assistants, it is not appropriate among Shona speakers for woman to appear to be too clever financially. If male spouses believe their wives are earning pocket money, there is no threat to the perceived dominant male financial position. However, should a vendor distinguish herself as earning well, husbands might appropriate a vendor's income.

Another reason was rendered for not accurately reporting incomes. If a woman is earning well, she may become the target of witchcraft accusations by her colleagues. As reported previously, those who sell most of their commodities daily are highly suspect because it is believed, even by the vendors, that no woman can do business that well. Excellence in vending can only come with the assistance of the supernatural. Thus, for both pragmatic and ideological reasons, I feel that incomes reported on the interview schedule are not reliable. I believe I achieved greater reliability from the daily records I kept of each vendor's purchases and sales.

The following, therefore, is an analysis of vendor cash flows based on gross margins obtained by subtracting wholesale cost from retail revenue. Trade in some 50 fruit and vegetable commodities is included in the calculations. Of these 50, vendors identified 16 as producing the highest profit: cabbage (drum head), covo, derere (okra), magaka (spiny cucumbers), onions (dry), potatoes, rape, sweet potatoes, tomatoes, tsunga (green, leafy), apples, avocados, bananas, guavas, lemons, and oranges. To discern the importance of all 50 crops in the daily transaction of business, the incidence of their availability is presented in Table 6.1.[2]

Table 6.2 illustrates the changes in gross margins for these 16 crops over the months of intensive research—March through July 1986. Amounts are expressed in dollars/cents per kilogram, although neither wholesale purchase nor retail sale are actually conducted using these measures. Measures used at the wholesale level include boxes, pockets, bundles, and heaps, and at the retail level, heaps, pieces, bunches, and bundles, all of which are measured "by hand" or "by eye." My research assistants and I ascertained per kilogram amounts by weighing all commodities purchased as vendors returned from the wholesaler, and then weighing out the commodities vendors displayed for sale.

Table 6.3 presents the average prices paid per wholesale unit purchased during the period of intensive interviewing, and its retail markup expressed numerically and in percentage terms.

A vendor must be very astute in purchasing her commodities in order that a deficit is not realized. This factor may be intuited by many women, but is not known as a fact because of the daily flows of business and women's inability to keep records. In my survey, only 54 of the 325 vendors interviewed (16.6 percent) said they kept any kind of record of their wholesale and retail transactions.[3] I personally observed only two actually recording anything.[4]

Table 6.1 Fresh Produce Being Sold at Retail Market Sites Throughout Harare

Commodity	Percent of Sites (n = 24)	Percent of Women Selling (n = 325)
Apples	58.3	30.9
Avocados	87.5	21.0
Bananas	95.8	41.0
Brinjals (eggplant)	4.2	0.3
Broccoli	4.2	0.6
Broccoli leaves	4.2	0.3
Cabbage (drum head)	70.8	34.0
Cabbage (sweet)	37.5	13.5
Carrots	20.0	5.8
Cassava	4.2	0.3
Cauliflower	8.3	0.6
Chibage (mealies)	20.8	1.9
Covo	70.8	18.2
Cucumber	45.8	13.3
Derere (okra)	58.3	23.5
Derere leaves	4.2	0.3
Gem squash	4.2	0.3
Grapes	4.2	0.3
Guava	50.0	16.0
Lemons	87.5	34.8
Madumbo	0.2	0.3
Magaka	58.3	22.4
Mangoes	16.7	1.9
Mapudzi	16.7	1.4
Masaui	8.3	1.1
Mauya	4.2	0.3
Mborah	16.7	3.6
Naartjies (tangerines)	29.2	9.4
Nyimo	16.7	1.1
Onions (dry)	91.7	50.3
Onions (spring)	37.5	21.8
Oranges	83.3	40.0
Peaches	8.3	0.6
Peanuts	8.3	1.1
Pears	4.2	0.3
Peas	12.5	4.1
Peppers	4.2	0.8
Pineapples	16.7	1.1
Piri piri (chili pepper)	54.2	9.7
Potatoes	79.2	49.2
Pumpkins	41.7	11.9
Rape	100.0	68.8
Rugare	37.5	7.5
Sugar cane	29.2	3.3
Sugar loaf	8.3	0.8
Sweet cabbage leaves	12.5	1.9
Sweet potatoes	70.8	19.3
Tomatoes	100.0	88.7
Tsunga	100.0	39.2
Watermelon	4.2	0.3

Source: Interview schedules.

Table 6.2 Gross Margins per Kilogram of Sixteen Crops, March 1–July 24, 1986

	Apples		Avocados		Bananas		Cabbage (drum head)		Covo		Derere		Guava		Lemons		Magaka		Onions		Oranges		Potatoes		Rape		Sweet Potatoes		Tomatoes		Tsunga	
	Charged/ Z$	% Increase	Charged/ Z$	% Increase	Charged/ Z$	% Increase	Charged/ Z$	% Increase	Charged/ Z$	% Increase	Charged/ Z$	% Increase	Charged/ Z$	% Increase	Charged/ Z$	% Increase	Charged/ Z$	% Increase	Charged/ Z$	% Increase	Charged/ Z$	% Increase	Charged/ Z$	% Increase	Charged/ Z$	% Increase	Charged/ Z$	% Increase	Charged/ Z$	% Increase	Charged/ Z$	% Increase
March 3–7	.68	221	-0.3	94	.33	158	.06	126			1.01	320			.25	181			.29	143			.22	185	.29	167			.04	104	.07	119
March 10–14	.45	187			.38	183	.20	205			1.17	241							.33	137			.95	575	.28	157			.92	251		
March 17–28	.53	204	.10	119	.42	175	.09	147	.44	238	.80	229			.61	405	.32	329	.79	189			.30	230	.27	166	.42	283	.74	268	.33	183
April 1–5	.58	184	.15	119	.44	173			.26	179	.80	205			.37	219			.52	163			.23	192	.31	167	.37	237	.20	120	.40	195
April 7–8	.55	171			.52	184			.27	159			.07	123					1.14	167	.60	250			.35	183			.49	226	.14	123
April 8–9	.39	165	.36	209	.34	163	.08	135			1.31	270	.55	467			.15	183	.33	124			.31	263	.17	133	.35	284	.57	195	.30	148
April 14–18	.36	157	.26	149	.43	190	.03	114			1.04	241			.34	289	.23	172	.52	140	.29	148	.19	163	.21	150	.03	115	.19	128		
May 19–23			.34	194	.33	192	.03	114	.69	277	1.12	227			.52	336	.36	325	1.86	374	.29	167			.68	262			.29	132	.62	227
May 22–30	.43	156	.36	172	.26	143	.18	190	.22	156	.81	190			.28	193			.55	147	.25	152	.36	238	.25	169	.62	370	.40	149	.08	116
June 2–6	-.19	86			.34	149	.10	124			.70	138			.21	200			.36	127	.19	140	.33	203	.24	156	.26	170	.19	121		
June 9–13							.07	130	.22	167	1.00	256			.35	240	.20	267	.48	155	.36	216	.26	181	.19	166	.26	237	.28	147	.21	164
June 16–18					.28	147	.12	175			.46	153							.67	177	.16	129	.40	267	.31	282			.38	158	.29	226
June 19–20					.48	189													1.70	559			.37	318	.42	268			-0.5	95	.16	167
June 23–26	.94	216	-.08	90	.46	194	.14	167	.26	174	1.72	234			.34	262			.74	237	.31	178	.24	183	.21	160	.22	173	.44	141	.12	136
June 30–July 4	.10	108	.26	160	.35	160	.08	142	-0.4	92					.29	221			.57	174	.15	133	.19	161	.11	131	.24	233	.11	111	.12	134
July 7–11			.10	123	.60	254	.11	173									.12	155	.78	215	.26	163	.25	200	.16	162	.37	370	.47	157	.22	192
July 14–15			.41	473											.54	345									.74	374			.80	245	.44	233
July 14–15																									.41	258					.37	254
July 16–17					.42	181	.04	113											1.13	292	.19	132					.16	162	.56	190	.35	240
July 21			.43	430	.74	251													.66	208	.38	175			.33	274			.53	208	.63	333
July 22					.75	400													.52	218					.35	294			.90	390	.31	241
July 22					.86	332													.84	295	.41	200			.31	207	.46	407	.70	235	.45	261
July 23			.18	134	.19	136	.03	113	.40	248					-.07	84			.21	122	.10	124	.11	128	.41	258	.14	152	.28	141	.26	174
July 24					.24	143									.51	343			.52	172	.32	184			.43	287	.31	282	.53	220	.33	214

Note: The Z$ amount charged is the price per kilo vendors charged for a particular commodity. The percentage increase represents the gross margin vendors realized after deducting the wholesale cost they paid for a quantity of the commodity.

The purpose of this table is to illustrate the range of gross margins a vendor received per commodity over the period of intensive research. If a commodity was scarce, vendors would experience a loss because the wholesale price was high. If a commodity was abundant, vendors would experience a higher gross margin because the wholesale price was low. The consistent factor was the price charged for a certain heap or bundle, thus adding to the variability of gross margins.

Table 6.3 Actual Wholesale Unit Purchased and Retail Markup

Commodity	Unit	Wholesale Price (Z$)	Retail Price[a] (Z$)	Gross Margin (Z$)	Percent Markup
Avocados	each	.20	.50	.30	150
Cabbage	head	.25	.60	.35	140
Chibage	dozen	1.20	2.50	1.30	108
Lemons	dozen	.50	1.20	.70	140
Magaka	dozen	.50	2.40	1.90	380
Onions (spring)	bunch	.80	1.20	.40	50
Rape	bundle	.50	.60	.10	20
Rugare	bundle	.50	.60	.10	20
Tsunga	bundle	.50	.60	.10	20

Source: Interview schedules.
Note: a. Retail prices are quoted for the sale of total subunits sold once the wholesale quantity has been divided, e.g., a bundle of rape will be tied into six smaller bundles that will be sold for 10 cents each; lemons will be sold for 10 cents each, etc.

▲ Six Case Studies

The following six case studies illustrate the variability of women's gross margins as recorded during each respective week of interviews. Following this, a summary of gross margin data is presented for the remaining cases for which complete wholesale/retail data exist.

Case 1: Amai Daniel[5]

Amai Daniel sells her fruits and vegetables in an area once called a "buffer" suburb—a township historically designated for "colored" people in between the white city center and the former African townships. She is 40 years old, is divorced with no children, and lives in the neighborhood of the Mbare wholesale market. Amai Daniel has received four years of primary schooling and has had some training in "homecraft," but this was insufficient to help her get a job. She left her home area of Masvingo in 1972 to migrate with her husband to Harare in search of employment. A few years after her arrival, her husband divorced her because she had had four stillbirths and no living children. Although her lobola had been set at Z$100, her husband had not finished paying it. Upon divorce, her in-laws did not request any part of the lobola to be returned. After being divorced, she returned to her parents, but came back to Harare shortly thereafter because she was not happy in the rural areas. In Harare, she is a lodger and lives alone.

Amai Daniel had been a produce vendor for 12 years when we interviewed her. She had been conducting her business from this same location the entire time (albeit when she began she positioned herself under a tree, as the marketplace had not yet been built).

While making her purchases at Mbare, she also purchases plastic bags of varying sizes in which to package her fruits and vegetables. Since customers in this suburb have electricity, they are able to purchase larger quantities of produce and can store them in refrigerators. By repacking her commodities in plastic bags, Amai Daniel can sell her packets at Z$1.00 each—this includes tomatoes, potatoes, onions, apples, and oranges. Smaller packets sell for half the amount. Amai Daniel was interviewed the week of March 3. Her gross margins are presented in Table 6.4.

This vendor can package larger quantities of commodities because her customers can refrigerate their purchases.

Table 6.4 Gross Margins for Amai Daniel, Week of March 3, 1986

Commodity	Wholesale Cost (Z$)	Wholesale Cost/Kg (Z$)	Kg	Retail Price/ Kg (Z$)	Gross Margin/ Kg (Z$)	Total Gross Margin (Z$)
Apples	7.00	.60	11.750	1.50	.90	10.63
Beans	4.00	.625	6.400	1.38	.755	4.83
Cabbage (drum head)	.40	.17	2.300	.30	.13	.29
Derere	.50	.59	.850	1.25	.66	.56
Lemons	.40	.33	1.200	.62	.29	.34
Onions (dry)	7.00	.72	9.700	1.67	.95	9.20
Potatoes	8.00	.26	30.400	.51	.25	7.50
Rape	3.00	.86	3.500	1.11	.25	.89
Tomatoes	33.50	.98	34.170	.87	−.11	−3.77

Number of commodities sold: 9
Total gross margin for week: Z$30.47

Case 2: Amai Tendai

Just one month later, we interviewed Amai Tendai, who is a Malawian selling in one of the high density suburbs. She reported that she is 42 years old, married for 26 years, and that she came to Zimbabwe some 24 years ago with her husband, who migrated in search of employment. Both she and her husband have never been to school, and she has not taken any training courses. Her husband works as a messenger and earns Z$250 per month. When he first came to Harare, he obtained employment as a domestic, and the family lived at his employer's residence. When Amai Tendai first arrived in Harare, she stayed at home to take care of the children.

Amai Tendai has given birth to seven children, but only one has survived. Complications during her last pregnancy led to the stillbirth of twins and blood poisoning. Consequently, she had to have her right hand amputated. This disability has not prevented her from conducting her business, however. Amai Tendai began her business in 1972 after she buried her sixth child. She has had an advantage in the conduct of her trade. Her son, who has a car, takes her to the wholesale market daily and brings her to the vending site. With her son's assistance, Amai Tendai can purchase greater quantities daily, so her stall is always well-stocked with fresh commodities. Amai Tendai has been selling at the site where we interviewed her for the past 14 years.

Amai Tendai was conducting a very brisk trade, probably better than any other vendor at the site. Her astute business acumen has led her to devise a system that virtually guarantees her customers—giving each a little something extra when they buy from her. During the course of the interview, I directed my research assistant to record all of the items this

With a grown son to help with transport, Amai Tendai is able to offer many more commodities than her neighbors and thus conducts a very brisk trade.

vendor gave away free. She found that for each customer, a tomato or two was provided.[6] While this practice is common for many vendors, what is different for Amai Tendai is that she gives away fresh tomatoes—those she purchased that very morning from the wholesaler—instead of those "going off." Her gross margins, presented in Table 6.5, are different from those of Amai Daniel.

Case 3: Amai George

Amai George sells her fresh produce from a market site located in one of the currently developing high density suburbs some 20 kilometers distant from the town center. She is 37 years old, has been married for 20 years,

Table 6.5 Gross Margins for Amai Tendai, Week of April 1, 1986

Commodity	Wholesale Cost (Z$)	Wholesale Cost/ Kg (Z$)	Kg	Retail Price/ Kg (Z$)	Gross Margin/ Kg (Z$)	Total Gross Margin (Z$)
Apples	37.00	.64	57.800	1.00	.36	20.80
Bananas	13.00	.66	19.700	.74	.12	1.58
Beans	6.00	.46	13.000	1.33	.87	11.29
Cabbage (drum head)	24.00	.09	268.500	.26	.17	45.81
Cabbage (sweet)	24.00	.21	116.400	.36	.15	17.90
Carrots	2.00	.30	6.760	.68	.38	2.60
Cucumber	3.00	.22	13.460	.40	.18	2.38
Derere	10.45	.84	12.470	1.82	.98	12.25
Guava	2.50	.24	10.400	.45	.21	2.18
Lemons	.60	.26	2.280	.53	.27	.61
Magaka	2.00	.16	12.630	.62	.46	5.83
Onions (dry)	25.40	.83	30.600	.67	−.16	−4.90
Peas	2.00	.67	3.000	2.94	2.27	6.82
Potatoes	22.25	.29	76.800	.46	.17	13.08
Pumpkins	4.00	.13	30.940	.30	.17	5.28
Rape	54.85	.51	107.520	.63	.12	12.89
Sweet potatoes	5.40	.24	22.580	.65	.41	9.28
Tomatoes	101.00	1.00	101.115	.83	−.17	−17.07
Watermelon	.60	.09	6.700	.27	.18	1.21

Number of commodities sold: 19
Total gross margin for week: Z$149.82

and has given birth to six children, the last of whom died when she was in third grade. The ages of her five remaining children range between 7 and 21. One lives away, and the remaining four live with her and her husband. Amai George also has her sister's son living with her.

Amai George attended school through Form Two and is as conversant in English as she is in Shona. She was born in an area well-known for vegetable production: Chiweshe. She left her area of birth in 1964 with her husband to look for work in Harare, some 30 kilometers from the Chiweshe communal area. She reported not having been very successful at finding work, and when she became pregnant she decided to give up the search. Now that her children are old enough to mind each other, and the costs of building a house are so high, she decided to try her hand at selling. Although she had been selling vegetables for only one year at the time of the interview, she was well connected to the trade.

Amai George reported that several of her family members also traded in fresh produce: her mother had been a vendor at Mbare Musika retail, and her two sisters were involved in wholesaling at Mbare with their husbands. (When I asked Amai George if she would be able to purchase her commodities cheaper from her relatives, she answered with an emphatic "no!")

The market site suffered from a number of anomalies: not all the houses in the adjacent community were inhabited, because they were in varying stages of completion; commercial farmers in adjacent areas sold their produce cheaper from farm kiosks; transport costs to and from Mbare were among the highest in the city; and the selling day really only began when people came home from work in the evenings. Since the marketplace did not yet have electricity, the absence of light made it difficult for vendors to operate. Amai George's gross margins are reported in Table 6.6.

Table 6.6 Gross Margins for Amai George, Week of May 19, 1986

Commodity	Wholesale Cost (Z$)	Wholesale Cost/ Kg (Z$)	Kg	Retail Price/ Kg (Z$)	Gross Margin/ Kg (Z$)	Total Gross Margin (Z$)
Bananas	18.00	.37	48.450	.95	.58	28.03
Derere	.60	.73	.825	2.86	2.13	1.76
Lemons	.60	.18	3.300	.80	.62	2.04
Magaka	1.20	.17	7.120	.53	.36	2.57
Onions (spring)	4.50	1.32	3.400	1.67	.35	1.18
Oranges	8.00	.38	21.060	.89	.51	10.74
Potatoes	4.50	.30	15.000	.54	.24	3.60
Rape	6.80	.42	16.340	.65	.23	3.82
Tomatoes	82.60	.89	92.820	.97	.08	7.44
Tsunga	4.85	.50	9.680	.94	.44	4.25
Number of commodities sold: 10						
Total gross margin for week: Z$65.43						

Case 4: Amai Dino

Amai Dino is 37 years old, has been married for 21 years and has six children, ages 6 through 20, all of whom are living with her and her husband. Two of her brother's children also reside with her.

Amai Dino was born in Mvuma, which she left to join her husband when she married in 1965. Together they migrated to Harare in 1966 so her husband could look for work. Her husband, who never attended school, currently works for the municipality and earns Z$250 per month. She completed six years of primary education but has never held formal sector employment. She has been selling at this site since she established her business in 1972.

Vendors at this site were coping with a recurrent weekend problem—the Friday evening arrival of farmers from the African commercial fruit and vegetable growing area of Mutoko. Their presence over the weekend less than a kilometer distant from the market site translated into decreased weekend sales for the vendors. Sales from Saturday to Monday, therefore, were not very good, because residents of this high density suburb could purchase from the farmers as much as they could carry that would keep without refrigeration.

Farmers from Mutoko give vendors too much competition on weekends.

Amai Dino places very high value on the education of her children. She reported that the sale of her vegetables had put all her children through school. She was concerned, however, about the kinds of jobs her children would find after finishing. She was especially concerned about one of her daughters who was being subjected to sexual harassment on the job. Amai Dino was perplexed about how men could continually try to take advantage of women, regardless of the professional levels they achieve. In spite of this problem, Amai Dino continued to sell her produce to educate her other children. Her gross margins are reported in Table 6.7.

Case 5: Amai Tatu

When Amai Tatu related her life history to me, I could not help being tremendously impressed by the way she has overcome the obstacles that brought her to the vegetable vending business. She is 32 years old, has been

Table 6.7 Gross Margins for Amai Dino, Week of June 9, 1986

Commodity	Wholesale Cost (Z$)	Wholesale Cost/ Kg (Z$)	Kg	Retail Price/ Kg (Z$)	Gross Margin/ Kg (Z$)	Total Gross Margin (Z$)
Bananas	3.00	.21	14.300	1.00	.79	11.30
Cabbage (drum head)	.60	.13	4.600	.22	.09	.41
Cabbage (sweet)	12.00	.19	62.000	.26	.07	4.12
Covo	.90	.22	4.120	.67	.45	1.86
Lemons	.30	.14	2.140	.67	.53	1.13
Magaka	.40	.11	3.650	.37	.26	.95
Onions (spring)	2.50	.55	4.550	1.08	.53	2.41
Oranges	12.00	.31	38.360	.70	.39	14.85
Potatoes	8.00	.27	30.000	.62	.35	10.60
Rape	7.25	.26	27.860	.33	.07	1.94
Sweet potatoes	1.75	.15	11.700	.59	.44	5.15
Tomatoes	18.00	.78	23.040	.83	.05	1.12
Tsunga	2.45	.27	9.000	.74	.47	4.21

Number of commodities sold: 13
Total gross margin for week: Z$60.05

married and divorced, and was remarried to her second husband eight years ago. She finished six years of primary school in her home area of Rusape. Because this region of the country was very active politically and felt the ravages of the liberation struggle early, she and her first husband felt they had to leave the area to prevent physical injury. She came to Harare in 1978 and has been selling vegetables only for a year, but because of her determination she has achieved a fair degree of success. But success and happiness have not come easily to her.

Amai Tatu told us that after marrying in the rural areas, she gave birth to triplets. Her mother-in-law, at whose homestead she was residing, accused her of giving birth like an animal. To prevent the murder of one or two of her children, Amai Tatu fled to a nearby mission, where she was collected by her father some months later. When the triplets were past the toddler years, Amai Tatu married a man who saw no problem with the triplets, and she was sent with her three children, as well as her husband's three children by a previous "city" marriage, to his parents' rural homestead. There Amai Tatu encountered two other "country" wives. Determined not to become another woman "left at home," she came to Harare with the six children in search of her spouse.

In the process of looking for people who could help her, she met with several ZANU-PF (Zimbabwe African National Union–Patriotic Front) leaders who took it upon themselves to help her. Once her husband was found, she continued her ZANU-PF relations and began selling fresh produce. She also became the head of the ZANU-PF women's club in her neighborhood. Additionally, because of the many social ties she created, she gained access to a parcel of land adjacent to her high density suburb home that either she or her children cultivate. The day we spoke with her, she had just harvested 43 kilograms of sweet potatoes from this plot, which she put on sale at the going rate. Her leadership of the ZANU women's choir provided a most enjoyable final day of research at this site, as the 20-plus members came to entertain us for an hour or so before our departure.

Amai Tatu currently resides with her husband and six children who range in age between 8 and 22. Three other children live with her (two belonging to her husband plus her sister's son). She reported that her husband, who completed a third-grade education, works for the municipality, but she does not know how much he earns.

Amai Tatu sells at a marketplace that has had its problems. When I first visited the market on the mapping exercise, I found no women selling from the market itself but from makeshift tables across the street next to the bus station. When I returned to conduct the intensive interview, several vendors had moved back into the market, but many decided to sell from the street because potential customers alighting from the bus would not cross the street to buy what they needed. Instead, they looked for other vendors selling closer to the bus stop. On a third visit, I found the roof of one set of stalls had blown away, leaving vendors unprotected from the elements. Concerned about their physical safety, vendors had set up some makeshift tables closer to the bus stop.

Amai Tatu, as a strategy to meet the demands of varying populations, also sold sweets to school children on their mid-morning break or immediately after school was out for the day at 1:00 P.M. I was unable to ascertain her earnings from these commodities. Her gross margins on fresh produce are presented in Table 6.8.

Table 6.8 Gross Margins for Amai Tatu, Week of July 7, 1986

Commodity	Wholesale Cost (Z$)	Wholesale Cost/ Kg (Z$)	Kg	Retail Price/ Kg (Z$)	Gross Margin/ Kg (Z$)	Total Gross Margin (Z$)
Avocado	3.65	.45	8.080	.45	0	0
Bananas	12.00	.38	31.516	.94	.56	17.63
Cabbage (sweet)	42.00	.24	175.630	.34	.10	17.71
Magaka	3.50	.23	15.440	.47	.24	3.76
Naartjies	9.00	.36	25.100	.79	.43	10.83
Onions (spring)	24.60	.69	35.700	1.58	.89	31.81
Oranges	4.75	.34	13.960	.73	.39	5.44
Potatoes	18.00	.30	60.000	.44	.14	8.40
Rape	25.70	.38	67.690	.38	0	0
Sweet potatoes	0	0	131.520	.21	.21	27.62
Tomatoes	168.70	1.05	160.650	1.56	.51	81.91
Tsunga	22.40	.37	60.960	.56	.29	11.74

Number of commodities sold: 12
Total gross margin for week: Z$216.85

Case 6: Amai Paul

The final case was obtained in our last few days of interviewing at an open-air market site adjacent to a shopping center in a low density suburb. Amai Paul had been selling at this location for three years. She had one job previous to establishing her own enterprise, and this was for less than a year as a domestic. She is 36 years old, has been married for 21 years, and has five children. She reported the eldest of these children is 20, but she was unable to recall the ages of the others, even though they all reside with her. No other residents occupy her home.

An open air market in the low density suburbs.

Amai Paul has never been to school, nor has she ever participated in any sort of training course. She was born in Buhera, which she left in 1965 to migrate with her husband to Harare in search of employment. Her husband, who has also never been to school, has a job as a gardener. Working for people of European descent, Amai Paul's husband receives his housing "free," but his salary is only Z$70 per month.

Amai Paul began selling fresh produce in 1983 and has held no other jobs since coming to Harare. She was very cautious in her purchasing and was selling only three commodities at the time we interviewed her. These three, however, were those constituting an integral part of the relish diet. These commodities are sold in the supermarkets across the street, but they are not kept very fresh. Africans in this low density suburb prefer to purchase their needs from the vendors because their commodities are fresher; customers know that the vendors go to the farmers' market daily and purchase directly from the farmers. From the exclusive sale of these commodities, Amai Paul was able to do as well as other vendors selling more. Her gross margins are reported in Table 6.9.

Table 6.9 Gross Margins for Amai Paul, Week of July 24, 1986

Commodity	Wholesale Cost (Z$)	Wholesale Cost/ Kg (Z$)	Kg	Retail Price/ Kg (Z$)	Gross Margin/ Kg (Z$)	Total Gross Margin (Z$)
Rape	12.30	.24	51.240	.53	.29	14.86
Tomatoes	41.00	.43	95.305	.88	.45	42.87
Tsunga	4.25	.25	17.080	.73	.48	8.22
Number of commodities sold: 3						
Total gross margin for week: Z$65.95						

▲ Analysis of Variability in Gross Margins and Financial Returns

In calculating the gross margins for 40 vendors for whom complete wholesale/retail information was available, the mean amount vendors paid wholesale for their commodities per week was Z$107.84 (with a range between Z$2.86 and Z$623.62). The mean return received per week by vendors was Z$170.91 (with a range between Z$7.09 and Z$920.16). This created a mean gross margin of Z$60.55 (with a range between Z$1.81 and Z$242.08).

Variability in gross margins among vendors documented over the research period is a consequence of (1) seasonal variation in wholesale price; (2) formal/informal wholesaler prices; (3) the number, type, and quantity of commodities sold; (4) physical properties of and vendor position within the marketplace (i.e., whether or not she is situated along a well-travelled pedestrian/consumer pathway); (5) physical position of the marketplace itself vis-à-vis other shops and services; (6) the number of years of selling at that market site (as a function of being known and thus having cultivated more customers); (7) how many customers a vendor has (partially as a function of her offering credit); (8) the amount of time a vendor must stay away from the marketplace owing to family matters (e.g., funerals, sick children, personal health, including pregnancy, etc.); (9) competition in the marketplace and in the surrounding area; and (10) labor.

Seasonal Variation in Wholesale Price

Seasonal supply is not just a matter of overall availability; it is also a matter of which market has the supply. In turn, who has the supply relates to who has produced the commodity—a white or an African farmer. White commercial farmers plant to harvest in times of scarcity in order to ensure premium prices. African farmers cannot always follow this pattern owing to production constraints.

While tomatoes are a commodity consumed by both white and African populations, during periods of scarcity they are not readily available either at Mbare Musika or the farmers' market; they are only available from the formal sector wholesalers or from U-Pick farms in the Harare environs. Given that supply is limited, the premium price requested is met by those retailers whose customers will bear an inflated price. When commodities are too expensive, vendors simply refuse to buy them (although in the case of the primary relish ingredients, i.e., tomatoes, rape, and onions, a vendor will do her best to have some supply to ensure she will retain her customers). This is mainly due to vendor retail pricing systems. Although wholesale prices vary seasonally, 29.5 percent (94 of 318 respondents) of vendors indicated they never changed the base price of a heap or a bundle, even though the size of the heap or bundle alters: the cost of the smallest heap of tomatoes remains 20 cents (50 cents since ESAP), although the size of the tomatoes varies seasonally. Likewise, a bundle of rape may consistently be priced at 20 cents, but the size of the bundle increases during times of glut (September and October), and decreases during times of scarcity (February and March).[7] Clark (1986) denotes 'these practices as quantity pricing, i.e., the price remains constant, as it reflects the inelasticity of family food budgets, while the variability in heaps changes according to wholesale/seasonal prices.

To illustrate price consistency, during a period of scarcity I suggested to one vendor that she increase the price of green beans from 30 cents to 40 cents per packet. She laughed, and as if by design, at that very moment, a young woman came to the vendor's stall, handed her 30 cents and said "beans." The vendor very knowingly looked at me, and then took pains to explain that customer expectation of price limited how much she could charge. Had the vendor followed my suggestion, she would not have sold her beans.

Clearly, the ability to generate a higher return is not solely a function of supply and demand. Rather, the complexity of the relationship of vendor to consumer, consumer price expectation, vendor ability to supply scarce commodities, and vendor willingness to supply "elite" commodities (i.e., if a vendor feels she must make a certain commodity available and it is not being sold at Mbare Musika, she will no doubt incur the extra expense to buy what she needs from formal sector wholesalers) all contribute to the ability to cultivate customers and to the variability of gross margins among vendors.

Formal/Informal Wholesaler Prices

Wholesale prices vary from market to market and at several times during the day. Even though the Independent Market may have published a lower price for a given commodity than what is being charged at Mbare Musika, a vendor will no doubt pay the higher price at Mbare because she must purchase other commodities not available at formal sector wholesalers. This was reportedly the case for 79.4 percent of vendors who purchase exclusively from either the wholesalers or farmers at Mbare Musika. Only 4 percent indicated they purchase at the Independent Market, and these only when what they want is not available at Mbare.

Commodity Differentiation

Many vendors (43.2 percent of the 245 who responded) feel that if they had more commodities for sale they would be able to generate higher incomes than those selling fewer commodities. The theoretical rationale contends that diversification reduces risk and allows for greater customer appeal. I found, however, that specialization in a given commodity can provide a different type of return.

One vendor in a high density suburb sold only tsunga that she picked herself from a nearby garden plot. Although calculation of her gross margin indicated only a Z$3.49 weekly return, she has made other gains. In establishing her reputation as "Amai Tsunga," customers who want to cook this green leafy vegetable purchase their needs from her as the leaves are always fresh. Her desire to establish a place in the community apparently outweighed her need to generate higher returns at the time. No doubt, as her reputation spreads her returns will increase.

Physical Properties of and Vendor Position in the Marketplace

The physical design of market stalls and the surroundings of the market site often hinder increasing returns to labor. For instance, vendors who have lockers in which to store their produce overnight could, if a commodity shelf life was more than one day without refrigeration, reduce the number of times they must go to Mbare. Vendors who have to carry their unsold produce home every night are more conservative about the wholesale quantities they buy.

The locker this vendor has enables her to store overnight any stock she does not sell.

In certain suburbs, business does not really begin until lunchtime and ends only after completion of the homebound rush hour. At these same market sites, however, there is no electricity, and business must be transacted either in the dark or by candlelight.

Design of marketplaces is sometimes inappropriate: the roofs do not extend far enough to cover the customer so that, when it rains, customers are likely to get wet. This factor has been taken into consideration, however, in the construction of market sites in newly-developed high density suburbs.

Vendors at this market are well provided with amenities, water to wash their produce, and a roof that protects customers in the rain, but they are lacking lockers for overnight storage.

A woman's particular position within the market site also affects the amount of business she will conduct. In the larger markets, where up to 40 vendors sell in four rows, women who have a stall on the inner rows are likely to have fewer customers than those who sell at stalls on the outside or along the perimeter of the market. Also, where markets are adjacent to bus stops, those selling closest to where people alight are more likely to have a higher number of customers than those on the opposite side. As one vendor reported: "Those who are selling on the other side by the post office are doing better business. We are near the other market, the one where the street vendors are selling. By the time customers come here, they have already seen everything they want on the other side of the market."

Control over who is allocated which stall is largely in the hands of the municipality. Where there is a market chairperson, she might have the power to tell vendors where to sell. The power a market chair exerts over other vendors could be derived from a number of sources: (1) vendors who voted her in; (2) her relationship with ZANU, the political party; (3) her relationship with people at the municipality or local government; (4) her use of magic; or (5) her sense of fairness. One vendor reported having been chased from stall to stall because she had done well wherever she went. The chairperson, thinking she might sell better at other stalls, continually usurped the vendor's position. This went on for several months until the vendor no longer withstood the harassment and moved to another market site. When I asked vendors why they withstood this type of treatment, they replied they didn't want any more "problems," that life was difficult enough already. When I probed further, I learned that several who had been sent away were not the true "owners" of the stall, i.e., they sublet the stall from the vendor who actually paid the rent, but for one reason or another was not actively trading at the time.

Physical Location of the Marketplace

Proximity of the market site to major shopping centers also seems to influence volume of trade. Market sites adjacent to other shops or social services seem to do better business than those across the street or in more isolated locations. As one vendor reported: "Our market is right at the end of the location; nobody can come and buy."

In conducting the first phase of this research, I found two market sites overgrown with weeds, and one that contained stalls for 78 women but was occupied by only 13. The ambivalence of city planning authorities about providing the appropriate means for African women to conduct their businesses is manifested in the way some markets are haphazardly situated. Some of the older markets, such as those at Stoddard, Mufakose, and Highfield, are in shopping centers or are adjacent to offices where various social services are provided. Newer markets, however, such as those in Dzivarisekwa, Tafara, and Mabvuku, are situated adjacent to beer halls but nothing else. Bus depots may be close by, but vendors have found that unless the market is directly adjacent to the bus stop, customers are unwilling to go out of their way to purchase what they need.

It is critical that vendors be consulted on the placement of new markets (Smart 1988). In one high density suburb, I observed a new market under construction. I talked with the construction workers, who turned out to be members of a fledgling cooperative. When I asked if they had difficulty in finding a site for their market, they explained that the municipality had told them to build it in another location. They argued that the site was too far from the bus station and too near another market. They were successful in finding another site because of their close ties to local political leaders.

Duration of Enterprise

Vendors reported having established their businesses at the location at which they were interviewed between less than 1 to over 34 years ago, with a mean of 5.5 years. The preponderance of vendors (approximately 75 percent) began their businesses after independence when urban influx laws were no longer enforceable. Table 6.10 presents a summary of this information.

Table 6.10 Number of Years Vendors Have Been Selling at the Location Where Interviewed

Number of Years	Percent of Vendors	Number of Vendors
Less than 1	9.7	31
1	23.9	76
2	11.9	38
3	11.3	36
4	7.5	24
5	6.0	19
6	6.6	21
7	4.1	13
8	2.5	8
9	.9	3
10	1.6	5
11–15	6.3	20
16–20	1.9	6
21–25	1.3	4
26–30	2.5	8
31–34	1.9	6

Source: Interview schedule.

Vendors argue that their ability to do good business is premised upon the amount of time they have spent selling at a given site. They assert a correlation between the number of years at a site and the number of customers they have. Moreover, there appears to be a gender bias as to the types of customers one can have. As one vendor indicated, "Women customers become friends after two to three purchases; male customers are 'regulars,' as 'friends' has another meaning among us Shona people."[8]

When I asked vendors why they felt others had more or fewer customers than they did, 24.2 percent (n = 223) said they were "well known" and this explained their volume of trade. More than 50 different responses were given in answer to this question. The second most frequent was "it depends on how many things you order [purchase from the wholesaler]" (16.1 percent).

The customer pool for each of the market sites also affects the number of customers a vendor has. Table 6.11 presents a potential household/customer-per-vendor ratio, based upon the households and population living in a given high density suburb and the number of vendors enumerated for that suburb in 1985–1986.[9] While it would appear that the figure for Mbare diminishes any potential to increase returns, the position of these vendors

Table 6.11 Customer Pool for Selected High Density Suburbs, 1985–1986

Suburb	Population	Households	Vendors	Household/ Customer Ratio	Vendor/ Population Ratio
Dzivarisekwa	22,718	4,818	110	1:44	1:207
Glen Norah	45,668	11,265	145	1:78	1:315
Glen View	59,775	15,960	265	1:60	1:226
Highfield	73,501	19,201	362	1:53	1:203
Kambuzuma	25,521	6,607	95	1:70	1:269
Mabvuku	38,958	9,151	86	1:106	1:453
Mbare	59,366	14,211	1,209	1:12	1:49
Mufakose	44,703	9,291	244	1:38	1:183
Rugare	8,362	1,475	7	1:211	1:1,195
Tafara	21,069	4,602	109	1:42	1:193
Warren Park	13,672	3,301	58	1:57	1:236

Source: Interview schedules.

Note: a. Many demographic changes have occurred in Harare since the period of intensive research 1985–1986. According to the 1992 census, the population had almost tripled since the last census in 1982. New high and low density suburbs have been developed, and several low density suburbs were consolidated, giving the appearance that a few had expanded drastically and that others no longer existed. Additionally, the number of street vendors has exploded since implementation of structural adjustment policies and the relaxation of municipal laws prohibiting the establishment of ad hoc vending sites. This plethora of necessary income generating activity prevented me from counting vendors and thus from correlating the number of vendors with the population in a given suburb to ascertain a current customer/vendor ratio.

adjacent to the wholesale market guarantees them a higher number of customers from other suburbs. If consumers have other business to transact at Mbare, they may well purchase their food needs at either the retail or wholesale market. Under normal circumstances, however, customers purchase what they need from markets in their home neighborhoods. The Rugare figure looks very promising, but the plots on which housing for railway employees is situated are surrounded by open fields in which women cultivate their own daily needs. The customer ratio in Mabvuku also looks promising, but this suburb is inundated with farmers from Mutoko every weekend, thus decreasing the effective customer pool for vendors.

I tried to ascertain vendor perception of how many customers they had daily. This inquiry led to many blank faces as a response. I rephrased the question and asked how many regular customers they had. This precipitated a response between 1 and 40, with the mean of 9.8. "Regulars" were defined as those customers who, when they come to a market site, automatically go to a particular vendor each time to purchase what they need. When I asked vendors why customers were called "regular," anticipating a response that indicated kinship or friendship, they responded that "customers just like the quality of my goods" (59.1 percent of 264). Slightly more than 24 percent indicated their regulars were friends or neighbors, and only 3 percent said their regulars were their relatives. "Regulars" are accorded specific status, as the following discussion illustrates.

"Regulars" and Credit

While all the women interviewed reported that they were never given credit by farmers or wholesalers, 92.8 percent (of 265 vendors) said they provide credit to their regular customers. A credit range of Z$1.00 to Z$40.00 was allowed before vendors required they be paid. The average amount of time allowed was until the end of the month or whenever customers received their salaries. One vendor reported she does not provide credit at the beginning of the month because "people should budget their money so they can eat properly just after they get paid."

I could not ascertain the extent of losses vendors incurred in extending credit. I did learn that when a person fails to repay a debt within a tacitly understood period of time, credit would not be reextended. At one market site, a vendor kept very close tabs of who owed how much and for how long. I was present when a customer who owed the vendor more than Z$10 for several months came to try and purchase more produce on credit. The vendor not only refused to extend the line of credit further, but also shouted at the woman to go home and get her husband to pay off the family food bill.

Necessary Absences

Vendors find it necessary to be absent from their stalls from time to time, either due to their own ill health, to take care of sick children, to return to the rural areas to plow, to attend a funeral or other ritual observance, or to take care of household errands. Each of these absences impinges upon the ability of vendors to maintain their incomes. Vendor health suffers significantly during the rainy season and during the winter (frost was on the ground on many mornings when my research assistants and I arrived in the field at 7:30 A.M.). Outside marketplaces might be very appropriate in the warmer climates of other African countries, but in Zimbabwe when temperatures can go below freezing the outside market presents particular problems.

Vendors maintained rural kinship ties by going "home" to see their relatives. For 71.9 percent of the vendor population, this occurred between one and three times a year. Women travelled home with one or more members of their families usually during school vacations, at Christmas, or when women's labor was needed on the farm. Women must also return to the rural areas to participate in certain rituals, e.g., funerals, *kurova guva* (bringing home the spirit a year after someone has passed away), ritual cleansing if one has had major problems, and consultation with nganga for various maladies, among other reasons.

Many of those who do not go home were from Malawi (6.2 percent), Mozambique (5.2 percent), or Zambia (.06 percent). Up to a few years ago, family ties were maintained internationally via cash remittances. This practice was stopped, however, by government intervention due to foreign currency shortages.

Competition

Vendors do not generally perceive themselves as being in competition with each other, regardless of the number of vendors selling in one location. When I asked vendors whether there was too much competition, about 27 percent reported that competition was against street vendors or those who sold door-to-door. The women felt that others who sold outside of the marketplace were unfair competitors because they did not have to pay rent and thus could charge less.[10] This had become such a compelling problem by 1993 that in one site, of the 40 vendors interviewed, only 15 remained (8 had passed away) and 17 had taken to the streets in order to maintain their levels of income since the municipality was charging Z$43.50 per month to rent a stall.

Attempts to lure more customers to a stall do not generally include price reduction. Base prices for commodities required daily by consumers do not change—the smallest heap of tomatoes is 20 cents, a bundle of vegetables costs between 10 and 20 cents (depending on the market site), and the smallest onion will cost 10 cents.[11] Bananas and other fruits are normally price-fixed according to size, as is cabbage. What brings a new customer to a particular vendor is a composite of the vendor's display, her selling demeanor, and, perhaps, whether there is a neighbor/kinsman relation.

In several marketplaces, two or more generations of one family were competing with each other for customers. The women did not perceive themselves as competitors, however, because they sold from stalls somewhat separated from each other. Each also felt she had cultivated her own clientele.

Labor

Labor is not factored in as a cost of doing business. This is also true in marketing activities in Nigeria: "The minimum price is based on cost (which includes cost price and transport) plus profit margin, but rarely labor as most traders did not report costing their labor" (Johnson 1973:110).

Yet the number of hours a vendor occupies her stall, in addition to the time she takes going to the wholesaler and packing up her goods at the end of the day, far exceed the workday of a typical wage earner in Harare who puts in a 44-hour work week.

A pleasant demeanor goes a long way in cultivating customers.

An eye-appealing, well-ordered display can attract customers to a vendor in a middle row of a crowded market.

Vendors rely heavily upon their children for assistance after school and during school holidays. While most children who fulfill this role are girls who are at least 10 years old, occasionally I came upon a stall being tended by either boys or girls younger than 10. In two instances, husbands who were out of work were called upon to mind the stall when the wife had to be elsewhere for the day. In several other instances, when female relatives came to visit from the rural areas, they also were enlisted to help.

▲ Cost of Doing Business

Gross margins constitute the basis of vendor returns. Their actual or net returns are calculated by deducting the costs of doing business.[12] Costs include wastage, rent, and transport.

Wastage

The amount of any commodity vendors must discard due to spoilage was very difficult to ascertain. This was due to several factors: (a) as commodities "go off," vendors take them home to eat; (b) if business in a particular commodity, e.g., tomatoes, is not going well, vendors will cut up a portion to sun dry; and (c) vendors might themselves eat some of the commodities about to go off or give them to their children to eat when they come to the market from school.

We attempted to calculate wastage factors by weighing the commodities that had gone off and were about to be thrown into the dustbin, the rotten crops placed by makoronyera on the bottom of a box, and commodities not totally gone off that were set aside to be given away to customers. A sample percentage of wastage appears in Table 6.12. These proportions

Table 6.12 Sample Percentage of Commodities Discarded

Commodity	Percentage Discarded
Apples	11.0
Avocados	9.4
Bananas	17.8
Cabbage (drum head)	5.2
Cabbage (sweet)	5.8
Lemons	9.5
Onions	11.5
Oranges	4.0
Potatoes	16.1
Rape	7.0
Tomatoes	9.0
Tsunga	7.1

Source: Price schedules.

To prevent wastage, vendors display their greens in hand-made stone wells lined with plastic that keep the produce well watered.

represent the wastage factor for 61 (18.8 percent) vendors. I am reluctant to assign numerical values to these factors because they cannot readily be applied to all.

Rent

While rent may not constitute a severe constraint on some women, others who generate only minimal returns are strongly affected. Rent must be paid on a weekly basis, and generally necessitates a trip to the municipality. In some cases, market chairwomen collect all rents, travel to the municipality, and collect a receipt for each vendor.

Another way vendors get the most out of their commodities is to set them out in the sun to dry to be sold later as mufushwa.

Transport

The deepest cut into gross margins is transport. Amai Tendai does not have to bear this expense herself because her son drives her to and from the wholesaler, absorbing the cost of transport himself. Amai Daniel sells in a market site not too distant from the wholesaler, so she walks there. She is unable to carry her purchases this distance herself, however, so she hires a man with a wheelbarrow to walk them over.

Many women reported the necessity of taking two buses in each direction and of paying for parcels on each of the two return buses. Others reported the emergency taxi driver practice of gouging market women to carry them and their purchases from Mbare to their market sites. Given the distances many women must travel to purchase their commodities from the wholesaler, these expenses are out of proportion to their earnings.[13]

Table 6.13 presents the net returns for the six vendors in the case studies, while Table 6.14 presents this information on the other vendors.

Some 80.6 percent of vendors reported selling daily, with another 13.2 percent only taking off Sundays to go to church. The average selling day begins for 30.2 percent at 6:00 A.M., 39.7 percent at 7:00 A.M., 15.1 percent at 8:00 A.M., and 10.2 percent at 9:00 A.M. The selling day ends for 24.9 percent at 6:00 P.M., 54.2 percent at 7:00 P.M., and 17.8 percent at 8:00 P.M., making the average length of the selling day about eleven hours.

Table 6.13　Net Returns to Labor Per Week for Six Case Study Vendors (in Z$)

Vendor	Gross Margin	Waste	Rent	Vendor Transportation	Commodity Transportation	Ancillary Expenses	Net Returns
A. Daniel	32.44	0	2.45	0	7.00	.50	22.49
A. Tendai	149.82	35.96	3.15	0	0	0	110.71
A. George	65.43	4.49	1.75	8.89	2.00	0	48.30
A. Dino	60.05	3.10	1.40	7.00	1.05	0	47.50
A. Tatu	216.70	0	1.40	12.25	8.75	0	194.30
A. Paul	65.95	.80	1.05	14.00	8.40	0	41.70

Source: Interview and price schedules.

Table 6.14　Mean Net Returns to Labor for 40 Vendors (in Z$)

Mean gross margin		60.55
Mean wastage	n/a[a]	
Mean weekly rent	1.75	
Mean vendor transport	9.10	
Mean commodity transport	4.90	
Mean ancillary expenses	.87	
Total expenses	16.62	
Mean weekly net returns		43.93[b]

Note: a. As noted above, wastage figures were obtained for a very limited number of vendors. Since wholesale pricing varied considerably over time and between vendors, I was not able to calculate a representative figure for this factor.

b. This figure compares favorably to the minimum wage for industrial workers as specified in January 1982—Z$105 per month. This income figure differential might well represent one of the reasons why vendors perceive they are better off selling than working for a salary (see Davies 1974:217, for a similar favorable comparison at an earlier time).

Even if selling ends at 7:00 P.M., the workday is still not over as most vendors do not have lockers and must take their commodities home for overnight storage. For 59.1 percent the one-way journey takes less than 10 minutes; for 21.8 percent it takes between 10 and 20 minutes; for the remaining 19.1 percent, the trip takes more than 20 minutes. This amount of travel time is multiplied when not many commodities have been sold, thus necessitating more than one trip home.

Factoring in an hour for transport to the wholesaler, and another half hour to return home with unsold commodities, the average vendor workday is 12.5 hours. If a woman kept up this pace six days per week, her average work week would be 75 hours long. Dividing this average number of hours into the mean weekly net returns to labor (Z$43.93 divided by 75), the average hourly wage would be less than 59 cents.

Our calculations are only half finished, however. The amounts needed by vendors to maintain their families are also a part of this general equation to ascertain whether the incomes women generate through produce vending provide enough cash to meet household expenditures.

▲ Household Expenditures

Expenditures vary greatly according to the number of children and other people living in the household. Variables considered in this calculation include school fees (paid by term but calculated to reflect a weekly budget), school uniforms (paid by year, but also calculated for a weekly budget), other clothing for the family (estimated for the year, but averaged for the week), house mortgage or rent (paid by month but averaged for a week), electricity and water (paid by month, but averaged for a week), medical expenses, remittances to family members (reported by month, but averaged per week), food per week (including staples), cooking fuel/kerosene per week, family transport either to school or to work (other than vendor's), and other expenses (including laundry soap, household furnishings, etc.). Expenditures for the six vendor case studies are presented in Table 6.15. The mean weekly expenditures for all vendors are presented in Table 6.16.

Table 6.15 Weekly Expenditures for Six Vendor Case Studies, 1985–1986 (in Z$)

Expenditures	Amai Daniel	Amai Tendai	Amai George	Amai Dino	Amai Tatu	Amai Paul
School fees	0	0	.25	7.62	3.63	4.33
School uniforms	0	0	2.62	3.40	1.83	.88
Clothing	5.00	5.77	7.69	9.62	13.46	9.23
Rent	3.92	6.69	11.54	5.54	3.46	0
Electricity and water	0	9.46	0	12.00	3.46	0
Medical	4.62	1.00	6.00	2.00	1.00	0
Remittances	1.62	0	2.31	6.92	2.31	0
Food	6.00	50.00	40.00	14.00	30.00	40.00
Fuel/kerosene	0	1.00	10.00	2.00	0	0
Transport	0	3.24	0	4.20	0	0
Other	0	0	30.00	0	12.00	0
Total	21.16	77.16	110.41	67.30	71.15	54.44

Table 6.16 Mean Weekly Expenditures for All Vendors, 1985–1986 (in Z$)

Expenditures	Weekly Mean
School fees	3.88
School uniforms	1.91
Clothing	4.41
Rent	7.49
Electricity and water	4.21
Medical	1.53
Remittances	4.97
Food	26.89
Fuel/kerosene	3.26
Transport	6.19
Other	15.05
Total	79.79

While the evidence I have presented on incomes and expenditures in general reflects only one week of data collection per vendor, it would appear that some vendors do not generate sufficient income to cover weekly cash needs while others exceed their needs. The mean weekly net return of Z$43.93 could reflect, for some, the worst week of business, for others, the best, and for still others, a typical week.

▲ Additional Income

For those whose incomes do not meet their need, I hypothesized that vendors must have access to other financial resources.[14] In their study of Kambuzuma, Kanji and Jazdowska (1993) found that women earned income by sewing, knitting, crocheting, sale of small livestock, petty trading, hairdressing, baking and cooking, and selling fresh produce. When I asked vendors what other sources of income they had, if they were married they said their husbands provided some; otherwise their grown children or other relatives contributed.[15] Vendors reported that when business was bad they would stop selling until the end of the month when their working husbands or family members received their salaries and could stake them to resume their market activities. In most instances, this cash advance constituted a loan to be paid back when vendor business picked up again. In other instances, according to intrahousehold dynamics, vendors just took the money as their due.

When income is being generated on a daily basis, vendors can manage that income through daily contributions to revolving credit/savings societies. Amounts vendors contribute and receive per week cannot be counted as additional income, but are reported here to illustrate the lump sums vendors can receive if they participate.

Additional contributions made by spouses, kin, or other sources also appear in Table 6.17.[16] For the entire population, the mean of additional incomes is reported in Table 6.18.

Table 6.17 Other Financial Resources for Six Vendors (in Z$)

Vendor	Family Assistance	Credit Society	Other	Total
A. Daniel	0	(14.04)	0	0
A. Tendai	23.08	(42.05)	0	23.08
A. George	9.23	(7.00)	20.00	29.23
A. Dino	0	0	0	0
A. Tatu	0	(17.55)	0	0
A. Paul	16.15	(10.53)	0	16.15

Table 6.18 Weekly Mean of Additional Vendor Financial Resources (in Z$)

Family assistance (n = 131)	13.66
Credit society (n = 185)	(18.70)
Other (food contributions) (n = 29)	n/a
Total	13.66

Source: Interview schedules.

▲ Additional Expenditures

Vendors incur at least two additional expenditures: remittances and transportation to rural homesteads. As an aspect of maintaining rural ties, vendors remit an average of Z$172.89 per year or Z$3.32 per week. Additionally, vendors return to rural areas to visit their kin at least once a year and pay a mean of Z$8.66 for transport for each person. Accompanying vendors on their journey are generally two other people, bringing the transport bill up to Z$25.98 or a weekly average of 50 cents. Thus, in addition to household expenses, vendors incur expenses of Z$3.82 a week to maintain ties with rural kin.

To obtain a budgetary picture of the weekly cash flow of the vendors and our six case studies, the merging of incomes and expenditures is presented for the six case studies in Table 6.19 and in Table 6.20 for the total vendor population.

Table 6.19 Total Weekly Net Incomes and Expenditures of Six Vendors (in Z$)

Vendor	Net Returns from Vending	Additional Income	Household Expenditures	Additional Expenditures	Surplus/ Deficit
A. Daniel	22.90	0	21.16	2.66	−.92
A. Tendai	110.71	23.08	77.16	14.42	+42.21
A. George	48.30	29.23	112.41	.23	−35.11
A. Dino	47.50	0	67.30	.23	−20.03
A. Tatu	194.30	0	71.15	5.79	+117.36
A. Paul	41.70	16.15	54.44	.14	+3.27

Source: Interview schedules.

Table 6.20 Total Weekly Net Incomes from Vending and Expenditures of Vendors (in Z$)

Mean net returns from vending	43.93
Mean additional income	(32.36)
Mean household expenditure	79.79
Mean additional expenditure	3.82
Mean surplus/deficit	−39.68

▲ Summary and Conclusion

Based on the data presented in this chapter, we have an understanding of vendor business and maximizing behavior. Beset with the dilemma of needing to earn an income in the city with little means to do so, women build upon the skills they have and launch fresh produce microenterprises, generally with assistance from a spouse or kin. Maintaining the enterprise is an economic challenge. The transportation, marketing, and municipal governance systems all present problems to vendors, who restock their stalls daily in order to provide their customers with the freshest commodities possible. While these systemic problems reduce the amount of profit vendors can realize, they feel they definitely do realize a profit. This amount, whatever it may be, is what sends vendor children to school and provisions the family. However, for some (i.e., those who appear to be losing on their business ventures), it is highly likely that vendor husbands and families contribute more to meeting household expenditures than reported and/or vendors have other sources of income that were not reported. For those whose profit margins are nonexistent, unreported sources of income are the only means by which vendor enterprises can be maintained.

Another issue requiring further exploration is that of cash flow versus "profit." It appears that vendors are concerned with "the money I have more than what I started with," but of greater concern is the amount of cash a vendor has at the end of the day. With this amount, she can purchase stocks at the wholesaler the next day, feed her family, and take care of incidental daily expenses. For larger expenses, e.g., school fees, rent, she depends on her intake at the end of the month when people buy more and on her returns from participation in a revolving credit/savings society. If the amounts generated through marketing or savings are insufficient, then alternative financial resources need to be found. Resources may be found within the family or in participation in activities not covered by this research.

Regardless of whether vendor-generated incomes are supplemented or not, the facts presented here on their financial returns clearly indicate that what they earn adds significantly to their ability to fulfill their economic roles and survive in an urban environment. It is important to note, however, that these returns do not constitute the only reason why vendors establish and maintain their businesses. Chapter 7 presents a discussion of these variables.

▲ Notes

1. A similar phenomenon was observed in the highland markets of Bolivia, especially in the La Paz market, where "farm people dismounting from lorries in the

area of the main wholesale and retail markets of La Paz are often seized by wholesalers or retailers and forced to sell their goods at a low price" (Preston 1978:118).

2. Baby marrow, chamollier (a green leafy vegetable), mazhanje (a wild fruit), mufushwa (dried, cut-up greens), papaya, and strawberries are not included, as these were sold at markets not a part of this analysis.

3. Research conducted on small scale manufacturing enterprises in several different countries produced similar results as to record keeping. In Jamaica, 16 percent of proprietors in this sector kept records; in Sierra Leone, 18 percent; in Honduras, 14 percent; in Egypt, 6 percent; and in Bangladesh, 6 percent (Liedholm and Mead 1987:33).

4. The women, however, expressed great interest in knowing how to keep track of their cash flows, and at one market site I was asked to teach them a simple means of recordkeeping. My inability to do this for nonliterate individuals caused me to seek assistance from the Zimbabwe Women's Bureau.

5. The term *amai* means "mother" in Shona. Women are referred to by the name of their first-born child.

6. Giving away commodities to ensure regularity of customers seems to be a common practice. In the markets of La Paz, "in addition to the payment for the eggs the La Paz dealer hands over either some sweets or, usually, a few onions and even some chili peppers or stale bread or a bun as a bonus" (Preston 1978:115). A similar practice is observable in the Kumasi market in Ghana (Clark 1986).

7. The heaps of tomatoes and bundles of rape are determined "by hand" or "by eye." An additional factor is considered, however, in measuring: how much of each is required for a meal. An interesting topic of future research would be to determine whether households buy more bundles of rape when, during times of scarcity, the bundles get smaller, or whether they make do with the smaller bundles and thus consume less.

8. Women and men among Shona-speaking people can have a ritual friendship, or *usawhira*. These friendships never include a potential for marriage or sexual relationship. If a female refers to a male as a friend, then the connotation is that a sexual relationship exists between them.

9. The particular characteristics of urban growth in Zimbabwe (e.g., creation of townships, vagrancy laws, food vending laws) explain why vendors have a more favorable customer ratio than in other countries.

10. At one market site, there were 22 vendors selling at stalls, and several others selling on the street about a block away. When queried about their prices, the street vendors reported similar prices to those recorded at the stalls.

11. Since ESAP, prices have changed. The smallest heap of tomatoes costs 50 cents, a bundle of rape costs between 50 and 80 cents, and the smallest onion can cost between 30 and 50 cents.

12. The formula utilized to calculate vendor net returns to labor is: $NR_{vw} = GM_{vw} - (W_{vw} + R_{vw} + T_{vw} + TT_{vw} + E_{vw})$, where NR = Net Returns to labor, GM = Gross Margin, v = Each vendor, w = Week of research, W = Wastage factor for each commodity per day, R = Rent paid per week for vending site, T = Transport paid weekly for vendor to/from wholesaler and to/from market, TT = Transport paid weekly for commodities from wholesaler to market, and E = Expenses incurred weekly ancillary to the conduct of business.

13. Transport is also a problem for women in Brazil and Mexico where it was found that "women were subjected to more prolonged, complex, and costly trips to work compared with men because [the] existing transport system did not address their particular productive activities" (Schmink 1986:20).

14. The incomes generated by other means could not be fully documented. Two other activities not ever mentioned by vendors are rent from lodgers and rent from subletting their stalls.

15. McPherson's study (1991) found that 45 percent of microenterprises generated 50 percent or more of household income.

16. Contributions made in kind to the urban household by visiting rural kin could not be calculated and included in this amount.

▲ 7

Noneconomic Variables in Microenterprise Development

Although women in Harare have established fresh produce microenterprises to generate income, other variables motivate them to continue in their trade and to withstand the problems they face in conducting their businesses. This chapter explores these noneconomic variables. The first part of the chapter analyzes the broad cultural, sociological, and urban contextual variables that necessitate women's economic activities. The second part analyzes individual reasons women reported why they became involved in this trade. These reasons include female employment opportunity structures, women's provisioning roles and the division of labor, the cultural value of the substance exchanged, exercising "psychic control" over an urban economic activity (including reducing dependence on males), other incomes and professional bonds arising out of the produce vending experience, and women's needs and childcare.

▲ The Cultural Ethic of Work

African women view themselves as active economic household contributors, whether they are in rural or urban areas:

> The goals that women set themselves are defined by their position within the overall social system and by the resources that they themselves possess. The strategies they use involve attempts to maximize these resources by manipulating the opportunities that they perceive in their environment (Dinan 1982:54).

The ethic governing the daily lives of Shona-speaking women resounds in their song: *Shandira! Hapana chinouya chega!*—"Work! Nothing comes without it!"

Women in the rural areas of Zimbabwe invest their time in both agricultural and domestic activities to provision their families and provide for child welfare. Some women might also engage in off-farm employment to

133

generate income. In the cities, the constraints women face in finding suitable work constitute a complex of economic, social, and cultural problems because the field in which women try to meet their goals is characterized by gender bias, scarce capital, abundant unskilled labor, and a poorly developed infrastructure (Johnson 1973:4). In these restricted circumstances, they try to develop their own individual niches to satisfy their needs (Jules-Rosette 1982; Gladwin 1980).

The notion of women not working was not acceptable to vendors. In the rural areas, they worked on a constant basis in the fields, in their gardens, in domestic activities, fetching water, and fetching wood. In the urban areas, they wanted to be equally productive, but not in the same activities.

▲ Chaos of the City

One of the most difficult problems women face in urban areas is the need for cash on a daily basis. Women told me they had had expectations of an easier life in the city because they did not have to work in the fields, draw water, or gather firewood. However, they were troubled by how much everything costs—accommodation, food, water, transport, etc.

Women were also disturbed at what they saw happening to their husbands and families. Too often husbands would take their salaries directly to the municipal beer hall and drink away money required for household expenses. Many women also told me of their husbands' wandering eyes, and how salaries were spent on other women. Although 90.1 percent of married respondents indicated their husbands were living with them at the time of the interview, women were concerned about the steadfastness and reliability of the relationship and felt, as mothers, that they must take a more pro-active position to ensure the incomes necessary to cover household expenditures.

Vendors also felt incomes generated by their husbands were not adequate. Since occupations of many spouses largely fall into the "unskilled" category, their income levels were reportedly very low. While incomes have increased over the years, especially since independence and the passage of minimum wage legislation, women still feel their husbands' earnings do not adequately meet urban costs of living. When they first migrated to Harare, as now, women felt the need to contribute economically to the urban household.

When I asked women what they did when they first came to Harare, 60.5 percent said they stayed at home taking care of children (either their own or those of a relative) or occupied themselves with domestic activities. The remainder found it necessary to establish almost immediately some means of generating an income. Approximately 10 percent said they looked for work in the formal, salaried sector, in factories, tobacconeers, hospitals, schools, and the like. Some 15 percent looked for work as domestics, while the remaining 15 percent went directly into the informal marketing sector selling a number of commodities out of their homes, door-to-door, or from streetside tables.

The blend of problematic marital relations, lack of desire or inability on the part of spouses to support the family, and the lack of work opportunities for females contributes to women's perceptions of the city as chaotic. To reduce this cognitive dissonance, women seek to fulfill economic roles ascribed to them through socialization by creating their own strategies for control.

▲ Urban Contextual Variables

Urban families require cash on a regular basis to pay for rent/mortgages, water, electricity, transport to work, and food. Urban lifestyles and the distance one must travel between home and work require that a daily sum be set aside for transport and work site meals. All these demands make it necessary for monthly incomes to be generated. Obtaining employment to meet these cash needs, however, is difficult for both men and women.

Male Employment Levels

According to the 1982 census, some 18.5 percent of the adult labor force was classified as unemployed (for males the percentage was 15.5, but for females it was 26.8).[1] Vendors reported that 21.3 percent of their spouses were unemployed,[2] an increase of 5.8 percent over the male average. Thus, households in which a husband is not working, and households where there is no male spouse—represented by 45.5 percent (n = 148) of vendors—rely solely on the earnings of the vendors themselves or, alternatively, on financial assistance from relatives.

Of the vendors who said they were married, 78.7 percent (n = 177) reported that their husbands were working. Of these 177 working husbands, 93.2 percent (n = 165) were earning a salary on a regular basis. Some 59.9 percent (n = 106) of spouses knew their husbands' earnings. These were reported as ranging between Z$30 and Z$1,500 per month, with the mean at Z$172.73. Comparatively speaking, in 1984 the minimum monthly urban wage for an unskilled worker was Z$115, with an average annual income of Z$1,015[3] (Riddell 1984).

For males, the inability to find work is more directly related to levels of education achieved; for females, unemployment rates are higher regardless of the educational levels they achieve (Zimbabwe, CSO 1985:122–130). "The role of education in preparing a child for a working life is highly defective and gives young men a better edge in the choice of professions while relegating young women to jobs they have traditionally been identified with like nursing and teaching" ("New Strategies Needed to Fight Sex Discrimination," *Moto,* No. 44, 1985:7). Table 7.1 presents educational level of males in Harare. Table 7.2 presents the educational levels achieved by male spouses of vendors interviewed.

Table 7.1 Educational Levels of Males in Harare

Age Group	At School	Left School	Never Attended	Not Stated	Total
0–4	—	—	48,457	—	48,457
5–9	21,221	203	14,688	39	36,151
10–14	28,643	538	398	40	29,619
15–19	20,249	10,370	395	66	31,080
20–24	4,125	38,932	920	77	44,054
25–29	715	39,843	1,254	87	41,899
30–34	244	28,342	1,408	45	30,039
35–39	128	20,737	1,491	36	22,392
40–44	73	18,195	2,399	37	20,704
45–49	46	13,919	2,320	35	16,320
50–54	17	10,616	2,416	37	13,086
Over 55	51	15,359	3,993	118	19,521
Not sure	38	1,005	424	40	1,507
Total	75,550	198,059	80,563	657	354,829

Source: Zimbabwe, CSO, *Census* (September 27, 1983) Table 13A.

Table 7.2 Educational Levels of Male Spouses of Female Fresh Produce Vendors in Harare

Educational Level	Percent	Number
None	18.9	45
Grade 1–3	8.4	20
Grade 4–5	13.9	33
Grade 6–7	26.5	63
Form 1–2	24.8	59
Form 3–4	3.8	9
More than Form 4	3.8	9

Source: Interview schedule.

Among vendor spouses some 18.9 percent had never gone to school, while the total urban percentage is 22.7. The unemployment level for vendor spouses in Harare is higher than that of the national average. Since no statistics on employment for Harare alone are currently available, I can only compare educational levels and unemployment on a national level (see Table 7.3).[4]

Table 7.3 National Educational Levels and Unemployment

	Employed				Unemployed			
	Males		Females		Males		Females	
Educational Level	Number	Percent	Number	Percent	Number	Percent	Number	Percent
None	158,580	57.0	65,640	25.9	32,270	11.6	22,370	8.8
Primary (1–7 years)	539,410	55.4	145,130	24.0	113,520	11.7	69,820	11.6
Secondary (Form 1 and over)	195,330	75.5	73,480	63.8	17,990	6.9	12,130	10.5

Source: Zimbabwe, CSO, *Main Demographic Features* (1985:120–121) Tables V.12 and V.13.

Male unemployment makes it imperative for females to generate their own incomes. Given that female employment opportunities are fewer than those for males, it follows that women's incomes must be derived from informal economic activities.

Cash Needs

The range of expenditures necessitated by urban living appear in Table 7.4.

Table 7.4 Average Monthly Expenditures for Harare Vendor Households, 1985–1986 (in Z$)

School fees	16.82
School uniforms	8.26
Clothing	19.12
Rent	32.45
Electricity and water	18.25
Medical	6.61
Remittance home	21.52
Food	121.00
Fuel/kerosene	3.26
Transport (not including vendor)	6.19
Other	15.05
Total	268.53

Source: Interview schedule.

I have already discussed the fact that some 45 percent of the population surveyed cannot rely on incomes from spouses, either because husbands are unemployed or because there is no resident spouse due to divorce or widowhood. For those spouses who are employed, Table 7.5 presents the salaries vendor husbands reportedly earn. The mean of monthly salaries is Z$172.73, representing a household expenditure deficit of Z$95.80. The preponderance of spouses (68, or 64 percent of the 106 reported incomes), however, make considerably less than the mean.

Table 7.5 Monthly Incomes Generated by Male Spouses

Incomes (in Z$)	Number	Percent
30–40	3	2.7
41–50	3	2.7
51–60	2	1.8
61–70	6	5.7
71–80	8	7.4
81–90	7	6.6
91–100	8	7.5
101–110	4	3.7
111–120	5	4.6
121–130	1	0.9
131–140	4	3.7
141–150	4	3.8
151–160	9	8.4
161–170	4	3.7
171–180	4	3.7
181–190	2	1.8
191–200	8	7.5
201–210	2	1.8
211–220	3	2.8
250	4	3.8
251–260	2	1.8
261–270	1	0.9
271–280	1	0.9
281–290	1	0.9
291–300	2	1.9
301–310	1	0.9
330	1	0.9
400	1	0.9
450	1	0.9
500	1	0.9
640	1	0.9
800	1	0.9
1,000	1	0.9

Source: Interview schedule.

ESAP has placed enormous financial burdens on urban households, in particular. Currency devaluation, deregulation, and inflation have tripled the urban cost of living for a family of four to Z$715 (Mudzengerere 1993:20) (and this does not include trips home, for which bus transportation has increased by 55.4 percent [Muchemenyi et al. 1993:15]). The highest cost increases have been in food, evidenced by the Consumer Price Index (CPI). In 1987, the CPI for foodstuffs was 276.0 for low income households; by September 1992 it had increased to 888.3 (Zimbabwe, CSO 1992b:9). In January 1993, the cost of food increased by another 71.8 percent (Mudzengerere 1993:21).

Thus, whether or not an urban household includes a male wage earner, it is highly likely that the incomes generated are inadequate to meet household expenditures. Women's businesses must thus be seen as critical to urban family survival. The financial burden women bear not only includes daily food provisioning, but also purchase of and payment for basic human needs, i.e., shelter, food, and water (see May 1979 for Zimbabwe; Kaba 1982 for Liberia).

The Myth of the Household Economy

It is assumed that household members (who can) contribute financial resources to meet the expenditures incurred for the benefit of its members. Indeed, incorporated in the definition of the household is the notion of it being a locus of income pooling (see Wallerstein 1984:20). This assumption requires reexamination.

Households require a more detailed analysis to determine *if* income pooling takes place, how the gender-based division of labor is reflected in the amount spouses pool, and the expenditures met through this resource sharing. If pooling is not a household ethic, then what are the individual financial responsibilities of each member—including conjugal, kin, and nonkin relationships—and what is the nature of the intrahousehold dynamic that promotes a "separate purse" rather than a "pooling" strategy?

In considering the household as a locus of relationships guided not by a physical boundary but by the cultural context in which this economic concept is derived, then we must view each individual within the household walls as a complex nexus of ascribed roles and those emerging as the result of economic development and social change. This nexus can be analyzed from many different angles, but my purpose in this volume is to consider gender roles in the contemporary urban household and determine how a predominantly female, income earning business affects the way financial resources are utilized. Two major cultural and historical elements must be brought to bear on this analysis: the responsibilities for food provisioning that women are culturally ascribed; and the labor reserve economy that contributed to the development of urban, gender-specific roles.

In the rural household established upon patrilineal, patrilocal marriage, men are granted usufruct rights over land, a specific portion of which is allocated to wives to cultivate garden crops for the family. Additionally, through labor in rainfed grain fields, wives are accorded a portion of the staple crop, also for family consumption. By their labor in these two domains, women provision their families. As the labor reserve economy brought more men to the urban areas for work, rural women assumed de facto food production responsibility. Ultimately, however, women also migrated and had to adapt their provisioning roles to the urban environment.

Cultural norms concerning provisioning in certain families were transformed, with males assuming full responsibility for household and family nurture. In most households, however, this was not possible due to the low salaries paid to male urban workers. Hence, women were required to earn an income. In so doing, they maintained their provisioning roles, while husbands met expenses that were a part of their culturally ascribed roles. To elucidate, at marriage, men were provided land for a homestead, food production, and cattle grazing. In the city, therefore, men pay for housing, including rent and utilities. To illustrate their commitment to extending the lineage, they also contribute to the education of their children by paying school fees. They might also enhance a wife's provisioning role by financially staking her to her first and any succeeding investment to establish and maintain a vegetable vending microenterprise, fully cognizant of the returns to the family the wife will produce—similar in function to providing rural women with their garden plots.

Inheritance laws reflect this separate purse theory. For instance, all property acquired since marriage has traditionally been claimed by a deceased husband's family, leaving a wife and children destitute. An assumption made by inheritance laws is that women's economic activities contribute to family nurture, while men's result in the purchase of assets. Assets, therefore, are owned by the lineage, as are children ensuing from the marriage (see Wilk 1989:35–39 for related arguments). Although inheritance laws have changed considerably, widows are not challenging the practice of looting the marital home.

The "separate purse" in Zimbabwe, therefore, has a triple heritage: culture, urbanization, and the labor reserve economy. An analysis of expenditures met by vendor households supports this notion. Out of the total number of women who are married, only 34 percent (79) reported that their husbands share their earnings in helping to pay for household expenses, school fees, rent, health care, and the like.

> In many households where the wife works she is expected to pay for food and clothing for herself and her children out of her earnings, with the husband making up as far as is necessary from his wages. The husband usually pays rent and probably school fees. This is the urban adaptation of the traditional practices in which the wife is largely responsible for the production at all stages of food for the family (May 1979:54).

Where incomes are generated by both men and women, each gender is expected to meet different expenditures. If the woman is working, she assumes responsibility for household food provisioning and family maintenance; if there is a husband in the household and he is working, he should pay rent and school fees. If this were indeed the case, what average expenditures would males have to meet, and what would females have to meet?

Using the monthly expenditures listed above, men would be responsible for paying Z$91.84 per month, or 34.2 percent, while women would be responsible for Z$176.69, or 65.8 percent. More men would be able to meet these expenditures with their salaries—66 percent of spouses employed (70)—if they were used to support the household. This is not the case for many vendor spouses, however.[5]

As an alternative to providing financial support to the household, I thought men might contribute purchased foodstuffs. I found that only 1.3 percent (3) of husbands provide this input for the family. Husbands' incomes are reportedly used to purchase their own daily work site provisions and to create leisure activities.

The concept of household economy in the urban areas requires redefinition in light of the data presented on low income households represented by vendors. Research conducted on this microlevel indicates that urban males may or may not find it necessary to share their earnings with their spouses or take responsibility for providing financial inputs for their children's well-being. Additionally, since women are purported to be the main provisioners of the household, the idea of a household economy where incomes are pooled seems erroneous. The inconsistency of contributions on the part of males, the disproportionate division of financial responsibilities according to gender in meeting household expenditures, and male unemployment all emphasize the need for women to generate a reliable income.

The Disintegration of the Family Unit

A final point on why women need to generate an income arises out of cultural beliefs about responsibility for stepchildren. Exacerbated by unemployment, social problems have given rise to a greater probability of marital dissolution, the rising incidence of children being born to single females, and greater cultural discord. If a woman marries, has children, divorces, and subsequently remarries, the second husband usually refuses to support the children of the previous marriage if the wife has custody. Custody of children will reside in women if bridewealth has not been paid (May 1983), if the children are under age 7, if the families of widows do not want the financial burden of the children, or if the husband refuses to take them after divorce. Thus, if a woman wants the children of her first marriage to be educated, she must find the financial means to do so. (Under the new Zimbabwean maintenance laws, a woman can have a man's salary attached—if he is employed—to obtain child support.)

▲ Why Women Become and Continue to Be Fresh Produce Vendors

The first half of this chapter considered why there is an increased need in the city for women to generate income. This section explores why fresh produce vending has been chosen by respondents.

Female Employment Opportunity Structures

Women in Harare employ a wide range of strategies to generate an income. For the preponderance of unskilled urban women, however, the range is limited. Educational levels limit employment options, although, as posited above, the structure of female employment opportunity more heavily influences the jobs women are allowed to obtain.[6] A similar assertion has been made for women in other places. In Latin America, "it is doubtful that increased education leads to better employment opportunities except at the higher levels of the occupational hierarchy, and here women are limited to those few "female" fields described earlier. Their wages are likely to be lower, and their mobility is more limited" (Schmink 1986:13).

A more forceful argument is posited for the women of Africa: "Societies are arranged in such a way that women's independent access to productive resources, to labor markets, to information, to political and legal rights are seriously constrained. Society permits them only limited control of their own productive capabilities" (Cloud 1984:44).

Parallel to the analysis of the male population in Table 7.1, Table 7.6 considers the educational levels achieved by females in Harare. Table 7.7 then presents the educational levels of female vendors.

Table 7.6 Educational Levels Achieved by Women in Harare

Age Group	At School	Left School	Never Attended	Not Stated	Total
0–4	—	—	48,588	—	48,588
5–9	22,612	227	15,061	47	37,947
10–14	30,123	1,073	603	52	31,851
15–19	16,339	18,931	1,324	67	36,661
20–24	1,597	38,101	2,163	78	41,939
25–29	284	28,485	1,998	45	30,812
30–34	132	18,007	1,674	42	19,855
35–39	76	13,221	1,699	29	15,025
40–44	34	9,720	1,740	17	11,511
45–49	21	6,625	1,425	27	8,098
50–54	20	4,916	1,061	21	6,018
Over 55	57	11,601	2,620	164	14,442
Not sure	32	363	357	36	788
Total	71,327	151,270	80,313	625	303,535

Source: Zimbabwe, CSO, *Census* (1983) Table 13A.

Table 7.7 **Educational Levels of Female Fresh Produce Vendors in Harare**

Educational Level	Percent	Number
None	18.8	60
Grade 1–3	14.4	46
Grade 4–5	21.9	70
Grade 6–7	27.2	87
Form 1–2	15.0	48
Form 3–4	2.5	8
More than Form 4	.3	1

Source: Interview schedules.

Of the total population of women in Harare, 26.5 percent have received no education, while 18.8 percent of female vendors are in this category. For females, the percentage who have no education more closely coincides with the percentage who are unemployed. I make this assertion on the basis of certain calculations made with documents supplied to me by the Census Department (Zimbabwe, CSO 1983: Table 19), which reports various employment information for all urban areas.

The only data I have to support my contention that female unemployment levels are higher than those for males in Harare are those extrapolated from the census figures appearing in the preceding pages. This information appears in Table 7.8.

Table 7.8 **Male and Female Unemployment Levels in Urban Centers**

	Male	Female
Unemployed	22,516	18,069
Not working	4,503	6,925
Homemaker[a]	686	83,426
Total reported	27,705	108,420
Total population	270,221	217,000
Percent of total	10.3	50.0

Source: Extrapolated from *Census* figures (Tables 13A and 19).
Note: a. According to the 1982 population census ten percent report, it is assumed that an indeterminate portion of the homemaker population is also seeking work or may be self-employed, in which case no statistics would be presented.

Of those who knew their ages, women reported they were between 16 and 73, with a converse relationship of age to education, i.e., the younger the vendor, the more education she had received. But years in school cannot be directly correlated to skills acquired. Colonial educational policies sought to create an African population with just sufficient knowledge to function in the colonial bureaucracy at a level settlers required. Skills training was not a part of the curriculum, so the job opportunities open to those with education were limited by what colonials determined educated Africans could do. While the educational curriculum is currently being revised to meet the skill needs of an independent Zimbabwe, the majority of vendors I interviewed had been a part of previous educational processes.

The exceptions to participation in the formal educational structure are the nonformal training schemes that 15.7 percent (51) of the female vendors had undertaken. Courses included sewing/dressmaking, first aid training offered by the Red Cross, and how to be a preschool aide, among others. But these training schemes did not prove adequate in securing vendors a long-term, reliable source of income. Indeed, after a brief foray into these fields, each endeavor was dropped in favor of fresh produce vending.

Vendors reported they had sought and found work in a number of enterprises: 22.5 percent (73) had been employed as domestics; of the remaining 35 who reported having worked for a salary, activities included working as a shopgirl, in a creche or nursery school, making greeting cards, sewing in a clothing factory, cleaning in a hotel, hospital, or office building, and as sorters and packagers at the tobacconeers.

The entrepreneurial economic activities women have developed for themselves include buying and selling clothing, knitting and selling sweaters, operating a tuckshop (kiosk), and crocheting and selling tablecloths and articles of clothing (see Brand 1982:42–44, for a further description of these activities). While each of these income generating activities provided vendors at one time with cash to purchase food, none was capable of sustaining them or their families over the long term.

Women's Provisioning Roles and the Division of Labor

African women have traditional domain over certain enterprises, whether they be in the rural or urban areas. Owing to the pattern of accommodation developed during the colonial period, many urban housing plots do not have adequate garden space. Moreover, due to the rising price of real estate, many families have been forced to become lodgers in other people's houses (Patel and Adams 1981). This status entails no rights to cultivate any land that may surround the house; such cultivation is conducted only by the owners.[7]

As asserted above, women do not discard the roles they are ascribed in the rural areas when they migrate to the cities. Women maintain their provisioning roles and are faced with a dilemma: how to provision their families without the productive means to do so. While wages and other income generating activities are considered the means to gain access to provisions for many women, establishing a food vending enterprise brings women closer to the food source. That is, by purchasing fresh produce wholesale from the earnings generated from prior sales, vendors can provision their families at wholesale cost, and generate an income at the same time. In this way, a cultural role is fulfilled in the process of meeting other economic objectives.

The Cultural Value of the Substance Exchanged

Valuing the substance of exchange has been elaborated on by Sahlins (1972). He draws an analytical distinction between use and exchange value in noncapitalist, nonmarket economies and asserts that investing value in articles of exchange is mediated by symbols ascribed with meaning in a given cultural context. That is, the commodity exchanged has value because it is used to fulfill certain objectives, and because it has symbolic value in the act of exchange itself (for example, establishing good relations between traders).

While Sahlins's arguments were made for precapitalist societies, I believe they can be applied to market transactions as well. Substance produced for exchange derives value from several arenas: the use of the item produced and exchanged, the social rewards achieved from the actual exchange, and the scarcity of the substance produced relative to its demand. What is missing from this evaluative process is the cultural meaning of the substance in and of itself, i.e., what meaning does the society ascribe to the substance itself? Indeed, does this sort of valuing exist?

Sahlins has attempted to ferret out these meanings and separate them from the "utility" of commodities exchanged. He posits that "meaning is the specific property of the anthropological object" (Sahlins 1976:x). Meaning, however, is derived from a system of codification that rests on yet another, more general debate on human behavior (i.e., nature vs. nurture). He states that the dichotomy is not trivial between

> whether the cultural order is to be conceived as the codification of man's actual purposeful and pragmatic action; or whether, conversely, human action in the world is to be understood as mediated by the cultural design, which gives order at once to practical experience, customary practice, and the relationship between the two. (Sahlins 1976:55).

He argues further that particular circumstances give rise to particular practices, which in turn are expressed through organization and codification, and that "codification expresses organization," i.e., codes are ascribed meanings that express certain human relations. I believe it is in this assertion that meaning can be ascribed to certain cultural symbols that are then related to others in a system of codification. The system would, however, express a wider social organization than that embodied only in the symbol.

Such a symbol for the vendors is in the fresh produce itself. In the countryside, a woman is allocated a well-watered plot on which to cultivate fruits and vegetables. This plot, essentially, has two purposes, one practical and one symbolic: to provision the family with continuously harvested crops; and to create a relationship between the woman who was "married-in" and the patrilineal ancestors of the husband.[8] Ceremonies are conducted to acknowledge the intervention of the ancestral (vadzimu) or clan (*mhondoro*) spirits in helping to bring about an abundant harvest of *mishashe,* green vegetables (Gelfand 1970). This ceremony is normally held in April when the summer greens have been picked, and again in September when the winter greens are harvested.

Since abundant harvests depend, it is believed by various Shona-speaking groups, on the relationship between the cultivator and the patrilineage ancestors, such a harvest is a symbol of the woman having been accepted by her husband's ancestors. The crops grown symbolize a relationship between the living and the dead. That women are responsible for the cultivation of these crops throughout the year seems not only a matter of economics and food provisioning, but also a continual indicator of a sustained relationship between a "foreigner"—a woman married-in—and an "insider"—a patrilineage ancestor.

The relationship of this discussion to that on the meaning of substance is that a woman in the rural areas who can trade her surpluses is making at least two statements: (1) that she has harvested abundantly enough to trade her surplus; and (2) that she has been accepted by her husband's ancestors, and continues to be so, as evidenced in what she has to trade. Surplus garden crops are thus a symbol of patrilineage acceptance and women's achievement of status within their husbands' families. Surplus garden crops are also an indicator of an underlying ethic that reflects hard work and diligence; a woman's personal status in the community is enhanced as she displays the fruits of her labor.

In the urban areas, it is more difficult to see the relationship between the substance of exchange and status. From a functionalist perspective, abundance of garden crops produced in the rural areas, utilized to nurture members of the patrilineage, symbolizes the protective care being exercised by the ancestors. In the urban areas the role of nurturing is continued but the type of labor in which vendors are engaged is not cultivating crops but cultivating customers. By exhibiting community provisioning behavior, the fruits of a woman's labor are seen in the number of sales she makes. Her sales efforts enable her to continue nurturing her family and currying the favor of the patrilineage. Her ability to relate to the broader community through vending is rooted in her socialization, which prepares her for her ascribed provisioning roles. In the city, therefore, the meaning of the substance exchanged remains—from a functionalist perspective—but the substance cultivated reflects the urban environment.

Similar to the failure of garden crops in the rural areas, when financial returns are insufficient (translated into insufficient "cultivation" of customers), a cause must be discerned. Some vendors indicated they did not sell much because they did not have much to sell; others said they had "bad luck." Bad luck is translated, for Shona-speaking people, into poor relations with the ancestral spirits.

The ability of women to trade in fresh produce is related to their continued, though tacit, good relations with those of the spirit world. Low incomes are attributable to no customers. If good relations prevail between vendors and their ancestors, ancestors would continually protect vendors from being "cursed" by other vendors and bring them more regular customers.

On repeated occasions, vendors reported that their stalls had been sprinkled with powerful herbs (*muti* or mushonga) that would prevent customers from purchasing from them, or that a vendor had sprinkled certain herbs on her own stall to attract customers. When there are no customers, there is no income, and no means to provision the family or send children to school. Customers, by analogy, have taken the place of abundant harvests as indicators of good relations with the ancestral spirits. Customers are also seen as the vehicle through which vendors generate the cash needed to nurture their families.

What is of underlying importance in this discussion is that women could not become very good vendors if they did not have some expertise in the crops themselves. This expertise is an integral part of the cultural system into which women are socialized. The knowledge they acquire in this particular cultural setting is brought to bear in conducting their trade.

Exercising Psychic Control over an Urban Economic Activity

Women in the city need to bring some order to their chaotic urban environment. By establishing and maintaining a business in the informal economy, women enhance their self-esteem by continuing to be able to contribute to the finances of the domestic unit. This same advantage was identified for self-employed petty traders in Nairobi:

> These advantages are: getting all the profits, which do not belong to anyone else; not being answerable to someone else; one cannot be sacked; no harassment or supervision; more incentive and effort; free disposition of time; free to stay home in case of children's illnesses; more initiative and motivation; more control over profit (Adagala 1986:25).

The women I interviewed exhibited a pride of professionalism in operating their businesses.[9] This pride is generated not only because they have carved out an economic niche for themselves in a relatively hostile environment, but also because they have achieved status in being able to solve the critical problems of daily food provisioning and cash needs. Moreover, they help to provide food access to others in the community by occupying the main provisioning link between producers/wholesalers and consumers. Without the very bold actions of female vendors to participate in this enterprise, purchasing daily fresh produce requirements would necessitate a bus ride to the nearest formal sector distribution point. As an alternative, retail shops would have to take on these additional commodities and charge accordingly. Thus, expenditure for stall rent and daily transport absorbed by female vendors purchased for them the status of produce provider not only to their own families but also to the wider community.

This pride of professionalism extended, almost to their detriment, to an extreme in delineating norms of behavior in the marketplace. For instance, when I asked women if they ever pooled their money to make bulk wholesale purchases, 100 percent indicated they did not. When I asked why not, some 48 different answers were given. Among the main reasons were: "we don't go to purchase at the same time" (16.9 percent); "we never could arrange to do that" (11.1 percent); "we don't have enough money to buy in bulk" (9.8 percent); and "no one ever thought of that" (9.2 percent). Interesting were the 10.8 percent who focused upon certain jealousies and distrust between vendors (e.g., use of magic, not being a member of the same ethnic group) and how this translates into lack of cooperative activity. The remaining vendors (42.2 percent) spoke critically about the inability to cooperate when finances are concerned, especially when expenditure must be incurred for transport and for commodities that are not price-fixed.

A critical aspect of vendor unwillingness to share with other vendors in purchasing is the individual perception that only the vendors themselves know their customers' needs and they know what commodities will sell. If others are sent to pick out commodities in bulk, individual vendors might be left with the quality of product their customers will not buy. It is not just a matter of buying a box of tomatoes; rather, the size, color, ripeness (measured in hardness or softness), as well as cost, all contribute to whether a vendor can increase the number of regulars by her display of commodities. Their pride of professionalism is measured in terms of how much they can sell each day, and this depends on their own business acumen in judging their clientele. It might also depend on the patrilineage ancestors.

Other Incomes and Professional Bonds

An additional opportunity to gain access to lump sums not readily available to women who earn incomes in other ways is the daily revolving credit/savings societies. Savings societies are vendor operated and entail the collection and distribution of cash on a daily basis. Their informal nature is not intimidating, as are the rigors involved in the establishment of formal cooperatives under the Ministry of Cooperatives. Depending on the number of people who participate, a woman could receive a sizeable lump sum at stated intervals. Those amounts could be saved to meet the financial requirements of school fees, funerals, household maintenance, etc., or could be used to purchase a larger quantity of commodities for resale. This strategy might be advisable at the end of the month when salaries are paid, or at Christmas bonus time when urban dwellers purchase more commodities to serve as gifts for their rural kin.

The professional bonding generated in sharing space over time has promoted a reliability among vendors such that when one must be absent another can sell for her. Some 36.9 percent (120) indicated that in their absence another vendor sells for them. Bonding has its limitations, however. The remaining vendors indicated that a relative or their children would come to sell for them, the reason being that in matters involving finances coworkers can be trusted just so far. In fact, this was also cited as one of the reasons why vendors do not cooperate in bulk buying—they do not trust each other. Sharing a purchase with one other vendor is acceptable, as one can pick which vendor to share with. Buying in bulk is not acceptable as it leaves too much room for doubt in the handling of finances.

Women's Needs and Childcare

If education limits female employment choices, then the presence of small children limits choices further. No formal sector workplace provides day care, and the economics of urban life diminish the probability of having a remunerated care giver continuously present in the home. While many vendors indicated the presence of other adults in their homes, the large numbers of small children observed in each marketplace attested to the absence of another caregiver. Thus, women whose families, friends, and neighbors have not been able to provide a social support network must identify an income-generating activity that is compatible with childcare.

▲ Summary and Conclusion

Women in Harare have had to find the means to generate an income because of many economic, cultural, and urban contextual reasons. The historical context in which work roles were defined was biased not only against Africans in general, but against African women in particular who were perceived as those who remained in the rural areas while their husbands migrated to earn an income. This bias is currently reflected in the pattern of urban unemployment. While many males are unemployed in Harare, a higher percentage of females fall into this category.

As a result of these biases, women have had to carve out an economic niche for themselves in self-generated, small scale enterprises. Similar

Selling fresh produce allows vendors to bring their children to work.

patterns of employment have been noted in Latin America (e.g., Harrison et al. 1974; and Schmink, Bruce, and Kohn 1986), throughout Africa (e.g., Robertson 1984; Adagala 1986; Brand 1982), in the East (e.g., McGee 1973; Jumani and Joshi 1984), in the Caribbean (e.g., Katzin 1971), and elsewhere (e.g., Harper and Kavura 1982).

With the cultural and sociological problems inherent in marriage, divorce, and widowhood, and the lack of concern on the part of many male spouses to contribute financially to household maintenance, it is necessary that women secure a steady source of income so they can at least satisfy their basic needs. The children women have serve as a further incentive to generate an income. Vendors reported the money they earn not only meets household provisioning needs, but also pays for school fees.

The particular choice women in Zimbabwe make to trade in fresh produce may have its ultimate rationale in their rurally-based link to garden production and thus to the ancestors who are seen as their protectors. Alternatively, the choice might be based more heavily in the economic theories of maximization since daily intake makes possible daily contributions to savings societies and the receipt of larger sums on a periodic basis. Or, the choice might depend on the age-old notion that women's work must be compatible with childcare, the marketplace being an acceptable location for young children.

Why a woman in Harare chooses to sell fresh produce as an income generating activity rests, ultimately, on her tacit goals of provisioning her family and caring for the well-being of her children, as well as on the employment opportunity structure. That a woman in Harare is limited in her choice of how to generate an income means that she must call upon what expertise she has to fulfill her goals. A woman's expertise is composed of what she has learned in the city and what she has acquired as having been socialized into a cultural, indigenous knowledge system. The combination of what a woman needs and the skills she has to fulfill those needs is different in every case. Some women choose domestic service because they feel other endeavors are too risky. Some women choose prostitution because they feel they can obtain the cash they need quickly and directly. Others choose fresh produce vending because such a business enables them to fulfill their traditional provisioning roles and accords them a certain status in the community that other microenterprises do not.

▲ Notes

1. The census used the following occupational classifications: professional, technical, and related workers; administrative and managerial workers; clerical and related workers; sales workers; service workers; agricultural, animal husbandry, and forestry workers; production and related workers; and workers not classifiable by occupation (Zimbabwe, CSO 1985). It would appear that the status "unemployed" was somewhat ambiguously assigned. The wording of the employment question—"Did this person work last week?"—is not defined and so was open to respondents' interpretation. While "Kind of Work" followed the above question, if the initial inquiry gave rise to a "no," then the reason for not working would have to be given. Ambiguity arises when working is defined as having a salaried job. The category would not necessarily include the many informal means Zimbabweans utilize to generate income. I would suspect, owing to the number of shoe repairmen, fishmongers, automobile mechanics, and others engaged in informal income-generating activities I observed, that the percentage of unemployed is really not accurate. The *Statistical Yearbook of 1985* (Zimbabwe 1985:47) reported that "according to the 1982 Census, about 130,000 or more than 9 percent of the labour force found themselves work in the informal sector. 90 percent of those were women. In total, 400,000 persons or almost 28 percent of the total labour force were either unemployed or found themselves work within the informal sector."

The 1986–1987 Labour Force Survey determined that, nationally, 22 percent of women and 52 percent of men were either self-employed or working for wages. For Harare, these figures shift to 29 percent for women and 69 percent for men (Kanji and Jazdowska 1993:13). In 1991, microenterprises in urban areas (Harare and Bulawayo) accounted for the employment of 506,276 people, or one-sixth of the population in these two cities (McPherson 1991:8). Due to ESAP implementation, the number of microenterprises continues to skyrocket because employment retrenchment has discontinued formal sector employment for thousands of workers, creating an unemployment rate estimated at 30 percent (McPherson 1991:1).

2. Employment or "working" was defined for this research as generating an income by any means, including earning a salary. Thus, when vendors responded

with the type of work their husbands were doing, they reported operating a tuck shop, repairing shoes, hawking, sewing, "general labor" (i.e., casual labor), and the like. Vendors see their husbands as being employed if they are generating an income in any way.

A similar argument can be made for the women themselves. When I asked vendors what types of jobs they had had before beginning their retail businesses, among the responses given were knitting, selling clothes, crocheting, making clay pots, hawking, as well as domestic employment such as cooking, laundry, and childcare.

3. I cannot report with certainty the basis for this wage figure. It would appear that salaries paid to white labor have been included. Riddell (1984) does not include in his analysis the differentiation of salaries based on race and skills, nor does he cite the source of his figures.

4. The total urban labor force for Zimbabwe (based on a 10 percent sample) for all people ages 15 and above is 692,330 (or 62 percent of the entire urban population of 1,116,760). Of these totals, 180,770 (26.1 percent) of the urban labor force are said to be female out of a total urban female population over age 15 of 493,250 (38.3 percent). The total number of unemployed females is 104,320 or 26.8 percent of the population, while the total number of unemployed males is 163,780 or 18.5 percent (Zimbabwe, CSO 1985:116).

5. Rae Lesser Blumberg has written a very illuminating report for the World Bank that analyzes how women's and men's incomes are utilized (Blumberg [draft] 1987).

6. Patriarchal ideologies also prevent women from obtaining formal sector employment (Drakakis-Smith 1984).

7. ESAP hardships have also altered these practices. In a recent survey of 90 households, it was found that "illegal" cultivation of vlei areas had increased significantly since 1985, harvests from which were used largely for consumption (Mudimu and Chigume [draft] 1993). Cultivation was not challenged by the municipality since regulations were not enforced.

8. David Lan (1986) found that the VaKorekore view life as a drying out process. Children are born wet, and as aging occurs, so too does drying out. The process is not exactly the same for men and women. Women's drying out occurs largely at menopause.

I find Lan's analysis particularly useful in considering the relationship of women to the land and women's agricultural roles. There is obviously a connection between water and fertility. Women are presumed wet and fertile when they marry; they are given wet and fertile lands to cultivate when they marry. Just as women prove their fertility in giving birth to children, the land they cultivate demonstrates its fertility in harvests. Fertility, however, is said to be enhanced by the ancestral spirits. Thus, a woman who cannot bear children, or a garden that does not produce abundantly, are each considered the result of a breach with the ancestors that must be healed through appropriate ritual.

9. Research conducted by Wild (1992:19–20) found a similar pride in all African proprietors of enterprises:

> A sense of pride, a notion of independence and achievement was implicit in the term "businessman." To be called a businessman conferred self-esteem and social status on the recipient. . . . Whether a wealthy transport operator or a small bicycle repairer, an established general dealer or a *female vegetable vendor*—they were all attributed with the prestigious name of "businessman" or "businesswoman." (emphasis added)

▲ 8

The Deconstruction of the Informal
Sector and the Gender Variable
in Microenterprise Development

The circumstances in which women fresh produce microentrepreneurs in Harare find themselves are a direct result of the many factors explored in this book: gender, culture, colonial imposition of the labor reserve economy, the informal economy, the horticultural subsector of the agricultural economy, the urban environment, and the broader political economy of the state. These provide both the context and causation for women vendors occupying the niche they do and withstanding the constraints they face.

In this final chapter, I will first discuss the far-reaching implications of these factors in facilitating microenterprise development, focusing largely on policy. I will then suggest an alternative approach to these enterprises based on resource entitlement. In concluding remarks, I will pull together the lessons learned from this research and identify ways they can inform women and development policies and projects.

▲ Market Women and Microenterprises: Implications of Women's Activities

When I asked vendors to compare ways they could earn an income, 72.9 percent (237) responded that fresh produce vending was the best. When I asked why, they responded with a variety of answers: "I have no education"; "I can't get any other job"; "I can't just stay home and do nothing"; "it's too long to wait for money until the end of the month"; and "if I were to look for work, who would look after the children?" Other respondents focused more directly on finances and food: they "can get money [quickly] to feed and support the family" (14.7 percent); they "never run short of money," or they "get money daily for food" (12.5 percent); if they don't sell much, they could "just pick vegetables from the stall and take them home to cook" or they "never go hungry" or they sustain "no loss" because they cook what they cannot sell (4.3 percent). Vendors also viewed the market as a workplace that did not conflict with caring for their pre-school-age children.

Despite vendor choice and the thousands of enterprises existing in the informal sector, little support has been provided to enhance their growth and development. There is a noted lack of credit, training, business information, infrastructural facilities, and equipment, as well as a strangling regulatory environment that stifles growth (Saito 1990:72–73). On their own initiative, fresh produce vendors have developed a path through this constraining morass in order to meet traditional food provisioning and child welfare roles. But vending satisfies more than these responsibilities. In the urban areas, it allows women to establish reference groups and sources for information exchange; to create a reputation for hard work and fair play among a community of strangers; and to engender a certain status in the community through facilitating the availability of food commodities.

Historically, the labor reserve economy was the impetus for this expanded view of womanhood, triggered by women's migration to an alien and hostile environment that demanded multiple income-earning activities. Vegetable vending was perhaps the closest approximation to women's rural roles. In patriarchal terms, it extended their domestic functions into the marketplace.

The market arena women entered was one not formally recognized by the state. Viewed for several decades as an urban subsistence sector, informal enterprises were denied access to state resources through the imposition of policies and local level by-laws designed to control expansion. After independence, when state resources had to meet the needs of the majority, fiscal and financial difficulties, in the context of global economic decline, culminated in structural adjustment. One aspect of these policies was the reassessment of the informal sector and consequent recognition of individuals who acted self-reliantly.

Fresh produce vendors illustrate why government may now tacitly recognize the informal sector's worth—to the household, the community, and the state.

Vendor Family Nutrition

Fresh produce vending assures family food provisioning. In Chapters 5 and 7, I asserted that a very large percentage of family income is utilized to purchase food. Lipton (1982) noted that the poorest people in many countries use as much as 80 percent of their family income to purchase 80 percent of their daily food requirements—the "double 80 rule." This rule may not be applicable in the case of people who have access to a variety of foodstuffs by virtue of their occupation.

Vendors reported taking food home daily to cook for their families. Are vendor families, therefore, nutritionally any better or worse off than other urban families? Sanders (1986:7) found that malnutrition was higher in families where there was no wage earning male contributor, or one in which the father is living away from the children. Would the opposite be found for vendor families? This empirical question needs to be posed.

Urban Household Provisioning

A second major implication of women's activities is the provisioning of the city itself with fresh produce. In Chapter 4, I discussed the structural relations between producers and wholesalers, and between wholesalers and vendors involved in the marketing of these commodities. Cultivating retail customers, of course, is the ultimate goal of these transactions.

The delicate balance vendors must maintain between the wholesale prices they pay for their commodities and the retail prices they can charge often puts vendors in a precarious income earning position as seasonal wholesale price fluctuation has to be buffered by vendors if they wish to retain their customers. During periods of scarcity, distribution of certain commodities favors the predominantly white, upper-class neighborhoods where premium prices can be obtained. The urban poor cannot afford to pay more for their daily foodbasket since wages for many unskilled and semiskilled workers are inadequate to meet household expenditures. Vendor ability to absorb wholesale price increases ensures the flow of commodities throughout the year. The economic data presented in Chapter 7, however, illustrate that vendors cannot realistically provide this buffer for very long nor can they do so for every commodity.

Urban Food Security

Vendor activities afford the urban poor a form of food security, defined as "the ability of a country or region to assure, on a long-term basis, that its food system provides the total population access to a timely, reliable, and nutritionally adequate supply of food" (Eicher and Staatz 1985:1).

The grain focus of food security research has provided information to policymakers on how to modify the food production and distribution system in order that an ever-increasing number of people can have access to food on a continual basis. How can these policies be generated without knowing anything about the other commodities in the family foodbasket?

Fruits and vegetables are produced largely by white commercial farmers and African women (with an increasing number of African men cultivating these crops commercially). These commodities are marketed either by women themselves or through a bifurcated marketing system. As illustrated in this study, data cannot easily be collected on either production or marketing. Yet, government policy seeks to change the nature of many of the marketing enterprises that meet urban food provisioning needs.

Considering the large population vendors provision, it is most important that food security research consider the range of food crops marketed through the informal sector and take into account the female fresh produce vendors.

▲ The Changing Policy Environment

The broader implications of women's role in urban food provisioning require further consideration, especially in light of ESAP. Concerning the informal sector, ESAP is acting upon a goal identified in the First National Development Plan: "Government will encourage self-employment by formalising the informal sector" (Zimbabwe 1986:18).

Although policies were not developed at the time to encourage this transition, government is now making credit available to "production" versus service-oriented enterprises. The hundreds—perhaps thousands—of individuals involved in marketing, therefore, will not have access to development-inducing inputs. The serious gap I see in this ESAP policy is the failure to reconsider the formal/informal economy construct. Any production system relies, ultimately, upon customers. Why is production singled out for assistance and not distribution? I would like to suggest one way the entire production-distribution chain could be assisted, especially in light of other ESAP policies.

▲ Resource Access and Entitlement

The wave of unemployment created by the ESAP policy of retrenchment has most strongly affected casual and unskilled workers, who develop any means necessary to maintain themselves and their families. The explosion of informal enterprises established to ensure survival has been fostered by a key phrase in the *Framework for Economic Reform:* "Regulations which come in the way of setting up of businesses will be relaxed" (Zimbabwe 1991:19). As a result, fresh produce vendors are now faced with an overabundance of competition since trade in these commodities requires a very low initial investment to get established. Other microenterprises are in a similarly disadvantaged position because changes in the regulatory environment affecting access to credit, training, education, and technology have not yet been effected. This means there has been an explosion in the number of microenterprises involved in distribution, but not in production.

Prior research links microenterprises closely to larger businesses (Tokman 1978a, 1978b; Liedholm and Mead 1987). ESAP polices ultimately seek to create more links by fostering the growth of technology producing microenterprises that can supply formal businesses. In effect, what researchers and policymakers are saying is that enterprises in both sectors, in order for growth to occur, must create interdependent partnerships. These partnerships, however, must consider not only production but also distribution. Production-distribution partnerships have been established, historically, in agriculture. Individual initiative created the system, but the labor reserve economy, the theoretical construct of the dichotomous economy, and the gender of most entrepreneurs relegated many of these initiatives to an undocumented, unvalued sector. Enterprises were not viewed as building the state but as challenges to the state, giving rise to an overregulated policy environment and a state structure that could provide resources only to formal enterprises, the operation of which benefited the state through foreign currency earnings and taxation.

Under ESAP, value is now being placed on microenterprises, but still within the context of the dichotomous economy. Would it not be more efficient to do away with this dichotomy and create a more uniformally-accessible resource environment through restructuring economic sectors? Would it not serve each respective sector—and the state—to consider the entire production-distribution system for related commodities under the same economic umbrella? Informal retail trade is already integrally linked to formal sector production for wholesale supply (this applies not only to fresh produce vendors, but also to other commodities). What prevents formal sector enterprises from recognizing and incorporating their informal distributive arm?

The partnerships I see ensuing from an incorporative focus on the production-distribution chain have far-reaching implications on resource access. Formal sector entrepreneurs can obtain capital, suitable business locations, a range of clientele, uninterrupted supply, and training; informal sector entrepreneurs are much more limited. If we were to construct a continuum of resource access (as opposed to a dichotomy), formal businesses would be placed on the higher end and informal enterprises would be on the lower. The following analysis of two female-owned enterprises in Harare is illustrative.

> Mrs. Kazoukas owns a shop in a low density suburb shopping center. She sells a range of fresh produce that appeals largely to her white clientele. She also sells frozen foods, all manner of packaged and canned foods (imported and local), cleaning supplies, housewares, gardening seeds and equipment, fresh bread and pastries, and cosmetics. She takes telephone orders and makes home deliveries. Mrs. Kazoukas has a cash register and so records all sales. She has employed a bookkeeper to tally her daily receipts and to prepare her monthly tax statements. She has a general dealer's license, and health inspectors visit her store twice annually to make sure her displays meet health codes. Her fresh produce is delivered three times per week by a wholesaler, who, incidentally, is a distant relative. She special-orders certain commodities when

they are in demand, and her relative has been known to travel to South Africa to purchase certain commodities for her exclusively for which she can charge premium prices.

Mrs. Kazoukas is doing such a flourishing business that she wants to expand her shop. Her business neighbor is not doing so well, but her neighbor owns the building in which Mrs. Kazoukas rents her shop space. She has decided to make the owner an offer to buy the building as she knows she can obtain a loan from the bank.

Amai Rufaro occupies a stall in one of the Harare City Council markets in a high density suburb near a bus stop approximately six kilometers from the city center. She sells 11 different fruits and vegetables, but her main moneymakers are the ingredients of the daily vegetable staple consumed by her African clientele: rape, tomatoes, and onions. She also sells sweets because her market is situated near a school, and children pass by on their way home to buy a piece of penny candy. Amai Rufaro tries to keep track of how many customers she has in a day and how much money she takes in, but her third-grade education limits her ability to keep records. It is also difficult for her logistically because she brings 18-month-old Rufaro to the market daily. Her attention to Rufaro diverts her attention from recordkeeping, but not from her customers.

At least four times per week, Amai Rufaro goes to Mbare Musika to purchase what she needs and then takes an emergency taxi back to her market site. There are no storage lockers at her site, so she must purchase wisely in order not to have too much to carry home at night, but enough to sell the next day if she does not have sufficient cash to go to Mbare again. Yesterday, she had to make a choice as to which wholesaler to go to. The previous day, there had been no onions at Mbare, so she went to the Wholesale Fruit and Vegetable Market. She bought high-quality onions that had been grown by a white farmer, and she paid a very high price for them. The profit she made on reselling them hardly made up for her extra transport expenses.

Amai Rufaro would like very much to expand her business into the adjacent vacant stall, but then she must be able to buy and display more commodities. Also, she knows that her market manager has been looking for a second stall for herself. She needs the initial capital to expand, and her husband has been earning well, but he rarely shares his salary with her, paying only for housing, electricity, and water, with an occasional new dress for her or clothing for Rufaro. Perhaps if she approaches him properly, he will lend her enough money to expand her business. Then she will have to find a way to approach the market manager.

These two case studies reveal resource accessibility for the formal business, but lack of access for the informal enterprise.

Capital

From these two business profiles, it is clear that Mrs. Kazoukas can obtain loans from financial institutions because she has collateral and a business record, as well as a license to conduct her trade. Amai Rufaro, however, could not access a bank loan because of the absence of this documentation, and because the loan she would require is very small. (Banks do not make small loans—under Z$500—because they are uneconomical.) Amai Rufaro must obtain informal financial support through her husband, her family, or, if she wishes to expose herself to usurious interest rates, from neighborhood moneylenders. Because she can access institutions in the formal economy, Mrs. Kazoukas would be placed with other business owners—large and small—on the upper end of the resource continuum, but Amai Rufaro would be situated at the lower end.

Business Location

While both businesswomen pay rent, Mrs. Kazoukas pays it to a friend under a contractual agreement, and Amai Rufaro remits funds to the city council. Because the city council's market facilities are limited, and the waiting list to obtain a stall very long, it is very unlikely that Amai Rufaro will be able to gain access to another vending site. Mrs. Kazoukas, however, is able to purchase the building she occupies and expand as she sees fit. Shop space in the low density suburbs, in the private domain, can be purchased or rented, depending on the financial resources of the proprietor. Market stalls in the high density suburbs, in the public domain, are insufficient to meet the demand.

Mrs. Kazoukas is located in a busy shopping center at two main crossroads where both whites and Africans transact business. The shopowners have pooled resources to hire someone to keep the area neat and clean so that more customers will find the center attractive. Amai Rufaro cannot afford such luxuries. Her stall is located in the center of the market, too far from the bus stop, and it is the city council's responsibility to clean the area once a week. Unfortunately, the entire marketplace always looks dirty since customers often discard rubbish on the market floor.

Business location, therefore, affects other resources accessed. On the continuum, Mrs. Kazoukas has wider options, placing her on the upper end, while Amai Rufaro is limited, placing her on the lower end.

Clientele

Mrs. Kazoukas's customers are both white and African. She services her clientele with items in demand and with specialty items obtained exclusively for her. She is able to occupy this niche because of her ethnic ties to importers of specific commodities and her access to markets in South Africa. Amai Rufaro sells her commodities only to Africans because only they frequent her market. She tries her best to provide all the commodities in demand; even during seasonal shortfalls, she spends extra money to purchase commodities from the white wholesalers. When she does this, however, her profit margin goes down. She employs this strategy because she does not want to lose the few regular customers she has, and she knows they will go elsewhere if she cannot supply what they need.

The majority of Mrs. Kazoukas's customers are employed and can well afford any seasonal fluctuations in commodity prices. The incomes of Amai Rufaro's customers fluctuate, as some are casual laborers. Her customers make demands on her to extend them credit until month-end when they are paid. She feels this is a service she must provide in order to retain her customers.

The ebb and flow of customers in each of these settings reflects income levels, the broader political economy of the city, and the historical development of high and low density suburbs. Marketplaces in Harare include as few as 5 vendors, but as many as 105. Each vendor wants to supply commodities in demand for daily consumption, as well as commodities that appeal to varying tastes and income levels. The structure of the marketplace, however, makes competition very stiff, and requires a vendor to be highly creative in how she chooses her commodities for sale. Mrs. Kazoukas supplies a number of commodities her competition sells, but that competition is more than a mile away. Moreover, she has the personal and financial resources to obtain specialty items that appeal to her higher income clientele. Using the clientele parameter, Mrs. Kazoukas would again be placed somewhere on the upper end of the continuum and Amai Rufaro on the lower.

Supply Accessibility and Flow

Ensconced in the formal market channels, Mrs. Kazoukas enters transactions for supplies in a standard business fashion, placing orders with wholesalers and receiving deliveries several times per week. The wholesalers all know the grade and quality of perishables she requires, and if the wholesaler with whom she has placed her order does not personally have an item, he will travel to other wholesalers to find what she needs. She either pays cash for her deliveries or pays each month after receiving a statement. The only supply interruption she experiences is when a commodity is not imported in a timely manner or when it is totally out of season.

Amai Rufaro must spend her own resources for transport and purchase what she needs directly. Thereafter, she must either carry her purchases on her head to her market, pay for an emergency taxi to deliver herself and her goods, or take several buses, thus cutting into her profit margin. The expenses she incurs to ensure a daily flow of fresh commodities to her stall are far greater than what Mrs. Kazoukas pays; volume is also severely limited owing to transport problems.

On the continuum, Mrs. Kazoukas would be situated again on the upper end because she rarely has to experience an interruption in her supply lines. Amai Rufaro's supplies are limited by cost and transport. Her need to rely on public conveyances puts her at a disadvantage because buses do not generally travel routes between high density suburbs; their routes generally lead from these suburbs to the light or heavy industrial areas where many people work. Again, Amai Rufaro is on the lower end of the business scale.

Training

If Mrs. Kazoukas wants to learn more about business management, she can take a course at a downtown business college. She might learn how to keep her business records on a computer, or about temperatures needed to maintain the freshness of perishables, or changes in government regulation of small businesses. In short, she can receive training in any aspect of her business she cares to learn more about. Amai Rufaro could, ideally, learn the same things, but she would first need some basic understanding of accounting principles, how to keep records, and the like. Instruction in these basic concepts is not available; most of the business acumen developed by microentrepreneurs in the informal sector is obtained through hit and miss techniques, very often at the expense of the enterprise.

Analysis of enterprises in accordance with the resources to which they have access will facilitate a change in the way we view businesses and business proprietors at the microlevel because underlying this conceptualization is an ideology of entitlement, of "socially and culturally recognized rights of specific categories of persons to particular resource shares" (Papaneck 1990:170). In the past, based on an ideology of colonial right, supportive (and even protective) institutions were established to promote growth of white-owned enterprises (e.g., commercial farms, mines, and industries) that constituted the formal or modern sector. Racial policies determined where people lived; they determined who could operate a business, who could obtain licenses, and where those businesses could be located; they determined bus routes throughout the city; and they determined who could work in the formal sector and at what level. African populations and enterprises, through a morass of discriminatory regulations, were effectively denied access to resources that would have enhanced their own economic development. The ideology of patriarchy further impaired the income earning capability of women since it assumed men would support them, the labor reserve economy notwithstanding.

At independence, the institutions that once supported a very small minority ostensibly became accessible to the majority. As full-fledged citizens, Africans had the right to access the resources once available to only a select few. Government, in an attempt to balance an agricultural economy based largely on white commercial production against the institutional resource needs of Africans, developed policies that sought to cater to all. Gender-specific laws sought to extend available resources to women in order that past inequities could be resolved. Providing to all that to which they are entitled, however, overtaxed the financial capacity of the state. In the last few years national resources have been diminished as the result of a severe drought and an imbalanced world economy. Women, in particular, are bearing the brunt of this resource shortfall because equity-based laws and regulations promoting the development of the informal sector have not been fully implemented (Chigudu 1988; Maya 1988; Chimedza 1990; Mvududu 1991; Brand 1992; and Mudzengerere 1993).

Each microenterprise, whether owned by a female or male, not only requires resources, it also creates them and disseminates them to others—as do firms in the formal sector (for a more lengthy discussion of this point see Bloch 1993:18). Formal enterprises, however, can easily access resource needs, while informal ones experience severe regulatory bottlenecks. How can both most efficiently be provided resource access? A more unified approach to satisfy resource demand is required.

To illustrate, fresh produce vendors have asserted their entrepreneurial skills to trade in horticultural commodities. These commodities fall within the purview of the agricultural subsector of the economy. Though many individuals share in the production and distribution of these commodities, only a selected few can access support institutions to enhance their development. Others are left on their own to form cooperatives and informal societies or make ad hoc arrangements targeting specific purposes. To bridge these gaps, incorporation of informal distributive mechanisms into the formal agricultural sector might result in a more efficient production-distribution system by making available to vendors and wholesalers expanded options on capital, credit, business location, clientele, supply, and training accessible through agricultural sector institutions. (A similar approach might be taken to other trading and production microenterprises.)

Reorienting our thinking from a formal/informal dichotomy to a more unified economy to facilitate greater resource congruence could potentially challenge traditional patriarchal practices. Since women comprise the majority of proprietors and workers in the microenterprise sector, incorporating these businesses under appropriate sector umbrellas would provide women access to resources that they could obtain only if laws preventing access were changed, including ability to obtain credit, own property, and enter into business partnerships or corporate agreements. Under the current legal structure, women find it difficult to be able to participate in these transactions. Legitimizing women's microenterprises by dismantling the formal/informal sector dichotomy could make the full range of business opportunities available to women, hence requiring their ability to act on their own behalf. This would have repercussions in the household—the locus of patriarchal control.

Power relations in the household determine the resources women can access (Papaneck 1990:170–171). Although once perceived in the labor reserve economy as a necessity, women's economic activities may now constitute a challenge to male economic dominance. If women's economic activities are viewed as an extension of their domestic roles, they are "entitled" to challenge all the constraints they face in pursuing these roles (i.e., in the case of vendors, harassment from police, makoronyera, and wholesalers, as well as responsibility to pay transport, rental, and amenities fees to the municipality). What other resources are urban women entitled to?

If they are single, widowed or divorced, women feel they are entitled to accommodation, food, and a means to earn an income to support themselves and their children. If they are married, women feel they are entitled to the first two by virtue of their husband's earnings, but may see the third as a necessity that challenges the domestic social order. Their perceptions of entitlement, however, may not correspond to those of males. What women seek is security for themselves and their children; what men seek may be very different.

To summarize this discussion, I would like to return to ESAP and its focus on maintaining the dual economy. An inherent assumption in many of the policies being implemented is that all are entitled to resources, but that the resource pool is very limited. Hence, each entitlement has been reduced. The policies acknowledge that each person is entitled to an income, whether from farming, industry, or personal enterprise. Since the economy is not able to provide employment to all who seek it, barriers to establishing income generating activities have been relaxed, leading to an exponential increase in the number of streetside vendors selling an array of commodities. To stimulate individual entrepreneurism, a number of separate institutions have been established to cater to informal sector needs for financial resources. These institutions parallel those available to formal sector enterprises, hence reproducing preexisting lending agencies. Instead of expending effort to create new institutions to cater to the informal sector, incorporating each enterprise into the appropriate economic sector (e.g., agriculture, industry, mining), with appropriately scaled institutional support, would reduce expenditures and integrate all sector-related activities. Reorienting economic sectors in this manner can also diminish patriarchy since it would legitimize women's enterprises and promote the transformation of constricting laws.

▲ Development Projects in a Unified Economy

Disadvantageous policies based in the theoretical climate of the informal economy—in which real people and real businesses operate—are preventing African producers, distributors, and retail outlets from achieving their potential. These policies define the parameters of informal sector enterprises, but are largely devoid of empiricism, despite the plethora of studies conducted in the past decade. If people who operate a trade in perishables define their activities as businesses, why can't researchers view them accordingly? All who establish an enterprise, no matter the size, do so with the expectation of making a profit to sustain themselves and their families. Like all businesses, they need start-up capital, a location to trade, a source of supply, clientele, and a supportive business environment. They also need to know about the market itself, how to establish prices, what commodities are in demand, if there is any patterned ebb and flow, seasonal supply, and the like. For people in corporations or large scale business, training is available at universities and other formal institutions. For smaller scale businesses, training in developing countries is not generally available. So, microentrepreneurs must learn through observation, from parents or relatives, or simply by hit and miss. The conceptualization of the informal sector, hence, prevents its development, but the need to generate an income mandates the existence of an environment that allows for microenterprise establishment, including supportive institutions.

Recent development projects supported by international donors have followed the lead of theorists and policymakers in defining microenterprises as part of the informal sector. As such, they have sought to develop separate institutions to cater to specific constituency needs, although several advocate coordination and collaboration with the "variety of agencies operating in Zimbabwe providing credit, training and technical assistance in support of small scale business" (Zimbabwe Women's Finance Trust and The Foundation for International Training 1990:4). The specific plans put forward to access donor funding are laudable in their intent to assist women, in particular, in achieving their entrepreneurial objectives (see, for example, Saito 1990). Many donors, however, have targeted their populations for assistance, not policies and institutional reorganization to meet the needs of microenterprises. The findings of two workshops, one sponsored by the Ministry of Community and Cooperative Development in 1992 and one by the Zimbabwe National Chamber of Commerce in association with the Friedrich Nawmann Foundation in 1993, identified the constraints to be removed and the supports necessary for the development of microenterprises. Many point to the actions entrepreneurs might take on their own behalf, while others suggest the creation of lending and other institutions to meet the low input needs of microenterprises. In and of itself, each recommendation is worth consideration. A cautionary note needs to be raised, however, concerning implementation to enhance sustainability, especially in light of Muchena's study. She found that some 8,237 projects targeted income-generating activities, with 125,242 female and 37,815 male participants. Despite these high participation rates in income-generating projects, few have stimulated sufficient incomes and few have proved to be sustainable (Muchena [1985] cited in Batezat and Mwalo [1989:62]).

In trying to achieve these latter two goals, it is critical that the stigma of "income generating activity" be removed from women's development efforts. Conceptualizing women in development projects needs to be elevated to a different plane, from one in which women are viewed as victimized and poverty stricken to one that views women as integral economic actors contributing to the well-being of their families, their communities, and the state. By creating appropriate institutional and sector linkages to access resources, women's (and men's) enterprises will have supportive environments to enhance their sustainability. What is required is a facilitative climate that does not rely on patriarchal and economic dichotomous theories to provide the basis for policy shift and project development; in short, a gendered approach to development that is not strangled in its infancy by theories based on perceptions of an old reality, but enhanced by theories based on the present.

▲ Conclusion

I have presented the vendors as they presented themselves to me—as positive actors discerning the best way they can to meet their food provisioning and income generating goals within the context of cultural, urban contextual, and economic constraints. I believe the problem orientation utilized in this research has provided an understanding of economic behavior not easily achieved through the lenses of a single discipline. A commitment to understanding the intricate nature of human behavior, how it changes over time, and how government policies and institutional actions affect it, however, are all matters of deep concern to anthropologists working in cooperation with others to help find ways to meet the needs of the urban poor.

It is indeed time for several paradigms to shift. The reality of women's participation in the work force and as business entrepreneurs dictates that, at least, we rethink what the conduct of business is all about. Globally, women occupy all levels of the workforce. To some extent, their contributions have not yet been recognized, as is the case with the Zimbabwe fresh produce vendors. Because they are women, and because they conduct their trade in a sector labeled as a residual of capitalist development, their contributions to urban food supply and the economy are overlooked. Yet, the way they, as women, conduct their trade ensures a degree of food security in an urban milieu in which Africans historically have been underpaid and unemployment rates are skyrocketing. The integral way in which they act as the end point in a production-marketing chain in perishable commodities ensures the flow of crops from the farm gate to the kitchen plate. Our responsibility to these and the millions of female (and male) microentrepreneurs is to recognize them for the contributions they make both to family survival and to national development.

▲
Bibliography

Adagala, Kavetsa. 1986. *Self Employment Women in the Peri-Urban Setting—Petty Traders in Nairobi: Conditions, Constraints and Strategies for Survival.* Paper prepared for the National Workshop on Policy and Planning in Kenya's Informal Sector, Nairobi, June 5–6.

African Training and Research Centre for Women. 1984. *Marketing in Ghana: An Analysis of Operational and Environmental Conditions.* Addis Ababa: United Nations Economic Commission for Africa (E/ECA/ATRCW/81/07).

Agency for International Development. 1989. *The AID Microenterprise Stocktaking Evaluation.* AID Evaluation Highlights No. 6. Washington, D.C.: AID.

Agency for International Development. 1991. *Women in Development: A Report to Congress by the U.S. Agency for International Development.* Washington, D.C.: Office of Women in Development, Bureau for Program and Policy Coordination, AID.

Agricultural and Rural Development Authority. 1985. *Mashonaland East Smallholder Fruit and Vegetable Programme.* Harare: ARDA.

Agricultural Marketing Council. 1953. "Fruit and Vegetable Production and Marketing." *Rhodesian Agricultural Journal,* Vol. 50, pp. 129–142.

Arrighi, G. 1973. "Labour Supplies in Historical Perspective. The Proletarianization of the African Peasantry in Rhodesia," in Arrighi, G., and John S. Saul (eds.). *Essays on the Political Economy of Africa.* New York: Monthly Review Press, 1973, pp. 180–234.

Ashe, Jeffrey. 1985. *The Pisces II Experience: Local Efforts in Micro-Enterprise Development.* Washington, D.C.: Agency for International Development.

Auret, Diana. 1990. *A Decade of Development in Zimbabwe, 1980–1990.* Gweru, Zimbabwe: Mambo Press.

Balleis, Peter, S. J. 1993. *A Critical Guide to ESAP.* Gweru, Zimbabwe: Mambo Press in association with Silveira House.

Barber, William J. 1967. "Urbanisation and Economic Growth: The Cases of Two White Settler Territories," in Miner, Horace (ed.). *The City in Modern Africa.* London: Pall Mall Press, pp. 237–251.

Barnes, Terri. 1987. *African Female Labour and the Urban Economy of Colonial Zimbabwe, with Special Reference to Harare, 1920–39.* Master's Thesis, Department of History, University of Zimbabwe.

Barnes, Teri, and Everjoyce Win. 1992. *To Live a Better Life: An Oral History of Women in the City of Harare, 1930–1970.* Harare: Baobab Books.

Batezat, Elinor, and Margaret Mwalo. 1989. *Women in Zimbabwe.* Harare: Southern Africa Political Economy Series (SAPES) Trust.

Batezat, Elinor, Margaret Mwalo, and Kate Truscott. 1988. "Women and Independence: The Heritage and the Struggle," in Stoneman, Colin (ed.). *Zimbabwe's Prospects: Issues of Race, Class, State, and Capital in Southern Africa.* London: Macmillan Publishers, pp. 153–173.

Beach, David N. 1977. "The Shona Economy," in Palmer, Robin, and Neil Parsons (eds.). *The Roots of Rural Poverty in Central and Southern Africa.* London: Heinemann, pp. 37–65.

Beach, David N. 1980. *The Shona and Zimbabwe, 900–1850.* New York: Africana Publishers.

Bell, Morag. 1986. *Contemporary Africa.* London: Longman.

Berger, Marguerite. 1989. "An Introduction," in Berger, Marguerite, and Mayra Buvinic (eds.). *Women's Ventures.* West Hartford, Conn.: Kumarian Press, pp. 1–18.

Bhila, H. H. K. 1982. *Trade and Politics in a Shona Kingdom.* London: Longman.

Bloch, Eric. 1993. "An Economic Perspective," in Zimbabwe National Chamber of Commerce and Friedrich-Naumann Foundation. *Development and Growth of Micro-Business Activity in Zimbabwe,* conference held 3–4 March, Harare, pp. 18–19.

Blumberg, Rae Lesser. 1987. *Income Under Female vs. Male Control: Differential Spending Patterns and the Consequences When Women Lose Control of Returns to Labor.* Washington, D.C.: World Bank (draft).

Blumberg, Rae Lesser. 1989. *Making the Case for the Gender Variable: Women and the Wealth and Well-Being of Nations.* Washington, D.C.: Office of Women in Development, AID.

Boserup, Ester. 1990. "Economic Change and the Roles of Women," in Tinker, Irene (ed.). *Persistent Inequalities. Women and World Development.* New York: Oxford University Press, pp. 14–24.

Bourdillon, M. F. C. 1976. *The Shona Peoples: An Ethnography of the Contemporary Shona, with Special Reference to Their Religion.* Gweru, Zimbabwe: Mambo Press.

Bourdillon, M. F. C. 1987. *The Shona Peoples: An Ethnography of the Contemporary Shona, with Special Reference to Their Religion* (rev. ed.). Gweru, Zimbabwe: Mambo Press.

Bourdillon, M. F. C. 1991. *Poor, Harassed but Very Much Alive: An Account of Street People and Their Organisation.* Gweru, Zimbabwe: Mambo Press.

Brand, Veronica. 1982. *One Dollar Workplaces: A Study of Informal Sector Activities in Magaba, Harare.* Harare: University of Zimbabwe, School of Social Work.

Brand, Veronica. 1986. "One Dollar Workplaces: A Study of Informal Sector Activities in Magaba, Harare." *Journal of Social Development in Africa,* Vol. 1, No. 2, pp. 53–74.

Brand, Veronica, Rodreck Mupedziswa, and Perpetua Gumbo. 1992. *Women Informal Sector Workers Under Structural Adjustment in Zimbabwe: A State of the Art Paper Written as Part of the Research Programme on the Political and Social Context of Structural Adjustment in Sub-Saharan Africa.* Harare: University of Zimbabwe, School of Social Work.

Brown, Ken. 1959. *Land in Southern Rhodesia.* London: The Africa Bureau.

Bush, Ray, and Lionel Cliffe. 1982. *Labour Migration and Agrarian Strategy in the Transition to Socialism in Southern Africa: Zimbabwe as a Case.* Paper presented at the Transition to Socialism in Africa conference, University of Leeds, May 7–8.

Business Herald, July 22, 1993.

Cheater, Angela P. 1979. "The Production and Marketing of Fresh Produce Among Blacks in Zimbabwe." *Zambezia,* Supplement.

Cheater, Angela P. 1986. "The Role and Position of Women in Pre-Colonial and Colonial Zimbabwe." *Zambezia,* Vol. XIII, No. ii, pp. 65–79.

Chigudu, Hope Begyendera. 1988. *The Impact of Structural Adjustment Policies on Women in Zimbabwe.* Harare: Ministry of Community Development and Women's Affairs.

Chimedza, Ruvimbo. 1990. *Zimbabwe's Informal Financial Sector: An Overview.* Working Paper AEE 4/90, Department of Agricultural Economics and Extension, University of Zimbabwe.

Christopher, A. J. 1977. "Early Settlement and the Cadastral Framework," in Kay, George, and M. Smout (eds.). *Salisbury: A Geographical Survey of the Capital of Rhodesia.* London: Hodder and Stoughton, pp. 1–28.

Clark, Gracia. 1986. *The Position of Asante Women Traders in Kumasi Central Market, Ghana.* Ph.D. dissertation, University of Cambridge.

Cloud, Kathleen. 1984. "Women's Productivity in Agricultural Systems: Considerations for Project Design," in Overholt, Catherine, Mary B. Anderson, Kathleen Cloud, and James E. Austen (eds.). *Gender Roles in Development Projects: A Case Book.* West Hartford, Conn.: Kumarian Press, pp. 17–46.

Collett, W. E. 1981. *Horticulture.* No. 15781. Harare: Commercial Farmer Union.

Collett, W. E. 1986. "Horticulture," in Van Hoffen, M. (ed.). *Commercial Agriculture in Zimbabwe 1985/6.* Harare: Modern Farming Publishers Trust.

Cormack, I. R. N. 1983. *Towards Self Reliance: Urban Social Development in Zimbabwe.* Gweru, Zimbabwe: Mambo Press.

Dalton, George. 1961. "Economic Theory and Primitive Society." *American Anthropologist.* Vol. 62, No. 1, pp. 1–25.

Davies, R. 1974. "The Informal Sector in Rhodesia: How Important?" *The Rhodesia Science News.* Vol. 8, No. 7, pp. 216–220.

Davies, R. 1978. *The Informal Sector: A Solution to Unemployment?* From Rhodesia to Zimbabwe 5. Gweru, Zimbabwe: Mambo Press.

Davies, R. 1979. "Informal Sector or Subordinate Mode of Production: A Model," in Bromley, Ray, and Chris Gerry (eds.). *Casual Work and Poverty in Third World Cities.* New York: John Wiley and Sons, pp. 87–104.

Dessing, Maryke. 1990. *Support for Microenterprises: Lessons for Sub-Saharan Africa.* World Bank Technical Paper No. 122. Africa Technical Department Series. Washington, D. C.: World Bank.

Devittie, Thomas D. 1974. *Africans in Urban Areas: Government and Municipal Policies, 1929–1939.* Master's thesis, Department of History, University of Rhodesia.

Dinan, Carmel. 1982. "Work, Marriage and Autonomy," in Allen, Chris, and Gavin Williams (eds.). *Sub-Saharan Africa.* New York: Monthly Review Press, pp. 52–57.

Downing, Jeanne. 1990. *Gender and the Growth and Dynamics of Microenterprises.* GEMINI Working Paper No. 5. Bethesda, Md.: Growth with Equity through Microenterprise Investments and Institutions, Development Alternatives, Inc.

Downing, Jeanne. 1991. "Gender and the Growth of Microenterprises." *Small Enterprise Development.* Vol. 2, No. 1, pp. 4–12.

Drakakis-Smith, D. W. 1984. "The Changing Economic Role of Women in the Urbanization Process: A Preliminary Report from Zimbabwe." *International Migration Review,* Vol. xviii, No. 4, pp. 1278–1291.

Drakakis-Smith, David, and Philip Kivell. (n.d.) *Food Production and Purchasing in Harare, Zimbabwe: A Preliminary Report.* Occasional Paper No. 13. Keele, U.K.: Department of Geography, University of Keele.

Drakakis-Smith, David, and Philip Kivell. 1988. *Urban Food Distribution Systems in Zimbabwe.* Keele, U.K.: Department of Geography, University of Keele.

Dulansey, Maryanne, and James Austin. 1985. "Small-Scale Enterprise and Women," in Overholt, Catherine, Mary B. Anderson, Kathleen Cloud, and James E. Austen (eds.). *Gender Roles in Development Projects: A Case Book.* West Hartford, Conn.: Kumarian Press, pp. 79–131.

Durant-Gonzalez, Victoria. 1976. *Role and Status of Rural Jamaican Women.* Ph.D. dissertation, University of California at Berkeley.

du Toit, Friedrich. 1981. *Musha: The Shona Concept of Home.* Harare: Ministry of Agriculture, Department of Agricultural, Technical and Extension Services.

Eicher, Carl K., and John M. Staatz. 1985. *Food Security Policy in Sub-Saharan Africa.* Paper prepared for the XIXth Conference of the International Association of Agricultural Economists, Malaga, Spain, August 25–September 3.

Eigen, Johanna. 1992. "Assistance to Women's Businesses—Evaluating the Options." *Small Enterprise Development.* Vol. 3, No. 4, pp. 4–14.

England, Kersten. 1982. *A Political Economy of Black Female Labour in Zimbabwe, 1900–1980.* Bachelor's thesis, Department of History, University of Manchester.

Epstein, T. Scarlett. 1982. *Urban Food Marketing and Third World Rural Development: The Structure of Producer-Seller Markets.* London: Croom Helm.

"Explosion in the Cities," *MOTO,* September 1982, pp. 5–8.

Fapohunda, Eleanor R. 1988. "The Nonpooling Household: A Challenge to Theory," in Dwyer, Daisy, and Judith Bruce (eds.). *A Home Divided: Women and Income in the Third World.* Stanford: Stanford University Press, pp. 143–154.

Feldman, Shelley. 1991. "Still Invisible: Women in the Informal Sector," in Gallin, Rita S., and Anne Ferguson (eds.). *The Women and International Development Annual, Volume 2.* Boulder: Westview Press, pp. 59–86.

Forman, Shepard, and Joyce Riegelhaupt. 1970. "Market Place and Marketing System: Toward a Theory of Peasant Economic Integration." *Comparative Studies in Society and History,* Vol. 12, No. 2, pp. 188–212.

Folbre, Nancy. 1988. "The Black Four of Hearts: Toward a New Paradigm of Household Economics," in Dwyer, Daisy, and Judith Bruce (eds.). *A Home Divided: Women and Income in the Third World.* Stanford: Stanford University Press, pp. 248–262.

Frolich, Willy. 1982. *The African Market System.* Vancouver: Tantalus Research (originally published in *Zeitschrift für Ethnologie* 1940).

Gallin, Rita S., Marilyn Aronoff, and Anne Ferguson. 1989. "Women and International Development: Creating an Agenda," in Gallin, Rita S., Marilyn Aronoff, and Anne Ferguson (eds.). *The Women and International Development Annual, Volume 1.* Boulder: Westview Press, pp. 1–22.

Gargett, Eric. 1977. *The Administration of Transition. African Urban Settlement in Rhodesia.* Occasional Papers, Socio-Economic Series No. 5. Gweru, Zimbabwe: Mambo Press.

Gelfand, Michael. 1970. "The Ceremony of *Mishashe* (Green Vegetables) Held in Mashonaland." *Zambezia,* Vol. 1, No. 2, pp. 9–11.

Gill, Margaret and Joycelin Messiah (eds.). 1984. *Women, Work and Development.*

Women in the Caribbean Project, Vol. 6. Cave Hill, Barbados: Institute of Social and Economic Research, University of the West Indies.

Gladwin, Hugh. 1980. "Indigenous Knowledge of Fish Processing and Marketing Utilized by Women Traders of Cape Coast, Ghana," in Brokensha, David, D. M. Warren, and Oswald Werner (eds.). *Indigenous Knowledge Systems and Development.* Lanham, Md.: University Press of America, pp. 129–148.

Gore, Charles G. 1978. *Food Marketing and Rural Underdevelopment: A Study of an Urban Supply System in Ghana.* Ph.D. dissertation, Pennsylvania State University.

The Greater Harare A to Z Street Guide Including Buildings and Industrial Areas. 1991. Harare: Munn Publishing.

Guyer, Jane I. 1987. "Introduction," in Guyer, Jane (ed.). *Feeding African Cities: Studies in Regional Social History.* Bloomington: Indiana University Press, pp. 1–54.

Harper, Malcolm, and Richard Kavura. 1982. *The Private Marketing Entrepreneur and Rural Development.* FAO Agricultural Services Bulletin No. 13. Rome: FAO.

Harrison, Kelly, Donald Henley, Harold Riley, and James Shaffer. 1974. *Improving Food Marketing Systems in Developing Countries: Experiences from Latin America.* Research Report No. 6. East Lansing: Michigan State University, Latin American Studies Center.

Hart, Keith. 1973. "Informal Income Opportunities and Urban Employment in Ghana," *Journal of Modern African Studies,* No. 11, pp. 61–89.

Herald (Zimbabwe), June 14, 1964; May 13, 1977; June 20, 1978; June 24, 1978; June 28, 1977; February 19, 1979; November 20, 1980; August 20, 1992; and July 22, 1993.

Hill, Polly. 1963. "Markets in Africa." *Journal of Modern African Studies,* Vol. 1, pp. 441–453.

Hill, Polly. 1970. "A Plea for Indigenous Economies: The West African Example," in Hill, Polly (ed.). *Studies in Rural Capitalism in West Africa.* London: Cambridge University Press.

Hodder, B. W., and U. I. Ukwu. 1969. *Markets in West Africa.* Ibadan: Ibadan University Press.

Holleman, J. F. 1951. "Some 'Shona' Tribes of Southern Rhodesia," in Colson, Elizabeth, and Max Gluckman (eds.). *Seven Tribes of Central Africa.* Manchester: Manchester University Press, pp. 355–395.

Holleman, J. F. 1952. *Shona Customary Law.* London: Oxford University Press.

Holleman, J. F. 1969. *Chief, Council and Commissioner.* Assen, The Netherlands: Afrika-Studiecentrum.

Horn, Nancy E. 1986. *The Informal Fruit and Vegetable Market in Greater Harare.* Working Paper 4/86. Harare: University of Zimbabwe, Department of Land Management.

Horn, Nancy E. 1988. *The Culture, Urban Context and Economics of Women's Fresh Produce Marketing in Harare, Zimbabwe.* Ph.D. dissertation, Department of Anthropology, Michigan State University.

Horn, Nancy E. 1991a. "Marketwomen's Strategies Buffering Urban Food Security in Harare, Zimbabwe." Paper presented at the annual meeting of the American Anthropological Association, Chicago, Illinois.

Horn, Nancy E. 1991b. "Redefining Economic Productivity: Marketwomen and Food Provisioning in Harare, Zimbabwe." Paper presented at the annual meeting of the African Studies Association, St. Louis, Mo.

"Housing: Keeping Pace with a Rising Demand," *MOTO,* No. 45, 1986, pp. 5–7.

Howard, Willam Stephen. 1987. *Social Strategies in Petty Production: Three Small Scale Industries in Urban Sudan.* Ph.D. dissertation, Michigan State University.

Howland, R. C. 1963. "The Market Hall—Salisbury's Oldest Building." *Rhodesiana,* No. 9.

International Labour Organisation. 1972. *Employment, Incomes and Equality: A Strategy for Increasing Productive Employment in Kenya.* Geneva: ILO.

Jambwa, M. L., and Colin Simmons. 1980. *Mining Labour in the Economy of Southern Rhodesia 1880–1965: Some Aspects of Recruitment and Organisation.* Conference papers on Zimbabwe. University of Leeds, Department of Politics.

Johnson, Eleanor J. 1973. *Marketwomen and Capitalist Adaptation: A Case Study of Rural Benin, Nigeria.* Ph.D. dissertatation, Michigan State University.

Johnson, Robin W. M. 1968. *The Economics of African Agriculture in Southern Rhodesia: A Study in Resource Use.* Ph.D. dissertation, University of Rhodesia.

Jules-Rosette, Bennetta. 1981. *Symbols of Change: Urban Transition in a Zambian Community.* Norwood, N.J.: Ablex Publishers.

Jules-Rosette, Bennetta. 1982. *Women's Work in the Informal Sector: A Zambian Case Study.* W.I.D. Working Paper No. 3. East Lansing: Michigan State University, Office of Women in Development.

Jumani, Usha, and Bharati Joshi. 1984. *Legal Status of Hawkers in India.* Ahmedabad, India: Self Employed Women's Association.

Kaba, Brahima D. 1982. *Profile of Liberian Women in Marketing.* Monrovia, Liberia: University of Liberia.

Kadenge, Phineas G. (ed.). 1992. *Zimbabwe's Structural Adjustment Programme: The First Year Experience.* Harare: SAPES Books.

Kanji, Nazneen, and Niki Jazdowska. 1993. "Structural Adjustment and Women in Zimbabwe." *Review of African Political Economy,* No. 56, pp. 11–26.

Katzin, Margaret F. 1971. "The Business of Higglering in Jamaica," in Horowitz, Michael M. (ed.). *Peoples and Cultures of the Caribbean.* Garden City, NY: The Natural History Press, pp. 340–384.

Kay, George. 1970. *Rhodesia: A Human Geography.* New York: Africana Publishers.

Kay, George, and M. Cole. 1977. "The Townsfolk," in Kay, George, and M. Smout (eds.). *Salisbury: A Geographical Survey of the Capital of Rhodesia.* London: Hodder and Stoughton, pp. 41–56.

Kay, George, and M. Smout. 1977. *Salisbury: A Geographical Survey of the Capital of Rhodesia.* London: Hodder and Stoughton.

Kosmin, Barry A. 1974. *Ethnic and Commercial Relations in Southern Rhodesia: A Socio-Historical Study of the Asians, Hellenes and Jewish Population, 1898–1943.* Ph.D. dissertation, University of Rhodesia.

Lan, David. 1985. *Guns and Rain. Guerrillas and Spirit Mediums in Zimbabwe.* Harare: Zimbabwe Publishing House.

Lewis, Barbara C. (ed.). 1981. *Invisible Farmers: Women and the Crisis in Agriculture.* Washington, D.C.: Agency for International Development, Office of Women in Development.

Liedholm, Carl, and Donald Mead. 1987. *Small Scale Industries in Developing Countries: Empirical Evidence and Policy Implications.* MSU International Development Paper No. 9. East Lansing: Department of Agricultural Economics, Michigan State University.

Lipton, Michael. 1982. *Poverty, Undernutrition and Hunger.* World Bank Staff Working Paper No. 597. Washington, D.C.: World Bank.

Logan, W. J. C. 1984. "Horticultural Crops," in Van Hoffen, M. (ed.). *Commercial Agriculture in Zimbabwe 1984/85*. Harare: Modern Farming Publishers Trust, pp. 88–92.

Luqmani, Mushtaf. 1978. *Improving the Effectiveness of Food Distribution in Developing Countries: An Analysis of Karachi, Pakistan*. Ph.D. dissertation, Michigan State University.

"Marriage Under Fire." 1985. *MOTO,* No. 41, pp. 4–5.

Marsden, Keith. 1990. *African Entrepreneurs. Pioneers of Development*. Discussion Paper No. 9. Washington, D.C.: International Finance Corporation, World Bank.

May, Joan. 1979. *African Women in Urban Employment*. Gweru, Zimbabwe: Mambo Press.

May, Joan. 1983. *Zimbabwean Women in Colonial and Customary Law*. Gweru, Zimbabwe: Mambo Press.

Maya, R. S. 1988. *Structural Adjustment in Zimbabwe: Its Impact on Women*. Harare: Ministry of Cooperatives, Community Development and Women's Affairs.

Mazur, Robert E., and Marvellous Mhloyi. 1988. *Underdevelopment, Women's Work and Fertility in Zimbabwe*. Working Paper No. 164. East Lansing: Michigan State University, Office of Women in International Development.

McGee, T. G. 1973. "Peasants in the Cities: A Paradox, a Paradox, a Most Ingenious Paradox." *Human Organization.* Vol 32, No. 2, pp. 135–142.

McPherson, Michael A. 1991. *Micro and Small Scale Enterprises in Zimbabwe. Results of a Country-Wide Survey*. GEMINI Technical Report No. 25. East Lansing: Michigan State University, Department of Economics.

Meredith, Geoffrey G., Robert E. Nelson, and Phili. Neck. 1982. *The Practice of Entrepreneurship*. Geneva: ILO.

Mezzera, Jaime. 1989. "Excess Labor Supply and the Urban Informal Sector. An Analytical Framework," in Berger, Marguerite, and Mayra Buvinic (eds.). *Women's Ventures*. West Hartford, Conn.: Kumarian Press, pp. 45–64.

Milimo, John T., and Yacob Fisseha. 1986. *Rural Small Scale Enterprises in Zambia: Results of a 1985 Country-Wide Survey*. Working Paper No. 28. East Lansing: Michigan State University, Department of Economics.

Mitchell, J. Clyde. 1969. "Structural Plurality, Urbanisation and Labour Circulation in Southern Rhodesia," in Jackson, J. A. (ed.). *Migration*. Cambridge: Cambridge University Press, pp. 156–180.

Moller, Valerie. 1978. *Urban Commitment and Involvement Among Black Rhodesians*. Ph.D. dissertation, University of Natal, South Africa.

Moran, Mary H. 1988. "The Market Feeds Me: Women and Economic Independence in Harper City, Liberia." *Liberia-Forum,* 4/7, pp. 21–34.

Moser, Caroline O. N. 1978. "Informal Sector or Petty Commodity Production: Dualism or Dependence in Urban Development?" *World Development.* Vol. 6, Nos. 9/10, pp. 1041–1064.

Moyo, N. P., R. J. Davies, G. C. Z. Mhone, and L. Pakkiri. 1984. *The Informal Sector in Zimbabwe: Its Potential for Employment Creation*. Harare: University of Zimbabwe, Department of Economics (draft).

Mpofu, Stanley. 1979. *A Design Criteria Proposal for Shopping Centres: Salisbury's Low Income Areas*. Master's thesis, University of Rhodesia.

Mshoperi, R. D. 1985. *ARDA NIJO Estate: Produce Market Study*. Harare: Agriculture and Rural Development Authority (draft).

Muchemenyi, Ishmael, Sihle Dube, Reginald Mazaiwana, Isable Mujuru, and Munyaradzi Saruchera. 1993. "Social Repercussions of Price Decontrol." A paper presented at the Southern Africa Winter School on the social dimensions of ESAP. Harare: University of Zimbabwe.

Muchena, Olivia. 1980. *Women in Town: A Socio-economic Survey of African Women in Highfield Township, Salisbury.* Harare: University of Zimbabwe, Centre for Applied Social Sciences.

Muchena, Olivia. 1982. *A Socio-Economic Overview: Zimbabwe Women.* Addis Ababa: United Nations Economic Commission for Africa. ST/ECA/ATRCW/ 81/10.

Mudimu, G. D., and Solomon Chigume. 1993. "Open Land Cultivation in Harare: Issues and Options." Harare: Department of Agricultural Economics and Extension, University of Zimbabwe (draft).

Mudzengerere, Nicholas E. 1993. "The Effects of Structural Adjustment on the Workforce in Zimbabwe." A paper presented to the Winter School on the social implications of structural adjustment programmes. Harare: University of Zimbabwe.

Murphy, Martin F. 1990. "The Need for a Re-evaluation of the Concept 'Informal Sector': The Dominican Case," in Smith, M. Estelle (ed.). *Perspectives on the Informal Economy.* Monographs in Economic Anthropology. Lanham, Va.: University Press of America and the Society for Economic Anthropology, pp. 161–181.

Mvududu, Sara. 1991. "The Impact of Structural Adjustment on Women and Other Vulnerable Groups in Zimbabwe." Class Research Paper, Department of Agricultural Economics and Extension, University of Zimbabwe.

Native Commissioner. Rhodesia. Umtali. *Report.* April 1, 1898. Harare: National Archives of Zimbabwe, File W9 (1) 1, NAH.

"New Strategies Needed to Fight Sex Discrimination," *MOTO,* No. 44, 1986, p. 7.

Obbo, Christine. 1980. *African Women: Their Struggle for Economic Independence.* London: Zed Press.

Omari, C. K. 1989. Rural *Women, Informal Sector and Household Economy in Tanzania.* WIDER Working Papers WP 79. Helsinki: World Institute for Development Economics Research of the United Nations University.

Ongla, Jean. 1978. *Structure, Conduct and Performance of the Food Crop Marketing System in Cameroon: A Cast Study of Yaounde and Adjacent Areas.* Ph.D. dissertation, University of Florida.

Orlove, Benjamin S. 1986. "Barter and Cash Sale on Lake Titicaca: A Test of Competing Approaches." *Current Anthropology,* Vol. 27, No. 2, pp. 85– 106.

Osirim, Mary J. 1990. *Characteristics of Entrepreneurship in Nigerian Industries That Started Small.* Ph.D. dissertation, Department of Sociology, Harvard University.

Osirim, Mary J. Forthcoming. "The Status of African Market Women: Trade, Economy and Family in Nigeria and Zimbabwe," in House-Midamba, Bessie, and Felix Ekechi (eds.). *African Women Traders and Economic Development.* Westport, Conn.: Greenwood Publishing Group.

Otero, Maria. 1987. *Gender Issues in Small Scale Enterprise.* Washington, D.C.: Agency for International Development.

Palmer, Ingrid. 1991. *Gender and Population in the Adjustment of African Economies: Planning for Change.* Women, Work and Development, 19. Geneva: International Labour Organisation.

Palmer, Robin. 1977a. "Agricultural History of Rhodesia," in Palmer, Robin, and Neil Parsons (eds.). *The Roots of Rural Poverty in Central and Southern Africa.* London: Heineman, pp. 221–254.

Palmer, Robin 1977b. *Land and Racial Domination in Rhodesia.* Berkeley: University of California Press.

Papanek, Hanna. 1990. "To Each Less Than She Needs, From Each More Than She Can Do: Allocations, Entitlements, and Value," in Tinker, Irene (ed.). *Persistent Inequalities: Women and World Development.* New York: Oxford University Press, pp. 162–181.

Parsons, Neil. 1977. "The Economic History of Khama's Country in Botswana, 1844–1930," in Palmer, Robin, and Neil Parsons (eds.). *The Roots of Rural Poverty in Central and Southern Africa.* London: Heineman, pp. 113–143.

Patel, Diana H., and R. J. Adams. 1981. *Chirambhuyo: A Case Study in Low Income Housing.* Gweru, Zimbabwe: Mambo Press.

Peattie, Lisa R. 1980. "Anthropological Perspectives on the Concept of Dualism, the Informal Sector, and Marginality in Developing Economies." *International Regional Science Review.* Vol. I, No. 5, pp. 1–31.

Pendered, A., and W. von Memerty. 1955. "The Native Land Husbandry Act of Southern Rhodesia." *Journal of African Administration,* Vol. 7, No. 3, pp. 99–109.

Phimister, Ian. 1977. "Peasant Production and Underdevelopment," in Palmer, Robin, and Neil Parsons (eds.). *The Roots of Rural Poverty in Central and Southern Africa.* London: Heineman, pp. 255–267.

Phimister, Ian. 1988. "The Combined and Contradictory Inheritance of the Struggle Against Colonialism," in Stoneman, Colin (ed.). *Zimbabwe's Prospects: Issues of Race, Class, State, and Capital in Southern Africa.* London: Macmillan Publishers, pp. 8–15.

Plattner, Stuart. 1985. *Markets and Marketing.* Monographs in Economic Anthropology, No. 4. Lanham, Md.: University Press of America.

Portes, Alejandro. 1983. "The Informal Sector: Definition, Controversy, and Relation to National Development." *Review,* Vol. VII, No. 1, Summer.

Portes, Alejandro, and Saskia Sassen-Koob. 1987. "Making It Underground: Comparative Materials on the Informal Sector in Western Market Economies." *American Journal of Sociology,* Vol. 93, No. 1, pp. 30–61.

Preston, David. A. 1978. *Farmers and Towns: Rural-Urban Relations in Highland Bolivia.* Norwich, England: Geo Abstracts, University of East Anglia.

PTA Consulting Services. 1982. *Study for the Agricultural/Rural Development of the Communal Areas of Mashonaland East Province.* Harare: PTA Consulting Services.

Ranger, Terrence. 1985. *Peasant Consciousness and Guerrilla War in Zimbabwe.* Harare: Zimbabwe Publishing House.

Reddock, Rhoda. 1990. "Caribbean Sub-Project," in Wieringa, Saskia. *Women's Movements and Organizations in Historical Perspective: Project Summaries and Evaluation.* The Hague: Institute of Social Studies.

Rhodesia. Ministry of Finance. 1979. *Urban Development in the Main Centres.* Harare: Government Printer.

Riddell, Roger C. 1974. "Poverty and the Wage Structure in Rhodesia." *The Rhodesia Science News,* Vol. 8, No. 7, pp. 201–204.

Riddell, Roger C. 1978a. *Alternatives to Poverty.* From Rhodesia to Zimbabwe 1. Gweru, Zimbabwe: Mambo Press.

Riddell, Roger C. 1978b. *The Land Problem in Rhodesia: Alternatives for the Future.* Gweru, Zimbabwe: Mambo Press.

Riddell, Roger C. 1984. "Zimbabwe: The Economy Four Years After Independence." *African Affairs,* Vol. 83, No. 333, pp. 463–476.

Rifkind, Malcolm. 1968. *The Politics of Land in Rhodesia: A Study of Land and*

Politics in Southern Rhodesia with Special Reference to the Period 1930–1968. Master's thesis, University of Edinburgh.

Roberts, Bryan. 1990. "The Informal Sector in Comparative Perspective," in Smith, M. Estellie (ed.). *Perspectives on the Informal Economy.* Monographs in Economic Anthropology, No. 8. Lanham, Md.: University Press of America and Society for Economic Anthropology, pp. 23–48.

Robertson, Claire C. 1984. *Sharing the Same Bowl: A Socioeconomic History of Women and Class in Accra, Ghana.* Bloomington: Indiana University Press.

Safilos-Rothschild, C. 1985. "The Persistence of Women's Invisibility in Agriculture: Theoretical and Policy Lessons from Lesotho and Sierra Leone." *Economic Development and Cultural Change,* Vol. 33, No. 2, pp. 299–317.

Sahlins, Marshall. 1972. *Stone Age Economics.* New York: Aldine Publishing Company.

Sahlins, Marshall. 1976. *Culture and Practical Reason.* Chicago: University of Chicago Press.

Saito, Katrine. 1990. *The Informal Sector in Zimbabwe: The Role of Women.* Report No. 9006-ZIM. Washington, D.C.: World Bank.

Saito, Katrine. 1991. "Women and Microenterprise Development in Zimbabwe: Constraints to Development." Draft. Paper presented at the annual meeting of the African Studies Association, St. Louis, Mo.

Salisbury. Municipal Council. 1932. *Salisbury: The Administrative Capital of Southern Rhodesia: A History and Description of the City.* Harare: Government Printer.

Sanders, David. 1986. Untitled draft report. Harare: University of Zimbabwe, Faculty of Medicine.

Santos, M. 1972. *Economic Development and Urbanization in Underdeveloped Countries: The Two Flow Systems of the Urban Economy and Their Spatial Implications.* Unpublished.

Schapera, I. 1928. "Economic Changes in South African Native Life." *Africa.* Vol. 1, No. 1, pp. 170–188.

Schildkrout, Enid. 1979. "Women's Work and Children's Work: Variations Among Moslems in Kano," in Wallman, Sandra (ed.). *Social Anthropology of Work.* ASA Monograph No. 19. London: Academic Press, pp. 69–85.

Schmidt, Elizabeth. 1987. "Women Are the Backbone of Agriculture: A Historical Assessment of Women's Role in Peasant Production in Zimbabwe, 1890–1939." Paper presented to the annual meeting of the American Anthropological Association, November.

Schmidt, Elizabeth. 1992. *Peasants, Traders and Wives: Shona Women in the History of Zimbabwe, 1870–1939.* Portsmouth, N.H.: Heinemann.

Schmink, Marianne. 1986. "Women in the Urban Economy of Latin America," in Schmink, Marianne, Judith Bruce, and Marilyn Kohn (eds.). *Learning About Women and Urban Services in Latin America and the Caribbean.* Washington, D.C.: Population Council.

Schmink, Marianne, Judith Bruce, and Marily Kohn (eds.). 1986. *Learning About Women and Urban Services in Latin America and the Caribbean.* Washington, D.C.: Population Council.

Scott, Gregroy J. 1985. *Markets, Myths and Middlemen: A Study of Potato Marketing in Central Peru.* Lima: International Potato Center.

Sethuraman, S. V. 1976. "The Urban Informal Sector: Concepts, Measurement and Policy." *International Labour Review,* Vol. 114, pp. 69–81.

Sethuraman, S. V. 1977. "The Urban Informal Sector in Africa." *International Labour Review,* Vol. 116, No. 3, pp. 343–352.

Sethuraman, S. V. (ed.). 1981. *The Urban Informal Sector in Developing Countries: Employment, Poverty and Environment.* Geneva: International Labour Organisation.

Sethuraman, S. V. 1989. *Women in the Informal Sector: A Review of Evidence from Developing Countries.* Geneva: International Labour Organisation.

Shaffer, James D., Michael Weber, Harold Riley, and John Staatz. 1983. "Influencing the Design of Marketing Systems to Promote Development in Third World Countries." Paper presented at the International Workshop on Agricultural Markets in the Semi-Arid Tropics by the International Crop Research Institute for the Semi-Arid Tropics, Hyderabad, India.

Shava, F. M. M. 1986. "The Worker in Zimbabwe." *Zimbabwe News,* January, pp. 6–7.

Smith, M. Estellie. 1990. "'A Million Here, A Million There, and Pretty Soon You're Talking Real Money,'" in Smith, M. Estellie (ed.). *Perspectives on the Informal Economy.* Monographs in Economic Anthropology. Lanham, Md.: University Press of America and the Society for Economic Anthropology, pp. 1–22.

Smith, R. Cherer. n.d. *Avondale to Zimbabwe.* Harare: Mardon Printers.

Southern Rhodesia. 1958. *Report of the Urban African Affairs Commission 1958* (Plewman Report). Harare: Government Printer.

Southern Rhodesia. 1945. *Report of Native Production and Trade 1944.* Harare: Government Printer.

Southern Rhodesia. Legislative Assembly. 1935. *Debates.* Vol. 15, Cols. 583–584.

Southern Rhodesia. Legislative Assembly. 1959. *Select Committee on Resettlement of Natives.* Harare: Government Printer.

Southern Rhodesia. Legislative Assembly. 1960. *Select Committee on Resettlement of Natives. Second Report.* Harare: Government Printer.

Stewart, J., W. Ncube, M. Mboreke, and A. Armstrong. 1990. "The Legal Situation of Women in Zimbabwe," in Stewart, Julie, and Alice Armstrong (eds.). *The Legal Situation of Women in Southern Africa. Vol. II, Women and the Law in Southern Africa.* Harare: University of Zimbabwe Publications, pp. 165–222.

Stoneman, Colin. 1988. "The Economy: Recognising the Reality," in Stoneman, Colin (ed.). *Zimbabwe's Prospects: Issues of Race, Class, State, and Capital in Southern Africa.* London: Macmillan Publishers, pp. 43–62.

Stopforth, G. 1972. *Two Aspects of Social Change: Highfield African Township Salisbury.* Harare: Institute for Social Research, University of Rhodesia.

Sudarkasa, Niara. 1973. *Where Women Work: A Study of Yoruba Women in the Marketplace and in the Home.* Ann Arbor: Museum of Anthropology, University of Michigan.

Sunday Mail (Harare, Zimbabwe). December 14, 1973.

Tanser, Tony. 1965. *A Scantling of Time: The Story of Salisbury, Rhodesia (1890–1900).* Harare: Stuart Manning.

Tinker, Irene. 1981. "New Technologies for Food-Related Activities: An Equity Strategy," in Dauber, Roslynn, and Melinda L. Cain (eds.). *Women and Technological Change in Developing Countries.* AAAS Selected Symposium 53. Boulder: Westview Press, pp. 51–88.

Tinker, Irene. 1990. "A Context for the Field and for the Book," in Tinker, Irene (ed.). *Persistent Inequalities: Women and World Development.* New York: Oxford University Press, pp. 3–13.

Trager, Lillian. 1976. *Yoruba Markets and Trade: Analysis of Spatial Structure and Social Organization in the Ijesaland Marketing System.* Ph.D. dissertation, University of Washington.

Tripp, Aili Mari. 1990. "The Informal Economy and the State in Tanzania," in Smith, M. Estellie (ed.). *Perspectives on the Informal Economy.* Monographs in Economic Anthropology, No. 8. Lanham, Md.: University Press of America and the Society for Economic Anthropology, pp. 49–71.

Tokman, Victor E. 1978a. "An Exploration into the Nature of Informal-Formal Sector Relationships." *World Development,* Vol. 6, No. 9/10, pp. 1065–1075.

Tokman, Victor E. 1978b. "Competition Between the Informal and Formal Sectors in Retailing: The Case of Santiago." *World Development,* Vol. 6, No. 9/10, pp. 1187–1198.

Truscott, Kate. 1986. "Socio-economic Factors in Food Production and Consumption." *Food and Nutrition,* Vol. 12, No. 1, pp. 27–37.

Turrittin, Jane. 1988. "Men, Women and Market Trade in Mali, West Africa." *Canadian Journal of African Studies,* Vol. xxii, No. 3, pp. 583–604.

Universalia. 1989. *Report on Zimbabwe Women in Development Entrepreneurship Project Identification Mission.* Harare: Canadian International Development Agency.

United Nations. Centre for Social Development and Humanitarian Affairs. 1989. *1989 World Survey on the Role of Women in Development.* Document ST/CSDHA/6. New York: United Nations.

United Nations Development Programme. 1990. *Women in Development.* Project Achievement Reports from the United Nations Development Programme. New York: UNDP.

van Onselen, C. 1976. *Chibaro: African Mine Labour in Southern Rhodesia, 1900–1933.* London.

Wallerstein, Immanuel. 1984. "Household Structures and Labor-Force Formation in the Capitalist World Economy," in Smith, Joan, Immanual Wallerstein, and Hans-Dieter Evers (eds.). *Households and the World Economy.* Beverly Hills: Sage Publications, pp. 17–22.

Waring, Marilyn. 1988. *If Women Counted: A New Feminist Economics.* San Francisco: Harp r.

Weinrich, A. K. H. 1975. *African Farmers in Rhodesia.* London: Oxford University Press.

Weinrich, A. K. H. 1979. *Women and Racial Discrimination in Rhodesia.* Paris: UNESCO.

Weinrich, A. K. H. 1982. *African Marriage in Zimbabwe and the Impact of Christianity.* Gweru, Zimbabwe: Mambo Press.

Wells, Julia. 1982. "Passes and Bypasses: Freedom of Movement for African Women Under the Urban Areas Act of South Africa," in Hay, Margaret Jean, and Marcia Wright (eds.). *African Women and the Law: Historical Perspectives.* Papers on Africa, VII. Boston: Boston University, pp. 125–150.

Werlin, Herbert H. 1981. "The Hawkers of Nairobi: The Politics of the Informal Sector," in Obudho, R. A. (ed.). *Urbanization and Development Planning in Kenya.* Nairobi: Kenya Literature Bureau, pp. 194–214.

"When 'Till Death Do Us Part' No Longer Means Forever," 1986. *Parade,* February, pp. 5, 22.

Wild, V. 1992. "An Outline of African Business History in Colonial Zimbabwe." *Zambezia,* Vol. XIX, No. i, pp. 19–46.

Wilk, Richard R. 1989. "Decision Making and Resource Flows Within the Household: Beyond the Black Box," in Wilk, Richard R. (ed.). *The Household Economy: Reconsidering the Domestic Mode of Production.* Boulder: Westview Press, pp. 23–52.

Wood, L. J. 1974. *Market Origins and Development in East Africa.* Occasional

Paper No. 57. Kampala, Uganda: Makerere University, Department of Geography.

World Bank. 1989. *Small Enterprises in African Development: A Summary.* Staff Working Paper No. 363. Washington, D.C.: World Bank.

Yudelman, M. 1964. *Africans on the Land.* Cambridge: Cambridge University Press.

Zimbabwe. 1985. *Statistical Yearbook 1985.* Harare: Central Statistical Office.

Zimbabwe. 1986. *First Five-Year National Development Plan 1986–1990.* Vol. I. Harare: Government Printer.

Zimbabwe. 1991a. *Zimbabwe: A Framework for Economic Reform (1991–95).* Harare: Government Printer.

Zimbabwe. 1991b. *Second Five-Year National Development Plan 1991–1995.* Harare: Government Printer.

Zimbabwe. Central Statistical Office (CSO). 1983. *Census.* Tables 13A, 19, and 30A. Harare: Government Printer.

Zimbabwe. CSO. 1984. *1982 Population Census: A Preliminary Assessment.* Harare: Government Printer.

Zimbabwe. CSO. 1985. *Main Demographic Features of the Population of Zimbabwe: An Advance Report Based on a Ten Percent Sample.* Harare: Government Printer.

Zimbabwe. CSO. 1992a. *Census 1992. Zimbabwe Preliminary Report.* Harare: Government Printer.

Zimbabwe. CSO. 1992b. *Quarterly Digest of Statistics 3.* Harare: Government Printer.

Zimbabwe. Ministry of Community and Cooperative Development. 1992. *Report of the General Workshop with National and International Organisations. Presentation and Assessment of Strategies and Approaches for SSE for Women.* Harare: Government Printer.

Zimbabwe. Ministry of Community Development and Women's Affairs. 1982. *Report on the Situation of Women in Zimbabwe.* Harare: Government Printer.

Zimbabwe Women Finance Trust and the Foundation for International Training. 1990. *Support Program for Women in Micro Enterprise Development Zimbabwe.* Harare: Canadian International Development Agency.

Zimconsult. 1983. *Final Report: Study of Musika Co-Operative Society Ltd. Mbare, Zimbabwe.* Harare: Zimconsult (provided by the Zimbabwe Women's Bureau in Harare).

Zinyama, Lovemore M. 1993. "The Evolution of the Spatial Structure of Greater Harare: 1890 to 1990," in Zinyama, Lovemore M., Daniel S. Tevera, and Sioux D. Cumming (eds.). *Harare: The Growth and Problems of the City.* Harare: University of Zimbabwe Publications, pp. 7–31.

▲
Index

▲
About the Book and Author

For the market women of Harare—for the most part first-generation migrants from rural areas—selling fruits and vegetables is serious business; to them, the cultivation of many customers is the equivalent of a bountiful harvest. According to government statistics, however, these microentrepreneurs are "invisible," and their contribution to income generation, family economic sustainability, and urban food security is ignored.

In this sensitively drawn ethnography, Nancy E. Horn shows that Harare's market women are indeed vital to Zimbabwe's national economy. She argues that these businesswomen consider profit for reinvestment and household maintenance as primary goals. They are business operators in the classic sense, and they should be treated as such by analysts and policymakers.

Horn offers an analysis of the meanings of commerce, work, and urban life to market women in Zimbabwe, presenting previously unavailable data on the daily weight and count of commodities bought and sold; daily, weekly, and monthly profit margins; and detailed household budgets. Weaving a complex account of culture and economics, she illustrates how the women bring to their trade a culturally based indigenous knowledge system in order to make economic sense of an often hostile urban environment.

Nancy Horn is a consultant at Michigan State University and is affiliated with the Institution of International Agriculture. She is currently working with Cornell University on a collaboration with the University of Zimbabwe that seeks to improve smallholder horticulture, including production and marketing.

DATE DUE

BRODART

Cat. No. 23-221